W9-AEW-236

GOOD NEWS TO THE POOR

WALTER E. PILGRIM

GOOD NEWS TO THE POOR

WEALTH AND POVERTY IN LUKE-ACTS

Augsburg Publishing House

Minneapolis, Minnesota

GOOD NEWS TO THE POOR

Copyright © 1981 Augsburg Publishing House

Library of Congress Catalog Card No. 81-65653

International Standard Book No. 0-8066-1889-2

All rights reserved. No part of this book may be used or reproduced in any manner whatsoever without written permission except in the case of brief quotations embodied in critical articles and reviews. For information address Augsburg Publishing House, 426 South Fifth Street, Minneapolis, Minnesota 55415.

Scripture quotations unless otherwise noted are from the Revised Standard Version of the Bible, copyright 1946, 1952, and 1971 by the Division of Christian Education of the National Council of Churches.

MANUFACTURED IN THE UNITED STATES OF AMERICA

To my wife
Jeanette
and daughters
Kathryn, Kristen, Karyn
In fond memory of our family year abroad

Contents

Acknowledgments

The major portion of the research and writing for this study was done on sabbatical leave in Tübingen in 1977-78. I wish to thank Pacific Lutheran University and the Lutheran Institute of Theological Education (LITE) for the leave opportunity. In addition, a scholarship for study abroad was granted by the Lutheran World Federation, which not only provided financial aid but also contact with persons from many parts of the globe and added to my sense of the urgent ecumenical mission of the church to and with the world's poor.

Many others helped bring this book to fruition, among whom my departmental colleagues, several pastor's study groups in Tacoma and Seattle, secretarial typists in the LITE office, and the Augsburg editorial staff deserve special mention. My grateful thanks for all their support and encouragement.

Introduction

The relation between possessions and the Christian life has always been a question of considerable controversy. In the history of Christendom there have been those who have advocated a total renunciation of possessions as the truest testimony to the faith, and there have been those who found no conflict in the amassing of wealth, rightly earned. Most Christians, of course, have lived somewhere between these two poles, but not without sensing the constant tension of needing and wanting possessions, and yet realizing their potential dangers to a faithful Christian life.

Perhaps today we sense this tension even more as we face the increasing discrepancy between the rich and the poor. This discrepancy may always be with us, but this fact dare not lead us to ignore the problems, or to passive acceptance of this gap, if we care at all as humans and Christians about our world. But what specifically can and should Christians do? The sheer complexity of the problem staggers the mind, since the question of poverty and wealth involves not only our own neighborhoods but also the entire world.

Christians instinctively look to the Scriptures for guidelines. But at least two considerations have made the Scriptures themselves seem inadequate for providing anything but the most general and obvious help on this issue to serious-minded Christians. One is the apparent discrepancy within the Bible itself, in which one can find support for both the total renunciation of wealth and also support for wealth rightly gained as a gift of God. Even in the Gospels where Christians most directly hear the words of their Lord and observe his manner of life, there appears to be more than one viewpoint regarding possessions, as we shall observe later. Beyond this, and perhaps weighing even more heavily on the minds of conscientious Christians is the fact that a gap of 2000 years separates us from the time of Jesus and the New Testament. We live in a new world, with new conditions, new cultures, new problems and new perspectives. Is there any way of moving directly and helpfully from first century Palestine and the Graeco-Roman world in which our Scriptures were produced, to the technological and complex world of the twentieth century?

Without making any claims to having discovered new insights or to having reconciled the many tensions within Scripture regarding possessions, I do think that a fresh look at the Gospel of Luke and the Acts of the Apostles can open up new possibilities for Christians and others who seek help on this fundamental issue. Much work has been done in the last decade alone on this topic, and I am indebted to these studies. Perhaps the impact of this book will rest mostly in bringing together some of the results of these studies in a systematic and intelligible way for the non-specialist. It has had this effect already for me. One cannot avoid the subject of possessions when one reads the Gospel of Luke and its sequel, the Acts of the Apostles. Only the brief Epistle of James has a comparable interest, but Luke's fuller volumes contain much more. It is my hope then, that this study can bring forcefully to the reader's attention the Lukan witness to the question of possessions, and in so doing provide a basis for further reflection and action by those who care—in Christ's name—for a hurting world.

Interpretive Approach

This study utilizes the basic insights and tools of modern historical study of the Scriptures. Perhaps a brief explanation of what this involves is in order.

Sources

Luke was not writing from scratch when he composed his two-volume work.[1] Scholars have identified at least three sources for this Gospel: the Gospel of Mark, a document called Q, and a source known as L. In the judgment of most New Testament interpreters, Mark was the earliest written Gospel and was used extensively by both Matthew and Luke (Matthew uses 90% of Mark; Luke uses 55% of Mark). The hypothetical Q source explains that material common to Matthew and Luke, even though no form of Q survives. While there has been a renewed effort in certain scholarly circles to challenge both the priority of Mark and the existence of Q, these "assured results," as they are often termed, still stand firm. In addition to Mark and Q, Luke also drew upon his own independent sources, known as L. We do not know whether it consisted of one or many sources or whether it was written or oral, but from it Luke undoubtedly found some of the most moving literature among all the gospel traditions. Each of these sources will be kept in mind as we do our study and seek to determine Luke's special contribution to the story of Jesus' life and teaching about the poor.

In Acts the matter is somewhat different. While Luke obviously had good sources, we have no certainty what they were, despite many attempts to identify them. Nor did Luke have any previous literary example to follow, as he did with his Gospel. So Luke is far more on his own in Acts and he pioneers the first attempt, so far as we know, of recording the church's founding and initial history. Nevertheless, by close comparison with his Gospel and by other literary means it is possible to recognize Luke's hand and his own distinct interests.

Methodology

Our primary interest is not with the historical life and teachings of Jesus. Our focus rather is on Luke's point of view and the way in which he shaped his sources and traditions, so as to present to his own believing community the challenge of the poor and the problem of wealth. It is our hope that by concentrating on the message of Luke for his time and place, we might then be able to recover a message apropos for our time and place, a message that will be *for* the poor and *against* a world in which the rich get richer and the poor get poorer.

In this study we will need to keep alert to several methodological concerns:

a) How does Luke alter his Markan sources? This can frequently provide a clue to his intentions.

b) How do Luke and Matthew utilize the Q source? While we may not be able to recover the original wording or even setting of a text, we can observe how Luke's version differs from Matthew's and then try to draw conclusions from this as to Luke's intent.

c) What comes from Luke's own L sources? After recognizing this material, we need to look for the similar content and themes which can provide us with insights into Luke's own special interests and concerns.

d) What traditional material does Luke preserve intact? The concern here is with the material Luke takes over unaltered from his source.

There are two further comments about methodology we want to underscore and both can best be made as words of caution:

The first is a caution about "spiritualizing" gospel texts. What we have in mind is a way of interpreting texts which restricts their meaning to the inner personal relationship between God and humanity. This has been a temptation particularly for Western Christians in their reading of the New Testament. This is the case, for example, when salvation is identified solely with the forgiveness of sins to the exclusion of other forms of human liberation and the redemption of the community and the world. Or this is the case when the biblical references to material realities, such as food and health, poverty and riches, are understood as non-material realities. The hungry become those hungering for God's Word, or the poor become the poor in spirit, or the sick and imprisoned those suffering from sin. In each case, salvation is interiorized and divorced from the material and social realm. While there are some tendencies to do this in the gospels, we need to keep our minds open to the full meaning of salvation in the Scriptures, which never divide the material from the spiritual, the soul from the body. Especially do we need to pay particular attention to the social dimensions inherent in given texts and in the life settings of the individual gospels.

There have been a number of recent efforts in New Testament studies to do just this.[2] What they have in common is their attempt to look beyond the purely theological meaning of a text to its broader social implications, and to move from a near-exclusive concentration on the personal dynamics of religious faith to the community of faith and its interaction with the surrounding culture.

What we are contending for is an interpretive eye that is open to all the meanings in a text, the spiritual and personal but also the social and communal. We are seeking a more wholistic understanding to help us overcome the prevailing spiritualizing tendencies of the past. Moreover we agree that this is a vital theological task since it has to do ultimately with the meaning of the gospel and Christian discipleship. To quote from a recent study on Luke: "Whoever restricts discipleship to an event in the hearts, the heads, and the privatized interpersonal relationships, limits the meaning of Christian discipleship and, in fact, makes Jesus harmless." [3]

The second word of caution concerns the perennial temptation to harmonize the gospels. Already in the second century A.D. a Syrian church leader, Tatian, had tried to replace the four gospels with only one. The church, however, rejected the diminished portrait of Jesus that resulted. But this temptation remains. A more subtle form of harmonizing occurs every time we read what we find in one gospel into another. Certainly we must compare the gospels with each other. Yet each gospel has its own integrity and must be dealt with on its own terms: Luke has his story to tell as he has been led to understand it and Mark and Matthew and John theirs. This provides the richness of the story, even if it makes us somewhat uncomfortable when we want only a single consistent story. The current practice in many churches to read lectionaries from only one gospel in sequence has been a very useful practice to help us overcome this danger of harmonization. Our point can be made with one simple, yet crucial example from Luke and Matthew. Whereas Matthew has Jesus say at the opening of his famous Sermon on the Mount, "Blessed are the poor in spirit" (5:2), Luke's opening line of his Sermon on the Plain reads simply, "Blessed are the poor" (6:20). The difference may seem small, yet the two are not the same and as we shall see, the difference between them tells us much about the separate intent of each evangelist and his understanding of the gospel.

Good News to the Poor

World hunger, global inequalities, human rights and diminishing energy resources have forced the church to come to terms with the Christian response to these issues. Liberation theologies from developing countries and the work of ecumenical groups such as the World Council of Churches have pressed the questions most urgently from within the community of faith. Thus the times themselves are especially ripe for doing all we can to listen anew to our sources, the Scriptures, and to such an evangelist as Luke.

This study will be limited in scope to the Lukan theme of "good news to the poor" and the related question of wealth and poverty.[4] However in the last 15 years alone there have been at least a dozen major studies of the Lukan attitude toward the poor and the problem of wealth.[5] Most of these were published in other languages or are in the form of doctoral theses not easily available to the general public. Our own work has drawn upon these labors with gratitude. Their numbers are indicative of the renewed interest in the social dimensions of the teaching of Jesus. It is our hope and intent to place before the interested reader what we and others find Luke to be saying to his generation about the poor, as a means of letting Luke speak to our generation as well.

Part I

GOOD NEWS
TO THE POOR

The first half of this book will explore the basic theme of Jesus' preaching according to Luke, the proclamation of good news to the poor. Two questions regarding this theme are fundamental: Who are the poor to whom the good news is proclaimed? And what is the good news proclaimed to them? As we shall see, our pursuit of these two questions will lead us deep into both the message of Jesus and the witness of the third evangelist. But first we must describe something of the background upon which Jesus' proclamation of good news to the poor occurs.

1

The Poor in the Old Testament and in the Intertestamental Period

As the background for understanding Jesus' proclamation of good news to the poor, we need to turn first of all to the Old Testament, the Bible of Jesus, and then to the literature written in the period between the Old and New Testaments. It will immediately become apparent that the concern for the poor and the questions about wealth have a long history in the religious family to which Jesus belonged and of which we are the heirs.

THE POOR IN THE OLD TESTAMENT

We will begin with a look at some of the major themes on this topic that appear in the Old Testament.[1]

Possessions as a Sign of God's Blessings

There is a continuous tradition running throughout the Old Testament that regards possessions as a sign of God's blessings. In this view, wealth and poverty are regarded as good gifts of God and the fact of possessing wealth, even great wealth, is interpreted as a sign of God's favor. This is true already in the patriarchal narratives of Genesis, which describe, often in great detail, the considerable wealth of Abraham, Isaac, Jacob, or Joseph in Egypt (Gen. 13:2; 26:13; 30:43; 41:40). With their large flocks and families and numerous servants and slaves, the patriarchs bear the covenant promise of God without any hint of God's displeasure over their wealth. Along with this, goes an emphasis upon their generosity and hospitality to friends and foes alike. But magnanimity and wealth are comfortably compatible in these early traditions.

This positive view of possessions is also apparent in the later Wisdom traditions. Although there is a sharp criticism of the rich as well, as we shall see, wealth is generally accepted as a self-evident blessing of life and given due praise. Even the gold and silver amassed by Solomon is credited to the Lord God of Israel (Sir. 47:18). The final editor of the Book of Job attributes the double restoration of Job's fortune at the end of his long period of testing to the hand of God (Job 42:10).

Conversely, there are some passages in the Old Testament which imply that poverty is a punishment from God. We see this in the legal traditions, where poverty is one of the threats used against the violators of the Law (Deut. 28:15-24; Lev. 26:14-26). Likewise the prophets can threaten evildoers with the loss of their treasured luxuries and a life of "sackcloth" instead of a "rich robe" (Isa. 3:24). The oppressed, too, threaten their persecutors with poverty (Ps. 109:10-12). This same negative view of poverty appears in a somewhat different form in the Wisdom literature. Here we find a number of criticisms against the poor that sounds all too familiar. The poor are lazy (Prov. 6:6-11), or drunkards and gluttons (Prov. 23:21), or carefree spenders (Prov. 21:17). In these cases, it is observed that poverty is self-inflicted. And beggars, who shamelessly display their poverty, are much despised (Sir. 40:28, "Better to die than to beg.").

Thus we find a consistent strain of thought in the Old Testament that appreciates wealth as a gift of God and regards poverty as a blight upon human life, either as divine punishment or as a self-inflicted wound. The problem of those who are victims of poverty due to the sins of others will occupy us at length in the remainder of this chapter. But it is important to note at the beginning this positive affirmation of wealth in the Old Testament tradition in order to grasp the radically different way in which Jesus approaches the question of wealth and poverty.

Yahweh as the Defender of the Poor and Needy

A more pervasive and fundamental theme throughout the Old Testament is the upholding of Yahweh as the protector of the poor and needy. This concept of divine protection of the poor is found nowhere else to the same degree in the religious literature of the ancient world. It is most important for our study that we stress a few of the high points in the development of this theme. Let us take a brief look at some of the key witnesses.

The Old Testament legal traditions. Built securely into the basic moral structure of Israel's covenant relationship with God are two commands: You shall not steal, and You shall not covet your neighbor's house, wife, man or maid servant, ox, ass, anything that is your neighbor's (Exod. 20:15, 17). While the specifics of these two commandments are spelled out from the viewpoint of a patriarchal and nomadic society, the essentials have continuing validity. Both commandments affirm the need and the right of the basic relational structures of human existence, such as home and family, as well as the need and the right of property and goods that are necessary for human life. Both commands also seek to protect these basic human and social rights and needs by forbidding others to take them in ways that are detrimental to the neighbor's well-being. Not only is outright stealing prohibited, no matter how it takes place, but the command not to covet gets at the root of the matter by exposing the evil scheming and greed of the human heart. On the positive side, both commands contain the injunction to work toward the welfare of one's neighbor, as Luther recognized when he wrote: "We should fear and love God, and so we should not seek by craftiness to gain possession of our neighbor's inheritance or home, nor to obtain them under pretext of legal right, but be of service and help him so that he may keep what is his." [2]

But what Yahweh wills and what in actual fact takes place among his people and his creation are never one and the same, which is the essence of the Fall. The needs and rights of human beings have been violated and one of the results is poverty. This is not what Yahweh wills. That is certain. Therefore we find in the various collections of legal traditions in the Old Testament the recurrent theme of Yahweh's love and care for the poor and needy, coupled with specific legislation on ways to remove poverty from the land and bring about more just and equitable conditions. We cite the three major legal traditions.

The Book of the Covenant (Exod. 20:22—23:33)

One of the earliest legal collections is connected with the giving of the Ten Commandments, as narrated in Exodus. In this material

Yahweh himself speaks to Moses and provides a lengthy instruction on legal ways to deal with violations of his commands. One of its basic assumptions is that all permanent or hopeless poverty is to be done away with. To fulfill this, the charging of interest is forbidden, the taking of clothing as a loan pledge is negated, bribery condemned and justice required (Exod. 23:6-7). Every seventh year slaves are to be released, the land is to lie fallow, the vineyards and olive orchards untended, all for the benefit of the poor (and also the wild beasts, Exod. 21:24; 23:10-11).[3] Singled out for special mention as the objects of Yahweh's protection are the stranger, the widow, the orphan and the poor (Exod. 22:21-27). The motive of Yahweh's defense of the needy is made unmistakably clear: Yahweh himself rescued his people when they were strangers and slaves in Egypt; hence his redeemed people should act in like manner toward the helpless in their midst (Exod. 22:21; 23:9). As further evidence of Yahweh's compassionate care for the poor and afflicted, he promises to hear them in their afflictions and to act (Exod. 22:23, 27).

The Deuteronomic Law Code

It is generally agreed that in the book of Deuteronomy we have an updating of the Mosaic legislation appearing in Exodus. If, as many scholars suggest, this was "the book of the Law" which prompted King Josiah's sweeping reforms in 621 B.C., then the contemporaries for which it was written date somewhere in the early 7th century B.C.[4] Some of what we read here simply repeats the earlier Exodus traditions, while other legislation goes beyond it. As before, there is to be no charging of interest, no keeping of a pledge from the poor, release of slaves, no cheating of hired hands (Deut. 24:10ff., 14ff.), no perversion of justice and no taking of bribes (Deut. 16:18-20; 24:10-22). The command to leave some sheaves or olives or grapes for the poor is extended beyond the 7th year to each harvest time and becomes an important welfare measure in Israel (Deut. 24:19-22). The Law of the tithe is spelled out, coupled with the admonition to care for the Levites, who possessed no lands (Deut. 14:22-29). At the Passover and the Feast of Booths, the celebration is to include servants, Levites, strangers, the fatherless and the widow. We note once again the mention of strangers, fatherless and widows (Deut. 24:14, 17, 19, 21). As in the covenant code, the theological underpinning of this regard for the poor is echoed in the repeated refrain, "You shall remember you were a slave in Egypt and the Lord God redeemed you" (Deut. 24:18, 22). With these words, Yahweh affirms his promise to come to the aid of the poor who cry out for relief and to punish evildoers.

In the midst of this legal material is a passionate appeal "Not to harden your heart or shut your hand against your poor brother but you shall open your hand to him, and lend him sufficient for his need, whatever it may be" (Deut. 15:7-11). This so-called "poor law" poignantly expresses the motivating forces at work in the legal legislation on behalf of the poor. The appeal to generous and ungrudging care is linked with the promise of the Lord's blessing to those who give freely (Deut. 15:10). Although it is recognized that the poor will always be around, nevertheless, "You shall open wide your hand to your brother, to the needy and to the poor in the land" (Deut. 15:11).

It is here, too, that we meet the concept of the Sabbatical Year, which figured so prominently in Israel's poor legislation. The Sabbatical Year required three things every seventh year: a) the land lies fallow (Exod. 23:10-11); b) all debts are remitted (Deut. 15:1-2); c) slaves are offered release (Deut. 15:1-6, 12-18). The purpose of the Sabbatical Year was to prevent gross injustices and oppression from taking root in society. It was Yahweh's desire that "there will be no poor among you" (Deut. 15:4). How faithfully the Sabbatical Year was carried out is a matter of considerable debate.[5] Most interpreters think that only the provision to let the land lie fallow was actually kept. Yet the warnings about refusing to lend money to the poor if the Sabbatical Year is approaching lends some credence to the evidence it was taken seriously, at least by some (Deut. 15:1-10). We can say this much with certainty, however; the Sabbatical Year existed as a powerful symbol to Israel of God's concern for the poor and for justice.

The Holiness Code (Lev. 17-26)

This collection is considered to be later priestly material, perhaps from the time of the Exile, even though it embodies many traditions that go back far into Israel's earlier history. Much of it repeats what we have already found, such as the command to leave gleanings in the field and grapes in the vineyard for the poor and sojourner (Lev. 19:1-10; 23:22) and not to oppose one's neighbor in any way

(Lev. 19:13-14, also the deaf and blind). Jesus was familiar with this section of Scripture, since from it he quoted the second of the two great commands upon which all the Law and prophets depend, "You shall love your neighbor as yourself" (Lev. 19:18).

It is in this legislation that we also encounter the concept of the Jubilee Year, which is particularly important for our study of Luke's gospel. The Jubilee Year is closely related to the Sabbatical Year. But it adds one further provision which makes it theoretically the most radical social legislation in the Old Testament. According to Leviticus 25:10ff., every 49th year the following is required: a) the land lies fallow; b) slaves are freed; c) debts are remitted; and d) the new Jubilee prescription, the ancestral land is returned. This additional provision of returning ancestral lands and possessions to their original families was obviously formulated to prevent great disparity in wealth and lands among the Israelites. Its theological premises are plainly stated: all the land belongs to Yahweh; he has given it to his people as a gift. Each has received an inheritance, and no one can sell his portion or keep another's in perpetuity. All have a continued right to their own land (Lev. 25:23-24). Obviously such legislation, unique in history, would prevent the accumulation of gross injustices, if carried out.

Yet it is highly doubtful that the Jubilee Year, heralded by the blowing of the shofar (ram's horn), was ever kept according to these provisions.[6] Nevertheless, the concept of the Jubilee was kept alive in Israel's memory as a reminder of the kind of just social and religious community Yahweh desires. And in the later prophets, especially Second Isaiah, it becomes the symbol of the eschatological age.[7]

In all of this legal material, one basic theme is woven throughout: Yahweh is the defender of the poor and needy. He desires justice and mercy on behalf of the poor, the stranger, the fatherless and the widow. His words are a call to remembrance: "I am the Lord your God, who brought you forth out of the land of Egypt . . . to be your God" (Lev. 25:38).

The Prophetic Tradition

Doubtless the most familiar sections of the Old Testament on the theme of the poor are the prophetic warnings and judgments addressed to the wealthy and powerful during the various periods of

Israel's monarchy. It was especially during this time of the monarchy in both the northern and southern kingdoms that greater and greater social disparities developed, bringing with them increasing oppression and exploitation. Out of this social and political period of crisis in Israel emerged one of the most unique religious phenomena in the world's history, the prophetic movement. In the name of the God of Israel, who had called them and sometimes compelled them to be his spokesmen, the prophets directed their words against the social injustices of the people and rulers and became the staunch defenders of the poor and powerless. It is to their message that we now turn, even though with great brevity.

The Early Prophets: Amos, Hosea, Micah, Isaiah

The eighth-century prophets became the earliest prophetic spokesmen on behalf of the poor. Their critique against the social abuses of their society was grounded theologically in God's covenant with Israel, his act of election. This covenant had called for faithful obedience, as expressed in the Torah. But Israel had become indifferent and unfaithful to the covenant, and this unfaithfulness was most clearly evident to the prophets in the trampling upon the poor and the neglect of the needy.

The citing of the evidence against the people is long and all too familiar—unjust courts (Amos 5:12; Isa. 10:1-2; Jer. 5:28), fraudulent trade (Amos 8:4-5), unfair taxation (Amos 5:11-12), theft of land (Mic. 2:1-3), violence against the poor (Ezek. 16:48), wasteful affluence amid poverty (Amos 4:1, 6:4f.), selling debtors into slavery (Amos 2:6; 8:6), and even suffocating tithes (Isa. 3:14-15). The list could go on.

Listen to a few of the prophetic indictments: By Amos, against the north, around 750 B.C.

> Thus says the Lord: "For three transgressions of Israel, and for four, I will not revoke the punishment; because they sell the righteous for silver, and the needy for a pair of shoes—they that trample the head of the poor into the dust of the earth, and turn aside the way of the afflicted; a man and his father go in to the same maiden, so that my holy name is profaned" (2:6-7).

> "I hate, I despise your feasts, and I take no delight in your solemn assemblies. Even though you offer me your burnt offerings and cereal offerings, I will not accept them, and the peace offerings of your fatted beasts I will not look upon. Take away from me the

noise of your songs; to the melody of your harps I will not listen. But let justice roll down like waters, and righteousness like an ever-flowing stream" (5:21-24).

By Hosea, shortly after Amos:

Sow for yourselves righteousness, reap the fruit of steadfast love; break up your fallow ground, for it is the time to seek the Lord, that he may come and rain salvation upon you. You have plowed iniquity, you have reaped injustice, you have eaten the fruit of lies (10:12-13).

By Isaiah, against the south, around 700 B.C.

"When you come to appear before me, who requires of you this trampling of my courts? Bring no more vain offerings; incense is an abomination to me. New moon and sabbath and the calling of assemblies—I cannot endure iniquity and solemn assembly. Your new moons and your appointed feasts my soul hates; they have become a burden to me, I am weary of bearing them. When you spread forth your hands, I will hide my eyes from you; even though you make many prayers, I will not listen; your hands are full of blood. Wash yourselves; make yourselves clean; remove the evil of your doings from before my eyes; cease to do evil, learn to do good; seek justice, correct oppression; defend the fatherless, plead for the widow" (1:12-17).

The Lord has taken his place to contend, he stands to judge his people. The Lord enters into judgment with the elders and princes of his people: "It is you who have devoured the vineyard, the spoil of the poor is in your houses. What do you mean by crushing my people, by grinding the face of the poor?" says the Lord God of hosts (3:13-15).

By Micah, a younger contemporary of Isaiah:

Woe to those who devise wickedness and work evil upon their beds! When the morning dawns, they perform it, because it is in the power of their hand. They covet fields, and seize them; and houses, and take them away; they oppress a man and his house, a man and his inheritance (2:1-2).

And I said: Hear, you heads of Jacob and rulers of the house of Israel! Is it not for you to know justice?—you who hate the good and love the evil, who tear the skin from off my people, and their flesh from off their bones; who eat the flesh of my people, and flay their skin from off them, and break their bones in pieces, and chop them up like meat in a kettle, like flesh in a caldron (3:1-3).

These prophets all agree that social injustices are most indicative of a falling away from the covenant God! Thus they speak God's judgment and issue a call to repentance. Not always do they live in hope of Israel's change, yet they hold out the promise of forgiveness and the hope of restoration in the coming new age. Of this one thing, however, they are certain; God is on the side of the poor.

The Later Prophets: Jeremiah, Second Isaiah

What we learned of the earlier prophets is true also of the later ones. Of course, the specific message of the prophet must change to meet the times in which he and his people live and to address the needs that emerge in their historical setting.

Thus when Jeremiah is called to prophesy, the fate of the southern kingdom is all but sealed (627-580 B.C.). Jeremiah speaks to this situation, but in judgment and in grace. He knows Judah's day of reckoning has come, yet the rulers and people live on under false hopes. And they continue their oppression of the weak in their midst. Therefore Jeremiah proclaims the true knowledge of God which expresses itself in a just response to the cause of the needy and afflicted. In a particularly powerful passage, Jeremiah condemns King Jehoiakim, the son of good King Josiah, because of his luxurious expansion of his already luxurious palace.

> "Woe to him who builds his house by unrighteousness, and his upper rooms by injustice; who makes his neighbor serve him for nothing, and does not give him his wages; who says, 'I will build myself a great house with spacious upper rooms,' and cuts out windows for it, paneling it with cedar. . . . Did not your father eat and drink and do justice and righteousness? Then it was well with him. He judged the cause of the poor and needy; then it was well. Is not this to know me? says the Lord. But you have eyes and heart only for your dishonest gain, for shedding innocent blood, and for practicing oppression and violence" (Jer. 22:13-17).

After destruction befalls Judah at the hands of Nebuchadnezzar, the cruel Babylonian oppressor, the people are carried off to exile in Babylon. During this time another great prophet comes to the fore, the unknown author(s) of Isaiah 40–66.[8] His words mark the high point of the prophetic movement. Even though he is preoccupied with bringing a word of comfort to his people and with search-

ing out the meaning of their future, he also makes a powerful appeal
for justice and the cause of the poor.

> "Is not this the fast that I choose: to loose the bonds of wicked-
> ness, to undo the thongs of the yoke, to let the oppressed go free,
> and to break every yoke? Is it not to share your bread with the
> hungry, and bring the homeless poor into your house; when you
> seek the naked, to cover him, and not to hide yourself from your
> own flesh? Then shall your light break forth like the dawn,
> and your healing shall spring up speedily; your righteousness shall
> go before you, the glory of the Lord shall be your rear guard. Then
> you shall call, and the Lord will answer, you shall cry, and he will
> say, Here I am" (Isa. 58:6-9).

It is this same Second Isaiah who envisions the coming new age
as a time when God will send his anointed servant with the news of
good tidings to the afflicted (Isa. 61:1-2). This eschatological hope,
as we shall see, becomes the primary vehicle by which Luke interprets the ministry of Jesus in his gospel, with the help of the text
from Isaiah 58:6, which we have just quoted.

This survey should suffice to remind us how central is the theme
in the Old Testament prophets that because Yahweh is the defender
of the poor and needy, loyalty to the covenant requires social justice.
Israel's judgment and grace are in large measure based on its fidelity to God's demand for justice and mercy. When we turn to the
critique of Jesus toward the rich and powerful in Luke's gospel, we
dare not forget this powerful prophetic tradition. A straight line links
the two together, both in Jesus' words of blessing upon the poor and
his woes against the rich.

The Psalter

The poor also occupy a special place in the Psalter. In a variety
of ways, a chorus of voices within the Psalter extol Yahweh as the
One who extends his hand of protection to the poor and lowly, as
they cry out to him.[9]

There are several types of Psalms which especially contain this
motif. For example, in the Royal psalms it is the king who is appointed as the representative of Yahweh to uphold justice and care
for the needy.

> Give the king thy justice, O God, and thy righteousness for the royal
> Son! . . . May he defend the cause of the poor of the people, give

deliverance to the needy, and crush the oppressor! (Ps. 72:1, 4, cf. 82:1-4; 132:15).

In the psalms of lament and other petitionary psalms, the speaker often identifies himself as a poor man, who is confronted by his enemies or by severe afflictions. In this situation he cries to God for help and makes his appeal on the basis of God's promise to rescue the afflicted.

> Incline thy ear O Lord, and answer me, for I am poor and needy. Preserve my life, for I am godly; save thy servant who trusts in thee. . . . In the day of my trouble I call on thee, for thou dost answer me (Ps. 86:1-2, 7).

Or again,

> The Lord is a stronghold for the oppressed, a stronghold in times of trouble. And those who know thy name put their trust in thee, for thou, O Lord, hast not forsaken those who seek thee. . . . Be gracious to me, O Lord! Behold what I suffer from those who hate me. . . . For the needy shall not always be forgotten and the hope of the poor shall not perish forever (Ps. 9:9-10, 13, 18).

Also in the psalms of praise, God is extolled for rescuing the needy and bringing the unrighteous to ruin. Psalm 146 seems almost like a text from Luke's gospel:

> Happy is he whose help is the God of Jacob, whose hope is in the Lord his God, who made heaven and earth, the sea, and all that is in them; who keeps faith for ever; who executes justice for the oppressed; who gives food to the hungry. The Lord sets the prisoner free; the Lord opens the eyes of the blind. The Lord lifts up those who are bowed down; the Lord loves the righteous. The Lord watches over the sojourners, he upholds the widow and the fatherless; but the way of the wicked he brings to ruin (Ps. 146:5-9).

In many of these psalms, a collective sense of the poor occurs. Here the beseecher identifies himself either with a group within Israel or with Israel itself, who see themselves as standing in dire need of God in the face of their enemies. "Remember this, O Lord, how the enemy scoffs, and an impious people reviles thy name. . . . Do not forget the life of thy poor for ever. . . . Let not the downtrodden be put to shame; let the poor and needy praise thy name" (Ps. 74:18, 19, 21). The poor and downtrodden in this Psalm are Israel itself, and the enemy rival nations. However, it is not always possible to distinguish between the individual or a group as the speaker frequently identifies himself with his people or a cause. The same self-description of the whole community as "the poor" reoccurs also in the Qumran community which produced the Dead Sea scrolls, as we shall observe below.

But who are these enemies who afflict the poor and needy? And what is the concrete situation of the afflicted? The petitioners describe themselves as the afflicted (Ps. 25:16), needy (Ps. 35:10), lowly (Ps. 147:6), downtrodden (Ps. 74:21), meek (Ps. 87:11), poor (Ps. 40:18), orphans and widows (Ps. 68:6), little ones (Ps. 116:6), and even barren women (Ps. 113:9).[10] In some instances we can be certain that the distress involves economic and political hardships, with their consequent oppression and suffering. Yet the circle is wider than these social ills, since it also includes sickness and different kinds of moral and religious conflicts (e.g. despair, guilt, persecution). But in all of these situations, except for the penitential psalms where guilt is the person's own responsibility, the poor of the Psalms see themselves essentially as victims who cry out to God for relief and vindication.

This brings us to the most unique feature about the poor in the Psalms, namely the merging of identity between the socially poor and the religiously pious.[11] In effect the "poor" and the "pious" become synonymous terms, and when this happens the meaning of the poor becomes "those who place their total dependence upon God." "God, my trust is in you!" (Ps. 88:1-2). This type of stance defines most profoundly the meaning of the pious/poor in the Psalms.

This new development in the concept of the poor carries over into later intertestamental writings and even into the New Testament. In fact, there are some scholars who have sought to identify these pious/poor as a distinct religious movement that emerged within Judaism, which they call the *anawim,* from a Hebrew word for the poor. It has even been suggested that Jesus' own social and religious background is best understood from within this movement.[12] Others, however, doubt whether any one group can be so precisely linked to this designation. Yet, as we shall develop later, the religious piety and social circumstances of the *anawim* in the Psalms and other literature does have a distinctly familiar setting within the Lukan infancy narratives.

One important fact should never be forgotten, however. Even though it is true that we find a spiritualization of the concept of the poor in the Psalter, that is not all. The social and political life-settings are still there. The situations of distress are still those of literal poverty, persecution, oppression, affliction and the like. The poor are truly the victims of life and their enemies the powerful and well-to-do. What makes them *anawim,* is the fact that their hope is in God and their cries reach out to Yahweh with confidence in his promised deliverance.

Wisdom Literature

This fascinating literature, which has been the object of intense study in recent years, also has much to say about the plight of the poor. We noted earlier in this chapter how the Wisdom literature shares a tradition that regards wealth as a good gift from the hand of God and correspondingly condemns the poor as lazy and careless, with beggars held in special contempt.

Yet this is not the full story. There is also a sharp criticism of the rich, coupled with appeals to share generously with the poor. The authors are keenly aware that the rich take unfair advantage of the poor. "A rich man will exploit you if you can be of use to him, but if you are in need he will forsake you." (Sir. 13:4, cf. vv. 3-7) "Wild asses in the wilderness are the prey of lions; likewise the poor are pastures for the rich" (Sir. 13:19). Or again, there is considerable sympathy for the poor man's plight, his loneliness and humiliation (Eccles. 9:16). Therefore we find frequent admonition to the rich to help the poor. Benevolence and almsgiving are praised, and stinginess reproved (Prov. 22:9; 21:13; Sir. 14:3; 4:1-8). Above all, God is recognized as the defender of the poor. "He who oppresses a poor man insults his Maker," while "He who is kind to the poor lends to the Lord" (Prov. 14:31; 19:17). "Do not rob the poor, because he is poor, or crush the afflicted at the gate; for the Lord will plead their cause and despoil of life those who despoil them" (Prov. 22:22f.; cf. Sir. 4:6).

Finally, in addition to these familiar themes, the Wisdom writers are fond of another motif, namely, the anticipation of a reversal of fortunes between the devout and the ungodly. This reversal motif often includes a change of status between the rich and the poor. For the present moment, the pious/poor may be in want, while the ungodly enjoy good fortune. Yet the day is surely coming, when the tables will be turned. Therefore we find repeated admonitions not to be upset by the present prosperity of the sinner. "Fret not yourself because of evildoers, and be not envious of the wicked; for the evil man has no future; the lamp of the wicked will be put out" (Prov. 24:19-20). Or we find reassurances that riches lead to sin and that the riches themselves will be taken away (Prov. 23:4-6; Eccles. 5:12-17; Sir. 11:18-19; cf. Luke 12:19). An extended argument of this same reversal theme occurs in Psalm 37, one of the so-called Wisdom psalms. To counter the discouragement of the godly poor in the face of the obvious prosperity of the ungodly, the author argues at length that soon the prosperous will "fade like the grass" (Ps. 37:2).

Thus the Wisdom literature, too, takes up the cause of the poor and challenges the life and practice of the rich. Yet there is an ambiguity about wealth that runs through much of this literature, so that it lacks a sense of radical justice, such as we hear from the prophets or the legal traditions. The afflictions of the poor are met primarily with the assertion that God will not let the righteous suffer forever. Practical experience, however, does not always match this "naive" assurance. In short, we find no eschatological vision which posits a faith in a God who will one day make all things right and new. This awaits the New Testament vision, as embodied in the person and message of Jesus.

THE POOR IN THE INTERTESTAMENTAL PERIOD

Although the Old Testament was the Bible of Jesus and the Bible of the early church, we dare not overlook the importance of the period immediately preceding the New Testament era.[13] Major historical events in Jewish and world history occurred during this time which directly influenced the New Testament. This period also gave birth to a number of crucial religious developments that shaped the message of Jesus and without whose knowledge we cannot fully bridge the gulf between the Old and New Testaments. Of special importance was the rise of distinct religious movements within Judaism—Pharisees, Sadducees, Zealots, and Essenes—as well as a new way of looking at the world and God's relation to it, preserved chiefly in the numerous apocalyptic writings produced in this period. We shall attempt a brief survey of this period's literature and its reflection of attitudes toward wealth and poverty.

Apocrypha and Pseudepigrapha

The attitude toward the poor in this literature [14] is not uniform.

Jewish apocrypha

One group takes up themes found in the earlier Wisdom literature, sympathizing with the hard life of the poor and demanding pity and the giving of alms. A passage seemingly echoed in the teachings of Jesus occurs in Tobit. Tobit advises his son,

> Give alms from your possessions to all who live uprightly, and do not let your eye begrudge the gift when you make it. Do not turn your face away from any poor man, and the face of God will not be turned away from you. . . . So you will be laying up a good treasure for yourself against the day of necessity. . . . Give of your bread to the hungry, and of your clothing to the naked. Give all your surplus to charity, and do not let your eye begrudge the gift when you make it. . . . Do not be afraid, my son, because we have become poor. You have great wealth if you fear God and refrain from every sin and do what is pleasing in his sight (Tob. 4:7, 9, 16, 21).

This passage is representative of Jewish piety of the highest sort as it existed in the intertestamental period. Almsgiving as an act of charity became prized as an unsurpassed meritorious deed. "For charity delivers from death and keeps you from entering the darkness; and for all who practice it charity is an excellent offering in the presence of the Most High" (Tob. 4:10-11). In other similar literature, examples of generosity are often cited and held up for pious emulation. Especially do ancient biblical figures become types of charitable models; Isaac, Joseph, and above all, Job.

Apocalyptic

Another group of writings singularly important for our purposes deals with poverty in an eschatological context. Most of this literature belongs to the apocalyptic genre, which flowered particularly in the intertestamental period. The essence of what they promise

is that in the coming new age all injustice will be set right by the
direct action of God. These writings are oriented to the imminent
end of the world. This includes the removal of poverty and divine
judgment against the unjust rich.[15] One writer, in the context of
the messianic woes preceding the end-time, envisions a period of
intense conflict between the rich and poor, princes and beggars,
until the poor are finally set above the rich (*Jub.* 23:19, 30). Even
the rabbinic literature preserves traditions that say poverty will
vanish in the coming age, though a few later traditions think
otherwise. In a moving Pharisaic work of the first century B.C., the
pious poor, who suffer martyr-like in this age, wait expectantly on
the Lord for their deliverance in the coming Age (Song of Sol.
5:2; 10:6; 13:10; 16:14-15).

However the most interesting piece of apocalyptic literature
comes from a writer who adopts the viewpoint of the oppressed
poor, and who eagerly anticipates the reversal of their social and
political status in the coming eschaton.[16] The poor with whom the
author identifies view themselves as the righteous *anawim,* who
live under severe oppression by the rich and powerful. But they
look forward to the coming judgment and its obvious reversal of
fortunes. A series of woes against the rich seem to parallel the
Lukan beatitudes and woes, though they are much expanded.

Woe to you, ye rich, for ye have trusted in your riches, and from
your riches shall ye depart . . . (*Enoch* 94:8).

Woe to you, ye mighty, who with might oppress the righteous,
for the day of your destruction is coming . . . (*Enoch* 96:8).

However one note is quite unlike the woes and teaching of the
gospels, and that is the note of revenge and obvious delight in the
coming judgment of the rich. The righteous poor are told, "Fear
not the sinners, ye righteous; for again will the Lord deliver them
into your hands, that ye may execute judgment upon them according to your desires" (*Enoch* 95:3). Or again, "Woe to you who love
the needs of unrighteousness; wherefore do ye hope for good help
unto yourselves? Know that ye shall be delivered into the hands
of the righteous, and they shall cut off your necks and slay you
and have no mercy upon you" (*Enoch* 98:12-13). Here is hope for

justice run riot, the cry for vindication become a cry for vengeance! While this is understandable in the light of cruel oppression and gross injustice, it is a motif that we do not find in the gospels, despite the common theme of a coming reversal. For now, it is important only to hear the expectation of a future eschatological reversal, which becomes even more explicit in the teaching of Jesus.

The Dead Sea Scrolls and the Qumran Community

A third group of writings from the intertestamental period are the Dead Sea Scrolls, whose writing and preservation was the work of the ascetic and apocalyptic community of Qumran, located on the northwest shore of the Dead Sea. Their discovery, beginning in 1947, constitutes one of the most exciting chapters in biblical archaeology and scholars and lay persons alike have expressed great interest in their life and beliefs, particularly since they existed as contemporaries with Jesus.[18] Most identify the community of Qumran with the Essene movement in Palestine.

Our interest lies in their attitude toward possessions. According to their basic document, the Rule of the Community (1QS), one who desired to join the community after a two-year probation was required to turn over one's entire wealth to a common fund (1QS 5:2). There were severe penalties for falsification and waste. This common treasury was controlled by the priestly hierarchy, "the sons of Aaron." Out of this fund all needs of the community were met; distinctions between the rich and poor were thereby erased. While the life-style of the community was monastic and ascetic, there is no indication in the scrolls that property was regarded as intrinsically evil. Rather, the renunciation of wealth and possessions was undertaken for the good of the community and the basic intent of this economic pooling and sharing of resources was a theological one: to reflect a form of life which God himself will establish in the coming age.

Interpreters have naturally been struck by the similarities between the use of property in Qumran and the description of the early church in Acts, which shared "all things in common" (Acts 2:44; 4:32). There may be some direct lines of influence; certainly the radical sharing of possessions and its distribution by leaders are common elements. Yet the monastic/ascetic life-style of Qumran is quite alien to the early church and, as we shall see, the reason for the common sharing in Acts is to take care of the poor, while in Qumran it is preparation for the coming age.[19]

According to Josephus and Philo, two contemporary Jewish writers, some Essenes also lived in the villages of Palestine and owned their own houses and worked at trades.[20] They often provided other Essenes with food and shelter as the need arose. So their attitude was not uniform.

Of special interest is the fact that in some of the Dead Sea Scrolls, especially the Thanksgiving Psalms *(Hodayot)*, we find the community referring to itself as "the community of the poor." Some commentators have singled this out as Qumran's favorite term of self-identity, or at least as a favorite of some members. This is unlikely, however, since the term is used infrequently and is only one of many self-designations of the community.[21] Nevertheless the use of the self-description "poor" is revealing. Like the term poor in the biblical psalms, it has here both a social and spiritual dimension. Socially, it points to their economic poverty, as well as their sense of isolation. This latter may also be linked to the community's acute sense of persecution. Yet the poor has definite spiritual overtones as well, since the poor are also called the "elect," the "righteous" and the "people of the covenant." Above all, these poor have placed their trust in God and he in turn acts on their behalf. When enemies press them, the poor know God will come to their rescue. At the end, a moment expected in this generation, it is the poor who will inherit the earth and rule over the nations (Ps. 37:9, 11Q).

Thus the poor of Qumran appear to resemble in many ways the *anawim* mentality of the pious poor, who look to God for the ultimate fulfillment of their deepest hopes and desires. However the expectation of Qumran, unlike the earlier Psalms of the Old Testament, is throbbing with eschatological intensity and anticipation. In this sense it comes closer to the piety of the *anawim* in the infancy narratives of Luke 1–2. Only the aspect of fulfillment is missing. In each case, the poor represent those who are socially, as well as spiritually, the lowly and who therefore place their confidence for the future in the promises of God.

The Rabbinic Literature

One further background resource for understanding the attitude toward the poor in the time of Jesus and the early church is provided in the rabbinic literature. None of this literature, which eventually grew to massive proportions, was put into written form until some years after A.D. 70, and the process of added interpretation and writing-down continued for centuries until its completion in the two great Jewish Talmuds, Jerusalem (A.D. 350) and Babylonian (A.D. 500).

Because of the great time span involved and the long period of oral transmission, it is extremely difficult to determine what traditions originated in the pre-A.D. 70 period and what followed. However we can make a few observations with some confidence concerning typical rabbinic attitudes contemporary with the time of Jesus.[22]

In the pre-70 period most of the rabbis were themselves economically poor, depending on their own trade and the gifts of their students and followers for financial aid. (Only later do some rabbis enjoy considerable wealth.) The famous Rabbi Hillel, e.g., came from a very poor family and worked throughout much of his career as a day laborer. So they understood the lot of the poor. But whereas one might think this would evoke much sympathy for the poor, the evidence is hard to come by. They seemed to regard their own poverty as an evil, often quoting Proverbs 15:15, "all the days of the afflicted are evil," or saying Job prayed for suffering rather than poverty!

But even more difficult is their attitude toward the poor masses, especially the *am haaretz*.[23] For two reasons at least, the rabbis and the *am haaretz* seem to be in conflict with each other. One is the plain fact that the *am haaretz* were simple, uneducated people, unlike the learned rabbis. The rabbis were thus tempted to look down on the illiterate masses, and were responded to in kind. The literature shows strained relationships between them as well as periodic outbursts of hostility. The second and more important point of conflict had to do with the failure of the *am haaretz* to observe the law. Since keeping the Law depended in large part on knowing the Law, the masses were often ignorant of what was required. And even with respect to what they did know, they often paid little heed. So we find more than once in rabbinic literature the words of contempt, "the cursed *(am haaretz)* who know not the Law." For this reason, too, some rabbis went out of their way to avoid dealing with them. In court, likewise, the poor man's word did not count. In truth, the masses' illiteracy and ignorance and struggle for physical survival made it all but impossible to know the Law, much less keep it.

It is probably not true, as some have conjectured, that the *am haaretz* were excluded from the true Israel or regarded as having no share in the life to come.[24] They were still "sons of Abraham." And it was in the post-A.D. 70 period that the conflict worsened between the increasing influential (and wealthy) rabbis and the *am haaretz*. Yet there seems to be little awareness in the earliest rabbinic literature that the poor are the primary objects of God's love and compassion. This particular awareness and its resultant special concern for their lot, did come to expression, however, in the life of at least one first century rabbi. This rabbi, in fact, became known for his compassion toward the multitudes, whom he saw as sheep in need of a shepherd (Mark 6:34). And it is this rabbi's life story in relation to the poor that we want to illumine in the next chapters.

We have sketched a rich, though varied, tradition regarding possessions and the poor in the Old Testament and late Judaism. Beginning with the positive affirmation of wealth as a blessing of God, we moved into the more central motif of this tradition, the portrayal of the covenant God as the defender of the poor and needy, a motif found alike in the legal, prophetic, hymnic and wisdom literature. The development of this basic affirmation included a word of divine judgment against the exploiters of the poor and the perpetrators of social injustice, as well as the divine promise of God's righteous vindication of the poor, which in the later literature offered the hope of a coming age of justice and righteousness. In the Psalter we also noted the emergence of an *anawim* piety, in which social and religious elements merge into a concept of the poor as those who live in complete dependence upon God. Finally, the picture of later Judaism becomes more complex, as the practice of almsgiving, a part of normative Jewish piety, mixes with apocalyptic hopes for a coming reversal and with a growing rabbinic separation for the poor. Let us now pick up the story of that one rabbi, around whom the hopes of many poor came alive.

2

Jesus and the Poor

In this chapter we shall describe something of the origins of Jesus and the movement that gathered around him from a social and economic perspective. While we are keenly aware that the Jesus-movement cannot be reduced to a sociological phenomenon, there is still much value in attempting to grasp some of the sociological factors at work in order to hear more clearly the message of Jesus, both as it provided words of comfort and hope to people in need and as it challenged others to reevaluate their values and securities in light of the coming kingdom.

Political and Social Unrest in First Century Palestine

To understand the first century A.D. we must know something about the period that immediately preceded it. Politically, the time from 167-63 B.C. was a proud period in Jewish history. The defilement of the Temple by the hated Seleucid ruler, Antiochus Epiphanes in 167 B.C. sparked a long-simmering revolt. Known as the Maccabean revolt, it succeeded in recapturing the Temple in 164 B.C. and restoring its ancient sacrificial worship.[1] Not long after, in 160 B.C., the Seleucids granted independence to Israel, a reality that existed until the Romans intervened in the civil strife that broke out in 63 B.C. This time of the Maccabean rule, however, though politically a source of pride, was not without severe conflict and social unrest. The Maccabeans' growing desire for power and territory conflicted sharply with the religious goals of their early supporters. Both the Pharisaic and Essene movements came into existence during this period largely as a protest against the political and secular direction of the upper classes, and sharp conflicts broke

out among them, including the ghastly crucifixion of 800 leading
Pharisees by the Maccabean tyrant, Alexander Jannaeus. The arrival of the Roman legions under Pompey was actually requested
by some leading Jews as a desperate hope for peace amid civil
strife.

Unfortunately, the Romans sacked the city, violated the sacred
precincts of the Temple and never relinquished their control of
Palestine again. From 37-4 B.C. they ruled through their loyal puppet, Herod the Great, by race Idumean, by forcible circumcision,
Jewish. Afterwards they ruled through a combination of appointed
tetrarchs, ethnarchs and procurators. The reign of Herod the Great,
though hated by most Jews and especially by the pious, actually
brought about fairly stable conditions in Palestine. Herod kept the
peace, brought a measure of economic prosperity, constructed
whole cities, among them the beautiful seaport, Caesarea, and built
a number of magnificent edifices which even his despisers had to
grudgingly admire, most famous, of course, the splendid restoration
of the Temple and its court area. But poverty and other social/po-
litical tensions were never far away, and the luxury of the Herodian
court and its pagan life-style, as well as the omnipresent threat of
Rome's legions, kept Jewish resistance simmering.

After Herod's death, things gradually changed for the worse, culminating in the Zealot revolt of A.D. 66, which led in four terrible
years to the destruction of Jerusalem and the leveling of the Temple
by the legions of Vespasian and Titus. To this day one can see the
evidence of the destruction, as Romans scarcely left one stone upon
another. Social upheaval is documented in many ways during these
increasingly tense and tragic years. The Roman census of A.D. 6 led
to the first recorded act of organized Zealot resistance, led by Judas
the Galilean, a man from Jesus' own province. Although it didn't
get far, the movement remained alive. Much of its zeal came from
its hope of repeating the triumphs of the Maccabees. Moreover,
the resistance increased not only because of the inbred hatred
against the Roman oppressors and their inept puppets, like Pilate,
but also as a result of unsettled conditions in the land. Many who
joined the resistance were unemployed, drifters, desperately poor,
even though Josephus, the contemporary Jewish historian who despised the Zealots, covers up this fact by calling them "brigands
and murderers." [2] Furthermore, the constant guerilla warfare left

the land in battered shape, and actually created the extremes of
poverty that fed the Zealot uprising.

Josephus also tells us that Herod Antipas, the son of Herod the
Great, who ruled Galilee from 4 B.C.-A.D. 39, built the beautiful city
of Tiberius, on the western side of the Sea of Galilee, and populated
the city with outsiders, including many beggars.[3] Apparently beggars were in plentiful supply. We also read about two great famines
that struck the land, one in 25 B.C. and another in A.D. 46-48 (cf.
Acts 11:27). Although they were caused by severe drought, their
seriousness was multiplied by the general condition of want that
existed from year to year and for which no provision was made.

Finally, we find evidence of constant tension between the upper
and lower classes. Already in Herod the Great's reign, constant
complaints were made against the opulence and splendor of the
royal court, in contrast to the growing economic decline of the
masses. We know of many tensions between the high-priestly families and other wealthy members of the Sanhedrin and the poor
priests and common people. Jesus' cleansing of the Temple was not
without its social appeal to the poor. Perhaps most revealing of conditions is Josephus' description of an event that occurred in Jerusalem at the outbreak of the Jewish War in A.D. 66. He tells us that the
first thing the Zealot leaders did to gain the support of the masses
and to conquer opposition of the upper classes was to raid the city
archives, where all the records of debts were kept, and to burn the
ledgers! [4] The significance socially of this act, perhaps intended as
a kind of Jubilee year proclamation, is not to be overlooked. The
people by and large were oppressed not only by the Romans but
by their own vested hierarchy, both religious and political.

It was in this kind of social and political scene that Jesus of
Nazareth lived and died. A Galilean, he must have heard with his
own ears the Zealot call to freedom and arms. And he must have
seen with his own eyes the grinding poverty of the many and their
exploitation by the few. The time was ripe for social upheaval and
revolution. Therefore Jesus' own words must be heard and understood as much as possible within this social setting.

Social Classes

But what was society like in first century Palestine? Who were
the rich and who were the poor, and what was their situation? We

can only offer a brief sketch of what is known, yet it should be enough to catch a glimpse of the class structure in Jesus' world.

There were, naturally, the rich. Out in front was the royal court, of which Herod the Great's court is the best example. We have already alluded to his affluent style of life. Even today visitors to Masada, the fortress built on top of a massive outcropping of rock alongside the Dead Sea, are awed by his three-tiered palatial residence on its northern tip, complete with baths and mosaics. In Caesarea, he lived in a palatial residence of white marble imported from Egypt. His Caesarean games, held every six years, attracted competitors and visitors from all over the Roman Empire. One could go on at great length to describe his royal life. His sources of income for his extravagant rule came from taxes, from personal property, from confiscated goods of leading men convicted of wrongdoing, from bribes and gifts and from a copper mine in Cyprus. Even a puppet ruler in poor Palestine found power an easy access to wealth. But subsequent procurators could not live like Herod's court or that of his sons. Yet their high level of living contrasted vividly with the populace.

Others belonging to the wealthy class were merchants and large landowners, tax-farmers, bankers and families of inherited means. We know, too, that the Sanhedrin had rich members, though this was not true of all. And then there was the priestly hierarchy and their associates, composed chiefly of the high priestly families. Their wealth came largely from the Temple tax required of Jews throughout the world, and from the sale of sacrificial animals and the profits of money changers. Religion paid, even though expensive bribes were necessary to stay in office. This group was well known for its love of feasts and banquetry, which consumed much of their income. In some cases they even practiced polygamy, which was permitted by law, but too expensive for most. Interestingly, the Gospels indicate that Jesus himself was no stranger at their homes or their feasts.

The middle class was not nearly as large as is normally true in western, industrialized societies, yet it did exist in its own way. Here we find the retail traders who kept the crowded shops in the bazaars, and the small tradesmen and craftsmen who owned and worked in their own shops. Each village, great and small, had some of these. However, the middle class in Jerusalem fared the best, due to the large influx of pilgrims for the feasts. To serve their needs a large catering trade existed for providing food, drink, clothing and animals. Perhaps it should be remembered that the feast days were times of celebration. For the Passover, it was commanded that the second tithe be spent only in Jerusalem, and that it be used on meat and strong drink or anything else they desired. Josephus says, "they feasted the seven whole days and spared no expense." [5] They were especially fond of wine and meats and the wives were often favored by gifts of fine white linen.

Perhaps the priests can be included in this middle sector as well. At least some priests and Levites were well educated and well off. Yet by and large the priests were honored, but poor. The law prescribed sufficiently for their needs out of the income from sacrificial victims and from the various tithes. But there was clearly a considerable gap between what was required by law and what was actually received. Josephus admits that the priests were often reduced to poverty because some of the people were indifferent. At times they were even forced by their poverty to go into the fields and try to demand of the people to pay their tithes! So their life was often lived on the thin edge of poverty, contrary to the status and wealth of the High priestly families.

The poor belonged essentially to two groups: those who sought to earn their own livelihood, and those who lived off subsidy. Among the former were slaves and day laborers. While the rural areas had few slaves, many lived as domestic servants in the larger cities. Jerusalem even had its own auction block. Whether there were Jewish slaves has been disputed, yet the evidence seems to say yes. Gentile slaves usually were circumcised, except in the royal court. However, the number of slaves was not large compared to other nations. The day laborers were far more numerous. They depended on each day's work for board and keep. They earned an average of one denarius per day, with keep. The famous rabbi, Hillel, once told how as a young student he did not eat the days he found no work.[6] The picture of day laborers in the Matthean parable, waiting patiently in the market place for work, was true to life (Matt. 20:2, 9). Among the poor living on the poverty line should also be mentioned the *am haaretz*, the people of the land. Either as small landowners or as tenants for large landowners, they did their best to get by with the minimum required for life and health. But they

were overburdened with taxes, tithes and rent and so often fell
hopelessly into debt.

Even worse off, however,, was the second group of poor, who
lived either partially or fully on relief. Lowest on the scale were
the beggars. Jerusalem in particular was filled with beggars who
gathered at the gates of the old city or near the Temple precinct.
They included the sick, blind, lame, lepers and the destitute. A
scrawny mother with her hungry babe in arms would plead for
help. Since almsgiving was encouraged, they often got something.
Pathetic, without hope, socially and religiously ostracized, beggars were constant reminders of one's inhumanity toward others.
We meet them often in Jesus' parables, in his healings, or at the
Beautiful Gate of the Temple (Acts 3:2-3, 10). From Josephus we
also learn that there were many unemployed poor and drifters,
people who were prone to follow any leader who promised them
board and a sword, and sometimes even a messianic revolution.

A different kind of poor were the fatherless and widows, the
victims of ill fortune, who needed social care and regularly received it. The orphan's inheritance was carefully kept, and widows had relief means open to them. As we will see, this concern
for widows carried over into the early church.

Here, too, the scribes or rabbis can be mentioned. They were
not paid for their teaching. Hence most had trades to assist them;
(e.g., Shammai, a carpenter; Hillel, day laborer; Paul, a tentmaker).
Yet they usually needed more and so accepted gifts and hospitality
for their services and sometimes even received aid from the poor
tithe. Jesus' indictment of the scribes, "who devour widow's houses"
(Mark 12:40; Luke 20:47) may not necessarily mean that they
cheated or defrauded widows, but they certainly imposed on their
hospitality.[7] At times, women of means provided regularly for their
care. Therefore, while the scribes do not belong in the same class
as the beggars and unemployed, they did constitute a class of people
who were largely dependent on others for their support.

From this description of the social classes of Jesus' time, we see
the extremes of wealth and poverty with the poor by far the majority. Their concrete needs and hopes would obviously be on the
mind of anyone who came to announce "good news to the poor."
But before we begin to look at this possibility, let us see how the
poor were provided for in first century Palestine.

According to Law, the poor must themselves pay the temple tax and the first-born tax. Yet other tax relief aid was provided for them. For example, the poor tax required that every third and sixth year the tithe of one's produce must be stored up for use by the poor. It was then to be distributed to those in need; widow, orphan, Levite, stranger. But it was often neglected. The rule also remained in effect in Jesus' time to allow the needy to pick the left-overs from fields and orchards and vineyards, and whatever grows during the Sabbatical year. All this must have helped.

Yet voluntary giving provided even more aid. Supreme on the list was the admonition to give alms. In rabbinic teaching almsgiving acquired a preeminent status and along with works of love was believed to gain merit in the next world. To give alms liberally was said to bring forth fruits in this world and to generate capital for the age to come.[8] A special mark of Pharisaic piety was generous almsgiving and the extension of tithes (Luke 18:12). In Jewish missionary preaching, proselytes were especially urged to give alms as a work of merit (Acts 10:2; Luke 7:5).

Voluntary giving was also practiced in other ways. One such was the custom to make a generous distribution to the poor at high feast days, such as Passover or the Feast of Purim (John 13:29). Another was the practice of spending up to one-half of the second tithe in Jerusalem for the poor. Still another was the existence of a number of religious groups who made it their duty to aid the poor, among them the Essenes, Pharisaic fellowships *(Haberim)* and hellenistic Jews of the diaspora living in Jerusalem.

Lastly, a systematic approach to helping the poor, begun in the diaspora, was also imported to Palestine, probably by the time of Jesus. The synagogue was the center for its practice. It consisted of weekly and daily care of the poor. The weekly care was given to the resident poor of the city, in the form of food and clothing. The daily care was provided to the transient poor in the form of food. Among the Gentiles, the Jewish practice of charity gained much admiration and helped attract many proselytes. It is possible that this system was in part also borrowed by the early church, as the charitable system described in Acts 6 indicates.

It can be seen that the poor were not without help in the Jewish society of Jesus' day. The commands of the Old Testament and God's repeated confirmation of his concern for the poor still had its power-

ful ongoing effect. Yet other signs indicate that the poor were not
receiving the attention, compassion and help, as God had plainly
intended. They were despised by the religious teachers and excluded from the most sacred precincts. They were far too overburdened
with laws and taxes and with systematic fleecing of their goods and
property. The rich and wealthy gave from their abundance, at best,
but not beyond. In fact, Jewish law itself set limits to the amount
of charity one could practice.[9] No one advocated total abandonment
for the sake of the poor or the cause of the needy! To go beyond
law and custom was not encouraged. This awaited, apparently, a
new impetus and a new motivation, something which came into
being in the preaching and teaching of a rabbi from Nazareth.

Jesus and His Disciples

Where does Jesus himself fit into the above description of the
social strata in Palestine? Jeremias has argued strongly that Jesus
should be identified with the lower classes and in particular with
the *am haaretz*.[10] As evidence he points to the fact that Jesus' Pharisaic opponents regard him as one of the "unlearned" and ridicule
his failure to keep the Law (John 7:15). Moreover, his own life-
style, without house or home and family and dependent on the daily
support of a few followers of means, show conclusively that he belonged to the poor, economically and socially.

But this conclusion has recently been challenged.[11] If the tradition that Joseph was a carpenter carries historical veracity, as we
have no reason to doubt, then Jesus' family actually belonged to the
middle structure of his society, to the small traders and artisans.
This does not necessarily mean that they had an easy or comfortable living, however. Their offering of two turtle doves at the time
of Jesus' presentation as the first-born would indicate that their income level qualified them to offer the poor person's sacrifice.[12]
Still, by vocation and by social status they fit into the lower middle
class of people who provided sufficient means from their own trade
for their necessities.

How Jesus should be regarded during his public ministry is another question. In Mark 6:3 he is called the carpenter, the son of
Mary, with brothers and sisters also living in his hometown. Most
likely he had adopted the trade of his father, which was customary
for the first-born.[13] But there is no evidence that Jesus practiced

his trade during his public ministry. The vocation most appropriate to his activity and life-style during this period is that of a scribe. And while the scribes were highly esteemed in the eyes of the people, socially and economically they belonged to the poorer classes, since they had to depend on charity for their primary means of support.

We know that Jesus and his disciples received and accepted hospitality as a regular means of support. When Jesus sent his disciples out to preach and to heal he made them fully dependent on the hospitality of those who received them, quoting a time honored principle, "the laborer deserves his food" (Matt. 10:10; Luke 9:4; 10:7-8; cf. 1 Cor. 9:14; Gal. 6:6). We also know it was considered meritorious to show hospitality to a scribe, as well as to offer him a share in one's property. Jesus' himself frequently accepted the hospitality of others, not only at banquets in the homes of the wealthy but in the homes of his own followers, as Peter's mother-in-law (Mark 1:31), or the sisters at Bethany (Luke 10:38-42; John 11:1). Moreover, Luke tells us specifically that Jesus and his disciples received financial aid from a group of Galilean women, whose support continued even when he went up to Jerusalem for the last days of his life (Luke 8:1-3; 23:49, 55; 24:1-2, 10, 22; Acts 1:14). We further learn that Jesus and his closest followers lived from a common purse. Without any private income of their own from the time they accepted Jesus' call to follow him, the disciples placed the gifts of others into their common fund and from this they purchased their daily needs, paid the temple tax, helped the poor and celebrated the great feast days. Judas Iscariot's role as pursekeeper is well-known (John 13:29).

Whether a common purse was practiced among other rabbis and pupils is uncertain; this may be an innovation on Jesus' part. Yet we know that there were Pharisaic groups which practiced communal sharing and distribution to the poor and that likewise Essenes shared freely of their substance with other Essenes, even though they still retained private property. What is important for us to see is that Jesus and his disciples belonged to those groups in society which did not produce their own economic sustenance, but rather by their unique service lived from the respect and gratitude and charity of others. This placed them socially and economically in the lower strata of society in the public years, and doubtless brought them into close identification with the conditions and life-style of the poor. In this respect they were essentially one with them.

While we have concentrated chiefly on Jesus' social status, we should also inquire about the status of his closest disciples. Of those whose former occupations are mentioned, the fishermen belonged to the lower middle class. Of the two pairs of brothers, Peter and Andrew, James and John, the latter's business seems more profitable, since hired workers were also employed (Mark 1:20). The tax collector, Levi/Matthew, was not a chief tax collector like Zacchaeus, hence probably was not wealthy. Although the reference to Simon the Canaanean, or Zealot (Mark 3:18; Luke 6:15) links him directly to the patriotic movement against foreign oppression, an interesting mix with a tax collector, it does not reveal his social class, though many who joined the movement were from the lower class.[14] Nor do we have any certainty about the origin of Judas Iscariot, other than his probable Judean origin.[15] His supervision of the common fund offers no helpful clues, other than to stress his greed. Of the rest we know nothing with certainty regarding their social status or origin.

What we do know is that their encounter with Jesus and subsequent call to follow him led to the abandonment of their former possessions and family relations, at least during the active ministry of Jesus. During their full-time discipleship, they shared Jesus' lifestyle, without any permanent place to lay their head or without any private income or property of their own (Matt. 8:20/Luke 9:58). They were poor by deliberate choice and by virtue of their call on behalf of the kingdom.

Jesus' Appeal to the Poor

Having sketched something concerning the sociological setting in Palestine in the time of Jesus as well as the place of Jesus and his closest followers within this setting, we now want to show by a careful study of the gospel traditions the degree to which the activity of Jesus attracted the poor to his cause. This is admittedly not an easy task for several reasons. In the first place, the attempt to describe the historical situation in Jesus' own ministry is a hazardous undertaking as contemporary New Testament studies have aptly demonstrated. We recognize the problems involved; yet we are not convinced that we can say nothing. Since historical reconstruction is always an inexact science, one can only state one's case on the basis of the evidence that is available.

Another reason for caution is that the gospel writers themselves provide us with only fragmentary insights into the social condition of those attracted to Jesus and the way in which his ministry met their needs. But Jesus' preaching did not occur in a vacuum and though its basic content had to do with the dawn of the Kingdom through his life and deeds, this content was filled with promise and hope for the lowly and needy. This we desire to demonstrate. A further caution stems from the fact that a primarily sociological reading of the texts has already been done more than once, with the results not always consistent with the gospel's intent.[16] With these cautions in mind, our purpose is to illumine more fully the sociological life-setting of the gospel texts, in order to understand more clearly the message of Jesus in its original context.

The evidence for the original Jesus movement as a movement among the economically and socially poor of Palestine comes from several directions.

The Multitudes

There is evidence at all levels of the gospel tradition, Mark, Q, L and M, that Jesus' fundamental appeal was to the masses. He was known throughout Galilee as a teacher and healer and his repute extended even to some neighboring Gentile territories (regions of Syrophoenicia, Decapolis). The description of Jesus' popularity as he moved from village to village, teaching in synagogues, debating in the marketplace and healing the sick brought to him, though preserved in forms shaped by two or three decades of oral preaching, still have the ring of authenticity. Striking, too, is the way in which the note of authority was recognized in Jesus' teaching, in comparison to other scribes and Pharisees, a fact commentators believe recalls historical truth.[17] This authority duly impressed, if not amazed, the crowds and other observers. Even his critics acknowledged his appeal and his concern to speak and do the truth, regardless of what others thought (Mark 12:14). As a result, the masses flocked to hear him, day after day.

Who were these multitudes? Obviously they included people of mixed social strata; yet the predominant evidence would indicate that they came largely from the lower, perhaps even uneducated classes. This is probably inherent already in the terms "people" or "crowd." But other lines of evidence point in this direction also. Josephus gives several examples of self-appointed prophets or messiahs, who suddenly appear, gather a following and stir up enthusiasm for their cause, until the Romans or others disperse them.[18] Although Jesus' appearance does not offer a perfect comparison, similar messianic enthusiasm by the multitudes seems probable at some points in Jesus' Galilean ministry (John 6:15). We should also recall that John the Baptist attracted a wide following during his wilderness ministry, a group consisting largely of those opposed to the religious and political authorities of the middle and upper classes. Crowds, tax collectors and soldiers are specifically mentioned by Luke in a passage that could well reflect Jesus' ministry (Luke 3:10-14; cf. 7:24-30).

The crowds often are composed of the sick and possessed. While sickness strikes everyone, it seems as though the most unfortunate persons are brought to Jesus, so that their sickness and poverty go hand in hand. The exceptions are duly noted by the evangelists, such as a centurion's servant or daughter of a ruler of the synagogue. Most of the sick are the suffering poor—the blind, lame, crippled, paralyzed—and the lepers who along with beggars cry out for mercy to the son of David. In a society where the sick largely stood under the shadow of guilt, these suffering poor appear to constitute the largest group responding to the ministry of Jesus. We also find that the gospels consistently distinguish the crowds from other groups in Galilee and Judea, such as the scribes and Pharisees, the Sadducees, the Sanhedrin, and other religious and political authorities. Jesus did not appeal to the upper classes; in fact, his ministry was perceived by those in positions of honor and esteem as a religious and political threat. Likewise, the most bitter attacks of Jesus are directed primarily against the establishment.

We see this especially in the final stage of his life in Jerusalem. All four gospels agree that Jesus' last days constituted a protest, if not an outright challenge, to the religious and political establishment in Jerusalem. Yet the authorities did not immediately lay their hands on Jesus because they feared the people (Mark 14:2). Jesus' popularity with the masses was too sensitive an issue; he must not be arrested publicly. Accordingly, the cleansing of the Temple was no innocuous event, but a personal protest by Jesus' against a sacred institution which he felt had been violated by greedy and power-hungry leaders. The charge "You have made it a den of robbers" was true and it must have evoked strong sympathy from those who heard about or saw the incident, especially if they belonged to the masses or poor pilgrims systematically fleeced by the religious authorities, whose power was bought at their expense.[19]

Among those in most frequent conflict with Jesus were the wealthy classes. We will see this in detail later in Luke's gospel, where this feature is greatly intensified. Yet Luke's development of this theme seems well-grounded historically. The danger of riches is anchored firmly in the tradition, as are some specific stories illustrating this danger (Mark 10:17-31). Certainly those persons possessing the most wealth were the least inclined to respond favorably to Jesus' teaching and Jesus was well aware of the difficulty caused by his call to choose between service to God and mammon. He was keenly aware of those who devour widow's houses, or who seek to practice the law in minute detail yet neglect the weightier matters of justice and mercy. He knew riches and pride were inseparable and could cause one to trust in earthly treasures rather than the pearl of greater price. On the other hand, if the rich found it difficult to respond, the poor found a warm reception. They were welcomed with open arms and many responded with enthusiasm. Thus the whole tenor of the gospel portrait is disposed most favorably toward the poor and against the rich.

Finally, the simple fact that Palestine was so poor, so that the poor constituted the majority of the people, points to the poor masses as the chief human source of Jesus' appeal. Even the footloose nature of the crowds who followed Jesus, sometimes quite unprepared for food and shelter, seems to presuppose people familiar with little or nothing and able to survive on meager resources. In sum, there is converging evidence that the main body of support for Jesus during his public ministry came from the multitudes, who constituted the lowest social and economic class in Palestine.

Tax Collectors, Sinners, and Others

Another line of evidence which affirms the thesis that the Jesus movement was a movement among the economically and politically oppressed can be found by examining the specific groups named in the gospels as follows of Jesus.

Tax collectors. The references to tax collectors as respondents to Jesus' ministry form part of the bedrock of historical tradition.[20] We find this not only in the call of Levi, the tax gatherer, and its sequel (Mark 2:13-17), but scattered references to tax collectors in all levels of the tradition combine to indicate how unexpected, nontraditional and offensive their response to Jesus was.

It is generally assumed that the tax collectors were both wealthy and hated because they consistently cheated and overcharged and because they worked for the Roman oppressor and his puppets. Hence they were socially and religiously ostracized in Jewish society. When Jesus, on the contrary, welcomed them into his community of disciples, his action occasioned great offense.

How accurate is this picture? There were in reality two levels of tax collectors: the tax farmer or overseer and the tax underling. The tax farmer had to buy his contract from the Roman administration or from free cities and then try to make a profit. It was a risky venture and open to much cheating. Some overseers got rich, yet it is questionable whether all or most did. The tax underling was an employee of the tax farmer, who did the actual day-to-day work at the tax office. Luke knows the difference when he calls Zacchaeus a *chief* tax collector (Luke 19:1). Most of the tax collectors referred to in the Gospels belong to the lower group of underlings. Perhaps this was the only work they could find, so they accepted it, despite its social disapproval. If the underling cheated, the profit most likely went to the boss.

The people as a whole were heavily, fearfully taxed. The head tax which the Romans required, usually in connection with a census, was the tax most hated by the Zealots and other patriots, but it was collected by the Jewish administration, not the tax collectors. It was the goods and services tax which burdened the people most heavily and which, in fact, caused the greatest economic hardship. We read of constant quarrels and complaints over taxes, especially from the small merchants and caravaners, as the tax collectors were everywhere trying to get their cut. Obviously the people hurt most by the excessive taxation responded with anger and resentment. However, it seems as though the scribes and Pharisees condemned them only if they cheated. The poorest part of the population, the daily wage earners and the slaves, paid little or no tax and thus had no strong feelings against them. Thus one cannot make a blanket statement to the effect that the whole populace despised tax collectors with equal intensity.

Still the Gospels and other sources do provide sufficient evidence that the tax collectors belonged to the socially marginal class as a direct result of their vocation. And religiously, they too were quite unacceptable to the Pharisees and other pious people. The listing of tax collectors with "extortioners, unjust and adulterers" in Luke 18:11 does not seem far off the mark. Moreover, the gospels agree that historically Jesus' association with the tax collectors was a chief cause of offense in his ministry.

Sinners. Alongside tax collectors, the gospels speak of "sinners" as an identifiable group associated with Jesus during his ministry. Who were they? Some have suggested that they were the *am haaretz*, the poor people of the land, the masses. Although the rabbis did refer to the *am haaretz* as people who know not the law, i.e., sinners, this general attitude is more appropriate to the post-A.D. 70 period than before it.

A more probable suggestion is that sinners refers to persons in despised occupations, or people with immoral life-styles, such as adulterers, prostitutes, murderers, robbers, defrauders.[21] The similarity between prostitutes and sinners seems apparent from Matthew 11:19 and Matthew 21:31, where they are interchangeable terms.

Yet another suggestion is that they were people who acted wrongly in their profession, as for example, shepherds, who were among the most frequently despised because they repeatedly led their flocks to graze on fields not their own.[22]

Both of the last two suggestions seem historically probable. At least we know enough to say that the persons designated sinners lived outside the law, and hence were religiously and socially ostracized. Again, as with the tax collectors, Jesus' appeal to them was at the heart of the offense caused by his ministry in the eyes of the pious. For his critics, the fact that Jesus associated with them was sufficient proof that his entire movement stood beyond the pale of respectability and was contrary to the intent of God and the good of the community. It is Luke who broadens this original and historical understanding of sinners into a statement about the condition of humanity before God (Luke 5:8; 18:13). But this is a later development of the gospel tradition.

Prostitutes. Prostitutes, too, find themselves welcomed into the new community gathered around Jesus. We see this not only in the touching story of the sinful woman preserved by Luke (7:36-50) or the tradition of the woman caught in adultery (John 8:1-11), but also in the striking saying preserved in Matthew, "Truly, I say to you, the tax collectors and the harlots go into the kingdom of God before you" (Matt. 21:31). Such associations were hardly the kind to be made up by the early church for publicity reasons! While the prostitute who anointed Jesus' feet may have had considerable wealth, as her expensive perfume indicates, most prostitutes were tragic victims. Controlled by a pimp, they normally worked in bordellos, often owned by respectable male citizens, who kept their identity hidden. The women came from the lower classes; slaves bought by owners, women forced by economic pressures to sell themselves, daughters of poor parents who sold or rented them for money, unwanted newborn girls now enslaved, war prisoners and infrequently adultresses punished by forced prostitution. The scene was as tragic then as now. Yet in their encounter with Jesus they met a friendship and acceptance and new lease on life that led them to genuine repentance and discipleship.

Poor, beggars, crippled and other handicapped. We shall group these persons together, as their differences socially and economically were minimal. We encounter persons in the Gospels living on both levels of poverty we discussed earlier, the subsidized poor and the wage earners. At the bottom level, we hear of people who live off of alms (Mark 10:21); we meet poor Lazarus, a crippled beggar who dies in poverty (Luke 16:19); we read of beggars who are lying around the street hungry invited to banquets (Luke 14:13, 21). A lame beggar at the Beautiful Gate gets an unexpected bonus from some poor Christians who help him literally to his feet (Acts 3:1-11). Beggars were a familiar sight to Jesus, as the Gospels report, and hence beggars found their way into his group of followers.

We also hear about the tough life of the poor one step above the beggar; the day laborer hoping to be hired, even after the day's work had begun (Matt. 20:3, 5-6) or a person in prison because he couldn't pay off his debt (Matt. 18:30) or in great economic need due to bad harvest or heavy taxes or huge debts (Luke 16:6-7) or landless tenants working for a wealthy absentee landowner (Mark 12:1). All of this reflects the authentic color of Jesus' time and all of these poor seem to be a part of his company.

In the oldest tradition, the poor and sick are mentioned in the same breath (Matt. 11:25); in Luke the poor are linked with the hungry and weeping (Luke 1:46f.; 6:20f.). We cannot always be sure in every case whether the poor are beggars, unemployed day workers or part of the impoverished land populace. But poverty there is. The gospel glimpses of the poor and hungry, the beggars, the sick and the lepers preserve a realistic historical portrait. And the ministry of Jesus finds its fullest response precisely among these people.

Our glance at the specific groups most closely associated with Jesus in the earliest gospel traditions demonstrates clearly that they belonged to the poor and marginal people of his society. Socially and religiously, the tax collectors, sinners, prostitutes, beggars and various kinds of sick constituted the class of outcasts, who were specific objects of Jesus' ministry. That the Jesus movement found its following among such people was both its shame to outsiders and critics, and its glory to insiders and followers (cf. 1 Cor. 1:18). Its roots in this social environment can scarcely be denied.

Anawim

A third line of evidence pointing to the emergence of the Jesus movement in the lower social and economic strata can be derived from its connection with the so-called *anawim* piety. While our source material is limited, a reasonable case can be made for the existence of an *anawim* piety, if not movement, in Jesus' day and for its significant role at the beginning of Jesus' activity.

We have already traced the origin of *anawim* piety in the Psalter.[23] These pious poor understood themselves as persons faithful to Yahweh, who in spite of enemies and persecution and afflictions entrusted themselves solely to his care and protection. Here the concept of poor and pious merge, the poverty taking on a deeply spiritual meaning. This same use of the "poor" occurs in the Pharisaic *Psalms of Solomon* and in the Thanksgiving psalms of Qumran, contemporary with Jesus. In the latter writings, the term "poor" acquires messianic expectations so that the *anawim* are the faithful elect who wait upon God for the coming of the imminent messianic age. This messianic piety constitutes the essence of the *anawim* mentality in Jesus' time.[24] While efforts to view the anawim as an identifiable religious movement in first-century Palestine and even as the movement out of which Jesus came have not succeeded, nevertheless their existence as a distinct type of religious piety in late Judaism seems highly probable. What is most significant for our purposes is to bear in mind that these *anawim* can never be severed from their roots among the poor in Palestine. Their spiritual outlook of absolute dependence on God reflected their social condition of privation and need. They were essentially the powerless, the exploited, the insignificant, and the economically deprived.

But where is the connecting link between the *anawim* and the gospel traditions? We will take up this question further when we discuss Jesus' preaching to the poor in Luke's gospel. For the present, we can only point to those places in the gospel traditions where the *anawim* mentality seems most evident: the milieu of the infancy narratives in Luke's gospel (Luke 1–2), the piety presupposed in the opening beatitudes of the two sermons from Matthew and Luke and those texts in which the theme of a coming eschatological reversal is clearly enunciated (see below). In each of these traditions we encounter a sense of spiritual poverty and need combined with a social setting of want and suffering which is characteristic of *anawim*. It is our thesis, supported by others, that these same circles of *anawim* nurtured in a special way the spiritual piety of messianic expectations and hopes, which for many pious Jews found their deepest fulfillment in the person and ministry of Jesus, the Anointed One of God (Acts 2:36).[25]

We have now described those lines of evidence which in our judgment enable us to affirm that from its earliest beginnings the movement begun by Jesus was a movement that appealed primarily to the lower classes, socially, economically, and politically. In this sense, one could call it a people's movement or a proletarian movement. The multitudes, the people comprising the motly collection of what the Gospels in abbreviated manner call tax collectors and sinners, and the *anawim* have this in common; that they comprised the lowest stratum of society, that they lived in various states of need associated with their humble circumstances, and that they found in the teaching and actions of Jesus a recognition of their needs and a reason to hope that through him God was already at work to make his promised kingdom a reality in their lives and in the world.

Oldest Traditions in the Gospels

Before taking up the way in which Luke's gospel depicts Jesus' ministry to the poor and the promise of the kingdom associated with it, we want to consider a few texts which a number of scholars have identified as part of the oldest tradition in the Gospels.[26] Our specific interest in these texts arises from the fact that they all contain the theme of a coming eschatological reversal, which we have identified above as a core belief of the *anawim*. If we are correct in the identification of these texts with the oldest traditions about Jesus, then they can tell us something about the people to whom Jesus spoke and something about the specific content of his message. Naturally the attempt to isolate pre-gospel traditions in the time of Jesus or the time of the church is an uncertain task. Yet it is necessary and useful, for it can help us sharpen our understanding of the historical setting of Jesus' ministry, as well as give us an appreciation of the process by which the remembered traditions about Jesus were used in the life of the church and later by the evangelists. What emerges is a dynamic view of a preached faith, which applied its confession of Jesus' lordship and the memories about him to new and changing situations, a view appropriate and necessary in every age, including ours.

What are the specific texts in the oldest Jesus tradition that preserve the theme of the coming eschatological reversal? Our task at this point is not to interpret these passages in detail, but to argue for their claim to belong to the oldest traditions and to state briefly the way in which they may have been understood within the earliest setting of Jesus' own ministry.

Luke 6:20-21/Matthew 5:3-9

This text belongs to the Q source common to Matthew and Luke. Thus it is older than the Gospels, and the fact that we have two quite different forms of the beatitudes in Matthew and Luke may further indicate that each had developed separately in the oral period preceding our Gospels. So the core sayings would seem to reach back into the earliest period of the gospel traditions. But what was the oldest form? Whether the direct address of Luke 6:20 "Blessed are you poor," or the indirect form of Matthew 5:3, "Blessed are the poor," is the earliest is debated, though the majority favor the Lukan form. The numerical expansion of the beatitudes in Matthew and especially their spiritualization (Matt. 5:3, "in spirit," 5:6, "for righteousness' sake") moreover, plainly reveal the hand of Matthew. Thus the Lukan form of the beatitudes appears to be the original.

The basic content of the beatitudes in their oldest form is a word of promise to the poor, built around the affirmation that the kingdom of God is theirs (Luke 6:20). The presupposition for this affirmation is the presence and authority of Jesus. In his messianic activity, the kingdom of God is breaking in and the end-time salvation has arrived. Thus he can offer the kingdom to the poor. But that is not all. The blessings upon the poor as recipients of the kingdom are made concrete in what follows; their present hunger will be satisfied, and their present afflictions will turn to laughter. The future tense offers the clue to its meaning. The coming of the kingdom, already begun in the appearance of Jesus, will find its fulfillment in the eschatological reversal of the present state of the poor! Now they are poor, hungry, weeping, yet as inheritors of the kingdom they will then be satisfied and full of joy. A total reversal of social status is envisioned, a point made even more vivid by the contrasting woes upon the rich in Luke's Gospel.[27]

How shall we understand this promise in its original setting in the life of Jesus? These words must have been addressed to the hungry, powerless, and socially dispossessed people around Jesus. His announcement of the kingdom, with its concrete promise of a better future, must have stirred up long latent hopes for a time when justice would prevail and their present hardships would be past. They saw their present life and condition as a scandal in the eyes of God. But they looked to the future to change this. In this manner the preaching of Jesus was a "revitalization of Messianic hope."[28] The establishment of God's kingdom meant God was already at work exercising his rule in the world, a rule of love, righteousness, justice, and peace, in which the will of God was done. And what had begun in Jesus' own ministry in his exercise of love and compassion for the poor and acceptance of sinners, was to be fulfilled at the completion of the eschaton, when the final establishment of God's rule would take place and the total reversal of social and religious status would occur. It was this kind of hope that those around Jesus took to heart, and thus understood themselves as the "little flock" who were heirs of the coming kingdom (Luke 12:32).[29]

Perhaps one can even be more specific about the content of the salvation-hope engendered by Jesus' preaching. The beatitudes promise satisfaction and laughter to the poor, which is exactly what the rich now have (Luke 6:25; 16:19). And this imagery of joy and abundance is also present in those gospel traditions where the image of the eschatological banquet comes to the fore.[30] At the meal in the coming kingdom there will be joy and laughter aplenty. What may be lacking now will then be provided. This also means that not only will the present condition of poverty and hunger and tears come to an end, but there will be a full settlement, a making-good of the present misery. While the Jewish imagery of miraculous food on the table in great abundance is not present in Jesus' teaching, one can imagine something of the fine bread from meal, and oil, eggs, honey and wine at the feast.[31] The hungry will be filled!

Luke 16:19-26

Another text which enunciates the theme of eschatological reversal which may go back to the earliest traditions about Jesus is found in the parable of the Rich Man and Lazarus. As the parable now stands, it has essentially two parts, vv. 19-26, the story of the reversal between the two men in the next life, and vv. 27-31, the theme of repentance.

It is the judgment of many commentators that the original parable is found in vv. 19-26, since the second half introduces the motif of repentance not present in the first half. We will discuss the arguments for this conclusion in Chapter Five.

But if this is so, then we have a parable in which two destinies are contrasted, that of a rich man and a poor man. While the parable is told in the singular, it is obvious that we are hearing about the separate fates of the rich and the poor respectively and not just a particular case. And while the point of death marks the transition between the two fates, the background of the parable in the teaching of Jesus would seem to link it directly to the coming eschatological reversal.

The parable itself draws an unforgettable contrast between the rich and the poor. The one has everything that could be asked for in terms of the good life. The other suffers everything. But at death their situations are irrevocably reversed. Lazarus enjoys the ultimate hope of every Jew. Every joy is now his while the rich man must endure the torment of hades forever. The reversal is total and complete.

Again, we must ask how this parable would have been understood by the original audience in Jesus time? Surely to the poor and suffering who gathered around him it would have been heard as unbelievably good news! They would have recognized the striking disparity between their grinding poverty and the favored existence of the rich and powerful. They scarcely needed a reminder of how unjust life was and how unaccountable were their afflictions, while their exploiters prospered. Yet here was a promise that this would not always be so and this promise came with the authority of One who claimed to speak and act for God. The dawn of the kingdom he announced would find its full brightness in the blessings upon the poor and the judgment upon the rich. The coming of the kingdom meant mercy, peace and righteousness. In some such way, we suggest, this parable would have been heard as a basic promise of hope to the poor in God's coming act of justice. Abraham speaks for God when he sets the hope of the poor to the fore, while at the same time speaking a word of warning to the rich: "Son, remember that you in your lifetime received good things, and Lazarus in like manner evil things; but now he is comforted here, and you are in anguish" (v. 25).

Luke 1:52-53

Yet another text echoing the same reversal theme as the previous two is embedded in the Magnificat, the famous song of Mary. The origin of all the songs in the Lukan birth narrative has been much debated by interpreters. Almost all commentators agree, however, that the songs are not verbatim utterances of the persons to whom they are ascribed in Luke. There is less agreement, though, on who is responsible for their composition. Judgments range all the way from Jewish sources in the Maccabean period to the work of Luke himself.[32] However, recent studies argue strongly for their origin in early Jewish-Christian circles, where belief in the redemption through the Messiah Jesus was vividly alive.[33] We find this view most persuasive, since the atmosphere of Jewish *anawim* piety combines with a sense of gratitude for salvation accomplished, so as to make a Jewish-Christian setting most likely.

In the Magnificat, the words of Mary give expression to the work of God the Savior in her life (vv. 46-49) and in the life of all those who fear him (vv. 50-55).[34] The key is Mary's exaltation by God (v. 48). Her low status in life has been transformed into blessedness. And this is exactly the way God continues to act. Verses 51-53 powerfully proclaim God's transforming, redemptive action in history: "He has scattered the proud in the imagination of their hearts, he has put down the mighty from their thrones, and exalted those of low degree; he has filled the hungry with good things, and the rich he has sent empty away."

How shall we understand the early composers and hearers of this great hymn? Were they not reflecting on their own experience of God's redemptive action in Christ and their hope in the ultimate consummation of the kingdom? Their place in society was among the little people, the insignificant, those who live frugally hoping for enough food and drink to get through the day. Yet through their faith in Jesus, the Messiah, their whole outlook and expectation had radically changed. Their insignificance no longer mattered, since they knew God through his Christ had come to their help. They were chosen for redemption and that meant that they already had gained a new sense of worth and dignity, along with a new community of loving and caring believers. But above all it meant the sure hope of God's mercy and justice in the coming age, when all the injustices and oppressions and burdens of this life would be gone. Then only good things would be theirs from the hand of God. In such a way, we think, these earliest believers grasped the message and promise of Jesus.

Mark 10:31/Luke 13:30/Matthew 19:30; 20:16

"But many that are first will be last, and the last first." Perhaps we can also include this brief saying among the earliest traditions that promise a coming eschatological reversal. In order to do so, we must first recognize that this is an isolated saying in the gospel tradition; that is, it has been loosed from its original context in the life of Jesus. We can tell this from the fact that it has several different settings in the synoptic gospels. It is apparent that either the evangelists or more likely the early oral tradition attached this independent saying to texts which seemed most appropriate, although its original context had been lost.

In Luke's gospel it is appended to a text in which Jesus warns his

Jewish hearers that unless they stop acting like "workers of iniquity," the Gentiles will take their place in the kingdom (Luke
13:22-29). The reversal of Jew and Gentile in the coming kingdom
is then confirmed by the attached saying, "some are last who will
be first and some are first who will be last." In Mark the context
is quite different. The contrast there is between the rich who will
not make it into the kingdom with their riches and the poor disciples, who have left everything to follow Jesus (Mark 10:23/
Matt. 19:23-29). Thus the reversal in the coming kingdom is not
between Jew and Gentile, but between the rich and the poor. Matthew gives it yet another context. He places it in relation to the
parable about God's undeserved grace, in which the workers employed for only one hour receive the same wage as those who toiled
and sweated all day. The point is the overwhelming generosity of
God, who gives his grace equally to all. At the end of this parable
Matthew then appends the saying on the first and the last, so that
it must be understood as a warning to those who want to restrict
God's grace to the righteous few.

The question that concerns us is what may have been the original
context for this saying. We suggest that Mark's gospel provides
the best clue, by setting it within the discussion of a coming reversal between the rich and the poor. But its original intent was not
that of a warning to the rich but as a word of promise and hope to
the poor.[35] It said something like this: "You who are least in the
eyes of others and by the measure of earthly standards have the
least, you will be abundantly blessed in the age to come." The
coming of God's kingdom meant the end to their lowly status and
God's vindication of their cause. As such, it was a message of hope
addressed to the little people and the sufferers who followed Jesus
and who thereby heard in his words the establishment of a new
order of life in which God's righteousness would prevail.

What we have attempted to do, admittedly as a tentative hypoth-
esis, is to point to a number of texts in the Gospels in which the
theme of a coming eschatological reversal is directed as a word of
hope and promise to the poor, who gathered around Jesus and responded to his message. It is our contention that these passages
give us some authentic clues about the nature of the earliest preaching of Jesus and the people who heard him gladly. As we have

shown in our survey of the historical period in which Jesus lived
and in our look at the specific groups of people mentioned in the
Gospels as the joyful recipients of his preaching and teaching, the
basic thrust of the Jesus-movement was to the lower classes, those
people living on the margin of society, socially, economically, politically, and religiously. What they have in common is a condition of
need and the desire for a more just and humane world. Some looked
to God for the fulfillment of their needs, others probably lived
without hope, crushed and broken by the burdens and injustices of
life; still others may have become bitter, defiant, or indifferent.

Whatever the specific human need and response, the appearance
of Jesus sounded a revival of hope and promise. Jesus announced
the dawn of the rule of God. Already in his words and deeds the
messianic signs of the kingdom were visible; the blind, lame, lepers, deaf and dead were returned to health and the poor heard
good news (Luke 7:22/Matt. 11:5). But this was only the beginning
of the reign of God. The fulfillment would one day surely come,
and then God would right all wrongs and heal all diseases and
bring his cause of mercy and righteousness to its completion.
Hence the promise of a coming reversal associated with the kingdom
would be God's way of making right the present social disorders
and injustices. Of course, this was a message to be believed and
obeyed. It meant placing one's trust in God for the present necessities of life and it also meant a commitment to seek God's kingdom
now as the operating principle in one's life (Matt. 6:33). But its
source was the promise of God, who in Jesus was already at work
calling the poor, the oppressed, the suffering, and the lost into the
community of the redeemed, who would one day sit at table in
the kingdom and enjoy the abundance of God, while the present
rich and mighty and proud would find themselves outside (Luke
13:27). In such a way, we suggest, the preaching of Jesus concerning the kingdom was heard by the poor. Perhaps it is an understanding we need to recapture in our own hearing of the gospel story, if
we are to be faithful to the full dimension of its redemptive and
social significance.

The Jesus-movement from its inception was rooted deeply in
the poverty of Palestine and its multi-dimensional poor. That can
be a starting point for us today, as we seek to be the heirs in faithfulness and hope of his message and mission.

3

Anointed to Preach
Good News to the Poor

With this chapter we now turn our attention to the distinctive
Lukan presentation of Jesus' ministry. Our primary goal is two-
fold. In the first place, we seek to demonstrate that the theme of
"good news to the poor" belongs at the heart and center of the
Lukan story. Beginning with the thematic text of Luke's gospel in
the synagogue at Nazareth, we will explore various other passages
which develop this theme throughout the gospel. The sum of our
investigation should confirm the centrality of this theme in the
third gospel.

In the second place, we seek to answer the simple, though crucial question of our study, the question of the identity of the poor
in Luke's gospel. Who are these poor concretely to whom the good
news is preached? Are they the socially or economically poor?
Are they the spiritually poor? Or does the term somehow include
all these dimensions in the mind of Luke? We find this question
to be decisive for understanding Luke's gospel and the social
dimension of Jesus' ministry embodied within it.

By carefully investigating these questions the way will be pre-
pared for our discussion in subsequent chapters of the particular
theme of wealth and poverty and its relation to the announcement
of good news to the poor.

The Announcement of Good News to the Poor (4:16-30)

No text is more important for understanding Luke's two volumes
than this one. Recent scholarship is in general agreement that here
we find the programmatic text for the Lukan writings.[1] These
verses introduce four major emphases:

64

- the announcement of Jesus' ministry as the fulfillment of God's salvation-time,
- a statement about the content of Jesus' ministry based on the quotation from Isaiah,
- the foreshadowing of Jesus' final suffering and rejection,
- the foreshadowing of the movement of the gospel from Jew to Gentile.

As this summary strikingly reveals, we possess in this text the entire outline of both the gospel and Acts in nuce. Therefore its importance cannot be overlooked. Luke is here introducing us to his two volumes and providing us with the glasses, as it were, by which we are to read all that follows.

The significance of this text is also underscored by the fact that in its present form and position within the gospel it is unique to Luke. A comparison with Mark reveals that Mark also has a tradition of Jesus' rejection in the synagogue at Nazareth (Mark 6:1-6). There are obvious similarities between the two accounts; yet the differences are also striking, especially in Luke's use of Isaiah 61 as well as two Old Testament stories which portray God's grace to Gentiles. How do we explain these differences? Has Luke rewritten the Markan text? Or does he draw upon his own independent source? Scholars have argued both ways. In our judgment, however, Luke is the one chiefly responsible for this version of the Nazareth event, as he seeks to utilize it for the "inaugural address" of Jesus in his gospel. But apart from the debatable problem of its source, there can be no doubt that Luke himself has chosen this text as his special vehicle for announcing to his readers the story of Jesus and the story of the church, and that he has positioned this text at the beginning of Jesus' ministry for this purpose.

Our primary interest lies with the first half of this text, vv. 16-21. Many commentators have all too quickly overlooked this section, a fact already indicated by the common heading given to both halves, "Jesus' rejection at Nazareth." A more appropriate title would be, "Jesus' announcement of the Salvation-Time." For certainly the opening section places the spotlight on the dramatic announcement of the arrival of the salvation-time, i.e. on the "today" of Jesus' appearance (v. 21). Furthermore, the content of this salvation-time is described by the quotation from Isaiah 61:1-2 (and 58:6). It is this prophetic word, therefore, which holds the interpretive key to Luke's understanding of Jesus' ministry. And if this is so, then we must try to relate this Old Testament text as carefully as we can to the actual ministry of Jesus portrayed in Luke. And we must also seek to determine the manner in which the original context of the Isaiah texts may have influenced Luke's understanding of Jesus' mission in fulfillment of these prophetic words.

In sum, we want to grasp as concretely as possible the way in which Luke interprets the announcement of salvation on the basis of Isaiah. Perhaps the crux of our question can be stated this way: Is the ministry of Jesus depicted by Luke as the fulfillment of Isaiah meant to be understood metaphorically or spiritually, or as literally as possible? [2] Or another way of asking it: Who precisely are the poor, captive, blind and oppressed to whom the good news is preached and for whom the acceptable year of the Lord has arrived? Most interpreters in the past have tried to spiritualize this text or have ignored its plain meaning. Perhaps another reading is necessary in light of Luke's gospel as a whole and especially in view of his undeniable concern for the poor and the oppressed. To attempt an answer to this fundamental question we need to examine first of all the basic relationship between these verses and Luke's entire gospel.

The Relationship Between 4:16-21 and Luke's Gospel

The "Today" of Salvation (vv. 16-17, 20-21). The verses that introduce and conclude the reading from Isaiah are generally regarded as Luke's own composition. They provide the setting for Jesus' dramatic announcement of the arrival of the final salvation time, and fix the eyes of the readers on the words, "Today this scripture has been fulfilled in your hearing." The word "today" is distinctively Lukan. It conveys for Luke the presence of salvation in the time of Jesus and also in the time of the church.[3] With it, Luke expresses his "realized eschatology," i.e., the view that salvation is primarily a present reality, and not some future hope. The drama of the entire scene is thus focused on the word "today." This word announces the final advent of what the Old Testament prophets and people had long awaited, God's coming in grace and mercy to begin his sovereign reign. And Jesus is the proclaimer and fulfiller of this "today."

The Spirit of the Lord is upon me (v. 18). The opening line from Isaiah 61:1 touches on another theme of special importance to Luke. In both the gospel and Acts the role of the Spirit is crucial. Jesus is conceived by the Spirit (1:35), baptized with the Spirit (3:21) and from his baptism on is empowered by the Spirit (4:1, 14, 18). During his earthly ministry he alone is the bearer of God's Spirit. His anointing by the Spirit is also remembered in the sermons of Acts (4:27; 10:38). And of course the entire story of the church in Acts is narrated by Luke as a continuation of the work of the Spirit begun in Jesus (Luke 24:49; Acts 1:4-5, 2:1ff.). Far from being a vague metaphor for Luke, the Spirit functions as the divine reality behind Jesus' life and mission and that of the church.

There is also a close link between the Spirit and Jesus' prophetic role. More than the other evangelists, Luke emphasizes Jesus' role as prophet and identifies this prophetic activity with his teaching and martyrdom (Luke 4:23; 2:39; 13:33-34; 24:19). We shall note later that the Lukan beatitudes and woes have the form of prophetic pronouncements (Luke 6:20-26).[4] Thus it is consistent with Luke's own portrayal of Jesus to identify the words of Isaiah 61 with the prophetic nature of Jesus' activity, in as literal a manner as possible.

He has anointed me to preach good news to the poor. We regard this phrase as the most significant in Luke. The idea of being anointed to carry out a divinely-commissioned task is central to the Old Testament, and in Isaiah is linked with the proclamation of good news to a captive people. Very early the term "gospel" was adopted by the church to express the good news about God's redemptive activity in Jesus (Mark 1:15). In this passage, the good news is said to be directed specifically to the poor. For some interpreters, this phrase is understood as both introducing and governing the following lines, in which case the poor is a collective term for the captives, blind and oppressed.[5] This interpretation rightly recognizes the importance of this phrase in the quotation. Yet it can also be argued that it should be taken independently, so that the poor are to be set alongside the captives and others as a separate group. While we favor this possibility, we cannot be certain. Of greater significance is the meaning of the term "poor" in Luke's gospel. But before we explore this large and crucial question, we want to complete our examination of the remaining phrases in the Isaiah quote.

He has sent me to proclaim release to the captives. If one compares Luke's quotation with Isaiah 61:1, it will quickly be noted that Luke's version omits the line, "he sent me to heal the broken in heart." This fact, as well as the later insertion of a line from Isaiah 58:6, points to Lukan (or earlier) editing of the text.[6] Who are the captives for Luke? Does Luke have in mind the miraculous release of Peter, John, and Paul from prisons in Acts (cf. Luke 21:24)? Others have suggested Luke may be thinking of the captivity of a crippled woman bound by Satan for 18 years before Jesus released her (Luke 13:10-17). In this case, all the exorcisms could be regarded as "release of captives."

However the word for release seems to provide the best clue to Luke's intention. In the Septuagint, "release" is used as a technical term for the Year of Jubilee ("Year of release" Lev. 25-27) or for the Sabbath year (Deut. 15:1; Exod. 23:11), so that it has the social and economic meaning of release of debts. But in Luke/Acts, apart from this Isaiah quotation, it has the primary meaning of "forgiveness." Moreover, this is a distinctive Lukan use of the term (1:77; 7:47; 24:47; Acts 2:38; 5:31; 10:43; 13:38; 26:18). Therefore, in both the ministry of Jesus and in the apostolic preaching, the word "release" is used specifically for the bondage of sin and evil which is removed through the forgiving power of Jesus. Still, its presence in the Old Testament quote from Isaiah may suggest that it retains something of its connection with the Jubilee hope of social and economic release.

Recovering of sight to the blind. Only once in his writings does Luke employ the metaphorical image of the blind, and that is in a text from Q (Luke 6:39/Matt. 15:14). In all other cases it has its literal meaning. The encounter between Jesus and the blind results in the joyful recovery of their sight (Luke 7:21; 18:35-43). We will soon observe this exact phrase quoted as one of the messianic signs fulfilled in Jesus' ministry, along with other acts of healing (Luke 7:22; cf. 14:13, 21).

To set at liberty those who are oppressed. Careful readers will quickly note that this line does not come from Isaiah 61:1-2, but from Isaiah 58:6. How did it get in here? Since it is hard to imagine Jesus or anyone pausing to have the scroll rolled back to Isaiah 58 while reading a selected text from Isaiah 61, the more likely explanation is that it was inserted by Luke or by the tradition before him. It was common for Jewish and Christian rabbis to enrich texts by the addition of phrases, often on the basis of catchwords.[7] Very likely, in this case it was the catchword "release" that caught the attention of Luke or some early Christian scribe, since the literal Greek behind the RSV translation of "set at liberty" is "to send away by release." In addition, the phrase from Isaiah 58:6 was peculiarly appropriate to the content of 61:1-2.

Once again we ask, who are the oppressed, set at liberty, or released? The literal meaning of the word for oppressed means "broken in pieces," which would suggest social injustices, and the context of Isaiah 58:6 supports this; yet we must be cautious. For the use of the word "release" by Luke points in the direction of the burden of sin which is removed by the gospel of forgiveness.

To proclaim the acceptable year of the Lord (v. 19). What may be in mind by the expression, "the acceptable year of the Lord?" The answer to this question has provoked a far-ranging discussion among recent authors.[8] In order to get at the specific meaning of this tantalizing phrase, we must now explore the Old Testament background of Luke's quotation.

Old Testament Context

As we have already observed, the quotation is a composite of Isaiah 61:1-2 and Isaiah 58:6. What can we learn about the original meaning and context of these passages? Chapters 40-66 of Isaiah are ascribed by modern scholarship to an unknown prophet living at the time of the exile.[9] His words as a whole brought a message of hope and comfort, centering on the promise of their return and restoration. In Chapter 61, the prophet adopts the form of the earlier servant songs (Isa. 42; 49; 51; 53) and announces the good news that God is about to free them from their captivity and restore them to favor. The message is one of promise and liberation to a defeated and oppressed people. But what has especially caught the eye of numerous commentators is the precise language that is used to portray the coming liberation. It is the language of the Jubilee Year.[10] This is so already in the announcement of good news to the poor and the release of the captives (slaves) and liberation of the oppressed, but above all in the reference to the acceptable year of the Lord (Hebrew "the year of the Lord's favor"). Then too, the fact that the word translated "release" by the Septuagint is the technical term for the Jubilee Year strengthens this imagery. Hence the conclusion seems correct that the prophet drew upon the Mosaic ordinance of the Jubilee Year in order to picture Israel's homecoming from its place of exile.

How is it with Isaiah 58:6? Throughout Chapter 58 we encounter a ringing rebuke against the people for their sins of injustice and oppression, in the best tradition of an Amos or Micah. Furthermore, the prophet appeals to the people to engage in just actions toward the poor, the homeless, the naked, and the debtors. Isaiah 58:6 holds the key. Four successive verbs express the one idea of supreme importance, the liberation of the oppressed. "Is not this the fast that I choose: to loose the bonds of wickedness, to undo the thongs of the yoke, to let the oppressed go free, and to break every yoke?" Thus the importation of this text into Isaiah 61:1-2, with its echo of the Jubilee Year call for social release, is consistent with both texts. And it obviously adds further weight to the prophetic dimension of the call to justice contained in the Lukan quotation.

This raises the critical question with regard to Luke's utilization of the Isaiah texts. How much of the original Jubilee Year motifs and the call to justice has Luke intended to import into his use of these two Old Testament texts? On this point interpreters are sharply divided. On one side we have the position popularized by a recent author that Jesus' own concept of the kingdom was borrowed extensively from the prophetic interpretation of the Jubilee Year.[11] In fact, the Lukan text of 4:16-30 is taken as prime evidence that Jesus began his ministry with the announcement that the final Jubilee Year had arrived, and that his audience so understood him. It is further argued that Jesus' announcement of the final Jubilee included the demand that its specific prescriptions for economic and social justice be taken with utmost seriousness. "It is really a Jubilee, conformed to the sabbatical instructions of Moses that Jesus proclaimed in A.D. 26, a Jubilee able to solve the social problems of Israel, by abolishing debts and liberating debtors whose insolvency had reduced them to slavery. The practice of such a jubilee was not optional. It belonged to the precursor signs of the kingdom. Those who refused to enter this path would not enter the kingdom of God."[12] A few other gospel traditions dealing with supposed Jubilee themes are also offered to support this interpretation.[13]

While it is necessary to consider the possibility that the Jubilee Year motif with its radical call for justice played a vital part in the teachings of Jesus, the attempt to do so in the way just described runs aground for several reasons. Not only is there the serious problem of attempting a historical reconstruction of the Nazareth episode, there is also the hard fact that there is no reliable evidence that the Jubilee Year was ever practiced. But the greatest difficulty has to do with the suggestion that Jesus appealed to the fulfillment of legalistic Mosaic prescriptions as the requirement for entrance into the kingdom.[14] Such a view runs counter to a number of bedrock traditions in the Gospels as well as the whole tenor of Jesus' preaching and activity.

The opposite view would be to reject or ignore altogether the call to justice and the promise of Jubilee liberation that is present in these texts used by Luke. This is often the case when the words are spiritualized or their social setting in Isaiah minimized, as though it would be out of place in the teaching of Jesus.

A more helpful approach to ascertaining the way in which these texts may have been understood by Luke is to inquire about their use in the New Testament period. Such an inquiry, which examines the use of Isaiah 61:1-2 in Jewish literature from the time of Second Isaiah through the later Talmudic writings, reveals that this text had become primarily an eschatological symbol for the new Age.[15] In the Dead Sea Scrolls the passage was associated with the end-time figure of Melchizedek, who on the final day would execute judgment against the forces of Belial and in effect establish "the acceptable year of Melchizedek."[16] What we find, then, is that in this later Jewish literature the Jubilee vision of Isaiah 61 is not interpreted literally as a kind of legal prescription, but as a symbol or vision of the new age. It seems right to conclude, therefore, that this is also the way it would have been interpreted by Jesus and by the early church, including Luke and his Jewish and God-fearing readers.

Our discussion about the background of Isaiah 61:1-2 and 58:6 thus enables us to say that it is not the Mosaic Jubilee which is announced by Jesus but the coming of the kingdom, which is then described in the language of the messianic and Jubilee vision of good news to the poor and release for the captives.

Does this eschatological Jubilee vision still possess any social and ethical importance in Luke's gospel? Before attempting to answer this important question, we need to return to our earlier discussion of the theme, "to preach good news to the poor." What other evidence do we have in Luke's Gospel about the centrality of this theme and its concrete meaning for the evangelist?

"Go and Tell John . . . The Poor Hear Good News" (Luke 7:18-23)

We shall look at this passage next because it repeats the same phrase found in Luke 4:18. There is no doubt that its source is Isaiah 61:1. However the origin of the text is pre-Lukan, since it belongs to the Q tradition (cf. Matt. 11:2-6). According to both texts, John the Baptist sent two of his disciples to inquire of Jesus, "Are you he who is to come or shall we look for another?" In the Lukan narrative Jesus initially responds with a series of healings and exorcisms and only then addresses John's disciples with a collage of references from Isaiah, among them "good news to the poor." The statement about the poor comes at the climax of the list, which suggests that it is either a summary statement or the one most emphasized. Both the deeds and the words of Jesus are understood as messianic signs of the kingdom's presence in Jesus. Indirectly, they answer with positive affirmation the question of John: Are you the expected eschatological Redeemer or not? [17]

That brings us to the key question about the identity of the poor in this text. It is important to recognize that Luke identifies Jesus' activity with concrete deeds on behalf of people in need, the sick, the demon-possessed and the blind. Likewise, the signs from Isaiah also point to concrete deeds toward a wide range of persons in need, the blind, lame, leper, deaf, dead, and the poor. If the "good news to the poor" serves as a summary statement, then the poor are the equivalent of the sick and the possessed. But if, as seems most probable in this text, they represent a distinct group among the needy, then the reference is to persons suffering from material want and deprivation. In either case, it is plain that the sick and the poor are not vague metaphors or spiritualized concepts. Rather, they represent persons in definite situations of need, who find their needs met by the power and presence of the one who is to come. The salvation-time effected by the ministry of Jesus is therefore manifest through his deeds of compassion and mercy toward the sick, the suffering, and the poor.

The text concludes, "Blessed is he who takes no offense at me" (v. 23). While this beatitude is addressed to John, its implications are much broader for Luke. The Baptist indeed may have been offended by the nature of Jesus' ministry of grace and healing to the sick and suffering. But in the subsequent section addressed to the crowds and in the gospel tradition as a whole, the primary offense of Jesus' ministry was his association with tax collectors and sinners (Luke 7:33-35). Luke especially, among the evangelists, underscores the offensive nature of this characteristic activity of Jesus.[18] Therefore we are again put on notice by Luke that the people to whom Jesus ministers are those living on the margin of society, socially, ethically, and religiously. To them the good news is proclaimed, a good news having something to do with the offer of a new status and worth before God and humanity.

Invite the Poor (Luke 14:13, 21)

Two further texts in Luke's gospel link us directly to the quotation from Isaiah 61 in Luke 4:18-19. Both occur in Chapter 14 and both are found within the Lukan narrative of Jesus' dining at the home of a leading Pharisee. His position as a ruler probably refers to his membership in the Sanhedrin (v. 1). In vv. 12-14 Jesus speaks directly to his host regarding those he should invite to his feasts. Those not to be invited are his friends, relatives or rich neighbors, i.e. those who can and will return the invitation. Instead, Jesus challenges him to invite the poor, the maimed, the lame and the blind, i.e. those who cannot repay him. This recommended list of invitees parallels the "poor and blind" of Isaiah 61:1-2 and is similar to the "poor, blind and lame" of Luke 7:22.

In the second text, the parable of the Great Banquet (Luke 14:15-24), which also has a Matthean version (Matt. 22:1-10),[19] Luke alone names those invited the second time as the "poor, maimed, blind and lame" (v. 21). The Lukan redaction is clearly seen through the comparison with Matthew's "as many as you find, both bad and good" (Matt. 22:10). Luke's invitation list here agrees exactly with v. 13, except for the inverted order of blind and lame.

It is obvious then that Luke has joined together in 14:13 and

14:21, as well as in 7:22, the recipients of the good news on the basis of Isaiah 61:1-2. Moreover, it is equally plain that in each instance the literal understanding of the recipients is intended.[20] They are examples of people in dire need, persons suffering from poverty and disease, who have no earthly means to repay their donors.

Furthermore, it is necessary to keep in mind the social and religious status of the "poor, maimed, blind, lame, lepers and possessed" in Jesus' day. At best, they existed on the edge of society. At Qumran, the crippled, blind, and physically blemished were excluded from the community altogether and were specifically designated as unworthy to join in the final eschatological battle between the elect and the hosts of Belial.[21] Also in the rabbinic literature of the time, illness and poverty stood under a cloud of suspicion. Within Palestinian society itself, lepers were outcasts and the blind, deaf, dumb, and beggars were forbidden from the Holy Place in the Temple. Thus we are envisioning here a segment of the populace that was religiously and socially apart and that lived in complete dependence on the goodness of others. Hence the good news must have something to do with a change of their status, both before God and within the fellowship of other human beings.

"Blessed Are You Poor" (Luke 6:20-23)

Among the most striking witnesses to the theme of good news to the poor are the Lukan beatitudes and woes. While no direct reliance upon Isaiah 61 can be demonstrated, nevertheless there seems to be general agreement that the beatitudes of both Matthew and Luke take their distinct theological character from an eschatological understanding of Isaiah 61.[22] Not only do we share this consensus, we also believe that the Lukan version of the beatitudes conforms most closely to the intention of Isaiah 61 and the Jubilee vision enshrined within it. For the moment we are concerned primarily with the beatitudes; yet the antithetical woes help illumine the meaning of the beatitudes and will figure prominently in our later discussion of Luke's attitude toward possessions.

It is important at the outset to grasp the similarities and differences between the Matthean and Lukan beatitudes. Just as the Matthean Sermon on the Mount begins with the beatitudes (Matt.

5:1-12) so does the Lukan Sermon on the Plain. Similar, too, is that in both gospels the sermon occupies a central position in setting forth the teaching of Jesus, though this is admittedly more true of Matthew than Luke. Nevertheless, it plays a thematic role for Luke also, and fills in much of the specific content of Jesus teaching.[23] But here the obvious similarities end and some crucial differences come into view. Let us see how this is so.

The Lukan beatitudes are addressed to the poor, the hungry, the weeping, and the persecuted. How shall we interpret this group? Or to put it more clearly, who are the poor of the Lukan beatitudes? There is an emerging consensus that in the Lukan beatitudes the audience differs fundamentally from that of Matthew's. There are two basic arguments for this consensus.

The first draws its force from a comparison with the Matthean beatitudes. The Matthean version offers a strongly spiritualized interpretation, particularly evident in those sayings directly parallel with Luke's. E.g., Matthew addresses the "poor in spirit" and "those who hunger and thirst after righteousness." Consistent with this are the blessings on the meek, the mourners, the merciful and the pure in heart. Repeatedly the hearer is directed toward the inward condition of the recipients of the divine blessing.

In Luke, however, it is quite otherwise. We find no spiritualizing additions to any of the beatitudes. The conditions described as blessed belong to the stark realities of life. The people addressed are simply and literally the poor, the hungry, the weeping and the persecuted. A respected scholar has summarized the differences succinctly in this manner: "Unlike Matthew's inward look to the condition of those whom God approves, Luke's beatitudes have the external elements of poverty in view. . . . They are characterized by an acute sense of the miseries of the oppressed class, and by the expectation of a reversal of conditions." [24]

The second argument supporting this interpretation is drawn from the Lukan woes (Luke 6:24-26). They are notably absent in Matthew's gospel. But Luke has constructed this key sermon so that the opening beatitudes have their antithetical counterpart in the woes. And if we were already able to conclude from a comparison with Matthew's version of the beatitudes that Luke has the literally poor and suffering in mind, this understanding is confirmed by the woes. For the woes are addressed to the rich, to those who

can laugh, and to the well-esteemed. In each case they are the antithesis to the poor and suffering of the beatitudes. The clear social
distinctions drawn here are between the haves and the have-nots,
the possessors and the impoverished, those favored by society and
those despised. The new and surprising element is the way in
which the norms and values of society are turned upside down.
The promised blessings belong to the suffering poor, while the
coming woes are pronounced upon the contented rich. According
to one commentator, this marks the first time in Jewish religious
literature that the poor are directly called the blessed.[25]

A related question of some importance for our study has to do
with the origin of the Lukan and Matthean versions. Perhaps the
majority of commentators have concluded that the Lukan version
of the beatitudes is the oldest or earliest form of the Q tradition.
Their arguments include the fact that Luke uses the form of direct
address ("Blessed are you . . ."), that his beatitudes are the sim-
plest and fewest in number, and that Luke would scarcely alter the
beatitudes in a non-spiritualized direction if they were originally
inward-looking. We find these arguments persuasive. However, there
are counter arguments which favor the Matthean version, among
which is the striking fact that the phrase "poor in spirit" has been
found three times in the Qumran literature, indicating its Jewish
origins.[26] Moreover the origin of the woes in Luke is an unsettled
question, to which a wide variety of answers have been given. If,
however, we are correct in viewing the Lukan beatitudes as the
earliest form, then it demonstrates all the more that Jesus directed
his ministry from the beginning to the socially and economically
deprived persons in society. Then, too, we can say it was a movement begun among the poor and dispossessed, to whom Jesus promised the good news of the kingdom and a coming time of social reversal. This, at least, is the way Luke understood Jesus' ministry,
according to the beatitudes.

But can we be any more precise about the identity of the poor in
the beatitudes? Are they the poor masses, or the poor disciples?
According to Luke, the sermon of Jesus was spoken in the presence
of a great crowd of both disciples and multitudes, who had come
to hear him and witness his healings (Luke 6:17, 7:1). Yet in Luke
6:20, the beatitudes are addressed specifically to the disciples. Thus,
although the people are not excluded, the disciples are the special

recipients of Jesus' teaching and the ones who are addressed as "you poor."

This has led to the suggestion that Luke views the poor of his beatitudes as poor believers, i.e., Christian *anawim*, whose status is one of both social and spiritual poverty. Or an even more attractive suggestion is that Luke has in mind "earthly disciples who abandoned their possessions and broke family ties for the sake of the kingdom." [27] Appealing as this is, especially because of Luke's intense interest in the demand to abandon all of one's possessions for the kingdom's sake, it seems too limited, since as we shall see not all of Jesus' followers are asked to give up their entire possessions. Yet all of his followers would seem to be included among the blessed poor of the beatitudes. Nevertheless, Luke does seem to imply that an inseparable connection exists between genuine poverty and faithful discipleship. For this reason, the poor are promised the kingdom of God.

In conclusion, we have argued that the Lukan beatitudes are addressed to people who are literally poor and persecuted. Yet their poverty is blessed within the context of their response to the ministry of Jesus and the call to the kingdom of God (cf. v. 22). Thus it is not just poverty or riches per se that is blessed or condemned, but poverty in the context of trust in God and riches in the context of rejection of God. The two go hand in hand for Luke. Nevertheless, there is still something of the powerful prophetic woes against the exploitive rich that rings loud and clear throughout this passage. And this sense of injustice and God's promised eschatological reversal is substantiated by other texts in Luke's gospel as well. Finally, we again must note the direct link between this text and Luke 4:16-21 in the theme of "good news to the poor." In fact, as a few scholars have recently suggested, the Lukan beatitudes may be a kind of early Christian commentary on Isaiah 61:1-2. [28]

The Poor Await the Good News (Luke 1-2)

We also find the theme of "good news to the poor" in the Lukan birth narratives. Recent studies have pointed to the traditions and themes in the infancy stories that reflect the *anawim* movement in Judaism. [29] In Chapter One we traced the emergence of this movement in the Psalms, and from there through the various intertesta-

mental writings, including the Qumran scrolls. As we saw, the basic
characteristics of the *anawim* was their self-understanding as the
pious poor, who lived in utter dependence upon God. While this
sense of spiritual poverty seems uppermost, it went hand in hand
with their lowly economic, political and social status in society.
Hence one can never remove the social realism of genuine poverty
and need from their self-identity.

Each of the actors and actresses in the Lukan Christmas pageant
are appropriately cast in the role of the *anawim*. The first pair,
Zechariah and Elizabeth, are described as "righteous" and "blame-
less" in the observance of the Law (1:6). Nothing specific is mentioned about their social status; yet as a member of the lower
priestly class we know they lived among the poor in Israel. However,
one special need is singled out, Elizabeth's childlessness, which was
a source of much shame (v. 25).[30] Thus when she finally gives birth
to a son, she rejoices that this reproach has been taken away. Zechariah, too, bursts into a prophetic hymn of exultation over the in-
breaking of the promised redemption. This early hymn also makes
references to political deliverance from one's enemies, thus reflecting
the ancient hopes of Israel for deliverance from their oppressors
(1:71).

Similar in many ways is the brief portrait of another pair, Simeon
and Anna. They also are righteous and devout, living in patient
expectation of the imminent consolation/redemption of Israel (2:25,
38). Simeon's vocation is not revealed but his glowing piety and
trust in the Spirit's guidance is manifest. His prayer of thanksgiving
envisions God's salvation embracing the world, but his prophetic
word to Mary points to the pain of Israel's rejection. Anna, whom
Luke calls a prophetess, has been a widow for many long years.[31]
We should recall that among Israel's poor, widows, orphans, and
strangers are those most remembered. But it is Anna's faithful devo-
tion in the Temple of the Lord that catches Luke's attention (v.
37). Thus in both of these exemplary models of male and female
Jewish piety, we catch a glimpse of the pious poor who wait upon
God for all their needs.

Of course the main figure in the Lukan infancy narrative is Mary,
the mother of Jesus. Joseph's role, unlike Matthew's account, is quite
insignificant, except as the partner of Mary. In Luke's drama, Mary
is the example par excellence of those who believe.[32] She receives

the word of her favored status with God in a spirit of humble faith and acceptance (Luke 1:38, 1:45). Of special significance is her self-description, "handmaid," i.e. slave-girl or maidservant of the Lord. The term itself conveys something of her humble circumstances. But its full meaning for Luke becomes apparent only in the great hymn ascribed to Mary, the Magnificat.[33] In the first part of the hymn, vv. 46-50, Mary marvels at God's regard for her, since, humanly speaking she is of such low estate (v. 48). She belongs in this respect to the little people, the nothings of our world. Yet God, the Most' Holy One, exalted her to become an instrument of blessing to the world. Then in the second part of the hymn, vv. 51-56, comes the application. God's exultation of Mary is indicative of the way God always acts. He is the one who puts down the mighty and exalts those of low degree. He is the one who fills the hungry with good things and sends the rich away empty (1:52-53).

With the coming of God's redemption in Christ the great reversal of status is underway and God manifests his bias for the poor and lowly. Thus we find anticipated already in the Magnificat the theme of the beatitudes and woes. Any attempt to spiritualize the text in such a way as to avoid its social impact will not do it justice. For it speaks unequivocally of the saving God who acts with justice to bring down the proud and oppressors and to exalt the lowly and oppressed. Mary, to be sure, represents the faithful people of God of all generations. But her faithfulness is rooted in the God who comes to the lowly with the promise of freedom and hope, and who is at work making this promise a reality.

In addition to the main characters in Luke's opening drama who personify the *anawim,* we find a few other traces of Luke's interest in the poor in the general plot of the story. The census mentioned in Chapter 2 brings to mind vividly Israel's political oppression, which in a few short years would lead to the tragic revolt and the destruction of Jerusalem and the Temple in A.D. 70. Joseph and Mary, as part of the subject people, must obey the bidding of Caesar and be enrolled for the hated head-tax.[34]

There are also several features in the actual birth story of Jesus which emphasize the lowly social status of his family. The offering they bring for the purification of Mary, a pair of turtledoves or two young pigeons, is that prescribed for the poor (Luke 2:22-24). The rich offered a lamb. This tells us that though Joseph was an artisan and so belonged to the middle class, his actual economic situation was something less. Perhaps even the lack of a room for them in Bethlehem may imply their inability to pay enough. The entire story of the manger birth evokes a sense of God's activity in the midst of earthly poverty.

This is even true of the story about the shepherds, named as the first recipients of God's good news to the world. Shepherds appear on nearly every list of despised professions in the rabbinic literature.[35] Despite their numbers and the seeming usefulness of their work, they were held in contempt because of their vulgarity and ignorance and especially because of their lack of moral character. By reputation, shepherds were thought to graze on lands not their own. The image of the "good shepherd," while biblical, seems rare. Rather, they belonged to the lowest stratum, if not among the outcasts. Yet surprisingly, Luke singles them out to hear the first preaching of the good news to the poor.

What we have tried to show is that the Lukan birth narratives present the opening drama of a God who puts down the mighty and the rich from their positions of eminence and raises up those of low degree. In these stories the revelation of the new age begun in Jesus the Christ is given to the poor and the lowly, as well as the pious and the not so pious. It does not seem too much to say that Luke is here already anticipating the good news to the poor embodied in Jesus' ministry throughout his Gospel.

Outcasts and Sinners Hear the Good News

A further identifiable group that we believe should be included under Luke's concept of the poor can be discussed broadly under the rubric "outcasts and sinners."[36] Two important facts concerning these outcasts need to be stated at the outset. One is the awareness that Luke's gospel as a whole concentrates thematically on this group. The familiar portrait of Jesus as the friend of tax collectors and sinners receives its most complete form in Luke. A second factor is the further recognition that this portrait is most characteristic of the special L traditions. While Jesus' association with outcasts and sinners is rooted in the Mark and Q sources (Mark 2:15-17; Luke 7:34; Matt. 11:19), its most powerful illustrations, within parables and stories, come from "L." It is not without good reason that Luke's gospel has often been characterized as the "gospel for sinners."

Who are the outcasts and sinners from Luke's perspective? The people most frequently named together are the tax collectors and sinners, whom we identified in Chapter Two.[37] Vocationally, religiously, and socially, they belonged to the culturally dispossessed in Jesus' day. At the same time, the poor and the sick, though mentioned separately from the tax collectors and sinners in the tradition, are brought together by Luke. For example, in Luke 7, Jesus' ministry to the poor and sick is both a messianic sign and a cause of offense to the Baptist and others (7:18-23). Similarly in the same chapter, both the Baptist's ascetism and Jesus' own friendship with tax collectors and sinners are a cause of offense to their contemporaries (7:31-35). In each case, Jesus' ministry is a stumbling block to others, as he seeks to bring good news and healing to those at the margin of his culture both religiously and socially.

Elsewhere in his gospel, Luke can refer to the outcasts and sinners as the sick who need a physician (5:31), a description which comes from Mark, or more characteristically as the "lost" (19:10). Luke, in fact, frames the entire public ministry of Jesus with the two christological sayings, "I have not come to call the righteous, but sinners to repentance" (5:32) and "the Son of man came to seek and to save the lost" (19:10). Obviously, the sick, the sinner, and the lost are the primary objects of God's redemptive good news for Luke.

This unique emphasis on the outcasts and sinners finds expression in a number of Lukan texts, such as the encounter with the sinful woman in the house of Simon the Pharisee (7:36-50), or the famous parable of contrast between the pious Pharisee and the repentant tax collector (18:9-14) or the story of Zacchaeus, the chief tax collector (19:1-10). However the central exhibit of this theme in Luke's gospel occurs in Chapter 15, a chapter sometimes described as "the gospel within the gospel."[38] Commentators have pointed out that each of the three parables in this chapter were originally spoken in defense of Jesus' association with the outcasts.[39] Luke has preserved the original context by introducing the parables as Jesus' response to his critics (15:2). His defense is simply this: he acts as God would act. His acceptance of outcasts and sinners reflect God's acceptance and forgiveness. Because of this, he directs his own attack against the pious who would exclude them from participation in the mercy and joy of the kingdom. The elder son who can't rejoice at his brother's return (15:25-32) or the Pharisee who prays in smug comfort, "I thank thee that I am not like other men" (18:11), or Simon the Pharisee, who doubts Jesus' authenticity as a prophet because he accepts the gratitude of a prostitute (7:39), all three represent a false religious piety which ostracizes itself from the people on the fringe and thereby separates itself from the joy of the Father's love. Conversely, Jesus' acceptance of these people into his fellowship points to his creation of a new community of those who were formerly on the outs with God and with other people. In this sense, "the first will be last and the last first," and God's promised eschatological reversal for the poor has already become a reality in the ministry of Jesus.

In this way the central depiction of Jesus' activity in Luke's gospel can be easily understood within the framework of the good news to the poor. The outcasts and sinners from a major part of those to whom the good news is proclaimed and who by virtue of this good news have found a new place to stand within the family of God and the family of humanity.

The Rich and the Poor

The final group that needs to be related to the Lukan theme of good news to the poor is perhaps the most obvious. These are "the rich and the poor." As we shall observe in Part II, Luke has a greater concentration of traditions about wealth and poverty than the other evangelists. In fact, one commentator has argued that Luke wrote his entire gospel precisely to deal with the problems caused by wealth and poverty within his own community.[40]

While that thesis may be too strong, the texts are there, as we will soon see. There are the parables of the Rich Fool, the Rich Man and Lazarus and the Dishonest Steward; there is the story of the rich tax collector Zacchaeus and the story of the economic sharing within the primitive community. These and more cry out for attention to the serious reader. And all of these, we suggest, are related to the announcement of good news to the poor. If this is true, then in these texts we have once again confirmed our findings that the poor for Luke are the socially and economically poor.

It has been our intention throughout this chapter to demonstrate the centrality of the theme of good news to the poor announced by the Lukan Jesus at the outset of his ministry, and then to show how Luke interprets this theme so as to include those who are poor in a social and economic sense. Luke does not allow us to merely spiritualize the concept of the poor. In fact, it is our contention that the weight of the texts falls on a literal understanding of the poor. As we have seen, the poor include those suffering from genuine poverty and need, who are sharply contrasted with the rich and powerful. These poor are promised a radical social reversal of their lot in the coming age. The poor also include the sick and the possessed, those living on the edge of society, who are offered healing and full acceptance within the fellowship gathered around the healer. They include as well the outcasts and sinners, those excluded socially and religiously because of despised professions and immoral lives, who are welcomed back into the Father's good graces, and offered a new status of full participation in the community gathered around Jesus and his disciples. They include even the disciples of Jesus, who have left all in his service, and who await with eager anticipation the coming deliverance, when the lowly will be exalted and the mighty brought low.

Plainly, the concept of the poor has a broad focus in Luke's gospel. For its particular meaning each text must be examined on its own merit. Nevertheless, this conclusion seems evident: the ministry of Jesus announced by the Isaiah quotation in Luke 4:16-21 is embodied in Luke's gospel in very real social and economic, as well as moral and spiritual dimensions. It identifies Jesus' redemptive ministry inseparably with the poor and the hungry, the sick and the afflicted, the captives and the oppressed, the outcasts and the sinners. For Luke's gospel, these include hard social realities, as well as deep spiritual needs.

But this is not all. If we are to interpret correctly the announcement of good news to the poor in Luke 4:16-21, we must add to the description of Jesus' ministry embodied in Luke's Gospel the significance of the Isaiah texts themselves. We have seen that Isaiah 61:1-2 proclaims the promise of freedom and restoration to the nation in exile. The enrichment of the text from Isaiah 58:6 carries with it a ringing call for justice and liberation. We have further seen that this promise of liberation in Isaiah 61 is expressed through the vision of the Jubilee Year. This brings to mind the radical restructuring of society toward a more just and humane system that the Jubilee Year set forth. However, since the Jubilee vision of Isaiah 61 was already transformed by late Judaism into an eschatological symbol, it seems highly unlikely that Jesus or the evangelists would understand it literally. Yet the Jubilee vision of Isaiah 61 persists, as both a powerful symbol of God's call to justice in the new age and as a stubborn reminder that the good news embodied in Jesus' ministry and that of his followers must reveal itself in concrete acts of love and liberation on behalf of the poor and oppressed. In this manner the Isaiah texts and the Jubilee vision in particular lend significant weight to the social dimension of Jesus' ministry to the poor, as announced in Luke 4:16-21 and fulfilled in Luke's gospel.

Another interpreter has written concerning Luke 4, "The Old Testament passages enable us—indeed force us—to understand that which God began in Jesus not simply as release from sin but as all those concrete kinds of physical, social and economic liberation of which the Old Testament speaks. At the same time Luke will not allow us to assume that those things which oppress the souls and minds and lives of people are tied wholly to their physical situation. The gospel reminds us that the freedom God intends through Christ is at root release from the entanglement and dominance of sin in our lives." [41] Both, we would claim, belong to the redemptive ministry of Jesus as depicted by Luke and announced by the proclamation of good news to the poor.

Part II

THE RICH AND THE POOR

In Part II of this study, we will examine those texts in the Lukan writings that bear on the question of wealth and poverty. Among the evangelists, Luke preserves by far the greater amount of material dealing with this subject. Obviously it has greater importance for him, not only as a part of the tradition about Jesus, but also as a message for the Christian communities with whom he is in touch and for whom he writes.[1]

Within his gospel, Luke has placed this subject in the broader context of Jesus' proclamation to the poor. As we have emphasized in the previous chapter, the Lukan Jesus is preeminently the Savior of the poor to whom the Kingdom of God is promised.

Thus it is upon the background of this total picture of Jesus' ministry that one must seek to understand the Lukan presentation of the theme of possessions. It is our thesis that Luke regards the subject of wealth and poverty as a practical test-case in the Christian realization of good news to the poor. As Jesus himself went to the poor with the good news of the kingdom, so his followers are to do the same. But this is no abstract or theoretical matter for Luke. Rather, it is one that affects among other things the way one regards and uses one's possessions. For the attitude toward one's possessions is a clear sign of whether or not one is fulfilling the mission of Jesus to the poor. Hence it is a topic of urgent significance for Luke.

His vital interest in this question is immediately apparent when one observes what he takes over from his sources. Luke includes all of the Markan texts on the rich and poor, except the anointing scene with its oft-abused remark of Jesus, "for you always have the poor with you" (Mark 14:3-9).[2] Similarly, Luke takes over all the Q texts on possessions. Most striking, however, are the many additional traditions of his own on wealth and poverty which Luke incorporates into his gospel.[3] It will be our task to examine this material

85

in order to determine the specifically Lukan attitude toward possessions that emerges from them. Our procedure will move along these lines: First, to carefully observe the alterations Luke may have made from the Markan and Q traditions and inquire about their significance. Second, to examine the L material, with respect both to its content and setting in the gospel. Third, to try to grasp the significance of all these texts for the community to whom Luke writes. This, in turn, can prepare the way for the contemporary question, namely, the meaning of relevance of these texts for the Christian community today.

Three major themes occur in the Lukan writings on the subject of wealth and poverty:

- The call to total surrender of one's possessions

- Warnings about the dangers of wealth

- Instructions and exhortations on the right use of one's wealth

Each of these themes will be examined at some length in the following chapters. We will begin with a consideration of the call for a total surrender of one's possessions.

4

The Call to
Total Surrender
of One's Possessions

There are a number of texts which bring to the fore the most radical solution of all to the problem of wealth, i.e., the call to total renunciation. Luke has clearly found this call in the tradition which he has taken over from Mark, yet he himself has sharply intensified this demand. Why has he done so? Does this represent Luke's own fundamental attitude toward wealth? A few have thought so. Or is there another reason for this emphasis? Again one can ask, to whom is this call directed or intended? Is it meant for all believers or only a few? For Jesus' time or for all time? There have been many answers suggested, as one might suppose. Before proposing our own understanding of these texts, however, we want to examine first the evidence in the gospel itself.

"They Left Everything and Followed Him" (Luke 5:11)

The core of this tradition on the call of the first disciples is found in Mark 1:16-20. But Luke's version has added a section centering on Peter's miraculous catch of fish, an addition that undoubtedly is intended to prefigure Peter's missionary activity in Acts (vv. 4-10).

However, the most revealing change to note for our purposes is the small but significant alteration at the end of the story. Whereas Mark says only that the disciples immediately left their nets and followed Jesus, Luke's version reads, "they left *everything* and followed him." The stress is clearly on "everything" *(panta)*, as subsequent texts will confirm. This seems to be Luke's own addition. He thereby wants to emphasize the totality of the call. The three fishermen left behind their job, their families, and all their possessions to follow Jesus. The break was complete.

87

Luke's description also allows us to glimpse something of what this may have meant economically. Fishermen belonged to the middle class. From Luke's version we can probably infer that the three fishermen were fairly prosperous, especially by the fact that they formed a partnership, an obvious business venture (vv. 7, 10). Hence the call to leave everything may have meant a considerable sacrifice.

The question has been raised as to whether the disciples were required to leave everything behind or whether they did so voluntarily. They were not forced, of course, to become disciples. Luke, in fact, omits Jesus' usual words of invitation, "follow me," though the invitation is implied (v. 10). But did Jesus require total abandonment of everything as a condition of discipleship or was this simply a voluntary act in imitation of Jesus' own life-style? While this question is not directly answered in this text or others, it seems as though at least the twelve disciples were asked to engage in a full-time discipleship with Jesus that allowed no exceptions during his earthly ministry.

In this text the call to total abandonment of one's possessions is limited to three persons, who become members of Jesus select circle of the Twelve. Are these, then, the only ones to whom this call is directed, or are there others? This question we will pursue further. For these three, at least, it is a call to complete renunciation of their possessions for the sake of a life of discipleship.

"He Left Everything . . . and Followed Him" (Luke 5:28)

The call of Levi, the tax collector, also emphasizes the complete separation from one's possessions. In Mark 2:14 and Matthew 9:9 we read that Levi simply rises from his desk at the tax office and follows Jesus. But according to Luke, "he left *everything* and rose and followed him."

Once more the break is total. In Levi's case, the economic sacrifice was probably even greater than that of the fishermen. While not all tax collectors were rich, and Levi was not a chief tax collector like Zacchaeus (Luke 19:1-10), who had persons serving under him, Luke stresses Levi's considerable wealth. In v. 29 he has Levi prepare a "great feast" in his house, to which a "large crowd" of tax collectors and others are invited (cf. Mark 2:15).[1] It was only the well-to-do who owned large houses who could afford a large banquet with many guests. So the call to Levi meant the abandonment of his possessions which supported a comfortable life-style that few in Palestine enjoyed.

Levi, too, joins the limited circle of the Twelve, who leave everything to follow Jesus. But in vv. 29-32 we catch a glimpse of a wider group of people who are being called into fellowship with Jesus, without any specific mention of the need to renounce all their possessions. These tax collectors and sinners are called to repentance but that is all.[2] So the question remains open whether or not more than the Twelve were asked to abandon all their possessions in response to the call of Jesus.

"Sell All That You Have . . . and Come, Follow Me" (Luke 18:18-23)

This story of the rich ruler, along with the subsequent section on the problem of riches, is also found in all the synoptic gospels (Mark 10:17-31/Matt. 19:16-30). The Lukan alterations are minor, yet they typically heighten the emphasis on wealth and the call to its surrender for the kingdom's sake. In Luke's version alone is the rich man designated a ruler (v. 18). It may be that Luke thinks of him as a member of the ruling council, the Sanhedrin. At any rate, the mention of his position as a ruler is doubtless meant to enhance his social and economic status in the eyes of the reader. Even more characteristic is the way Luke sets forth the demand which the ruler fails to meet: "Sell *all* that you have and distribute to the poor, and you will have treasure in heaven; and come, follow me." Once again, we encounter the Lukan "all" *(panta)* in the demand to follow Jesus (cf. Mark 10:21/Matt. 19:21, "sell what you have"). While the other versions may imply the need to leave everything behind, Luke alone specifies that Jesus meant all.

But to whom is this demand for the total abandonment of possessions directed? The rich ruler is not being called into the circle of the Twelve. Is he then being called into a wider circle of disciples, who must also sell all their possessions to follow Jesus? If so, is this demand true for all followers of Jesus? Or is this only an isolated case, in that only for this rich man was it necessary to break totally with his possessions, his trusted treasure, to gain the kingdom? The words of v. 22, "come, follow me," would seem to make this a call into a wider circle of Jesus' earthly disciples, similar perhaps to the seventy and others, who apparently lived in constant fellowship with Jesus (10:1). This possibility is strengthened by the words of Peter in v. 28, "Lo, we have left our homes and followed you." The reply of Jesus, "There is no man who has left house or wife or parents . . ." indicates that many more than the Twelve are included in Peter's words. Therefore it could be argued that the story of the rich ruler is a discipleship story, in which the command to sell all is not just a necessity for this one rich man but a command intended for all who are called into full-time discipleship with Jesus, at least during his earthly ministry.[3]

However, in vv. 24-30 the problem of wealth is not limited merely to those called into full-time fellowship with Jesus, but is expanded to apply to all rich people. Vv. 24-25 say bluntly, the rich can't enter the kingdom of God. Vv. 26-27 soften this only to the extent that God can do the humanly impossible. So the problem in these verses has shifted from the question of one rich man and his call to earthly discipleship to that of all rich people and their possibility of entering the kingdom of God. Obviously one can enter the kingdom of God without being or becoming full-time earthly disciples. But can one enter the kingdom of God without abandoning all one's possessions? Not only this one rich man, but all the rich are addressed with this question. Can the rich get in? That's the tough question raised by this text, and left open, though barely.[4]

In the concluding verses Jesus promises that those who have left all for the kingdom's sake will receive manifold in this age and eternal life in the next age (vv. 28-30). Compared with Mark and Matthew, Luke speaks in more general terms about the rewards, though he alone mentions "wife" in the list of what is left behind (cf. Luke 14:26).[5] However the same question arises here. Is the example of leaving all for the sake of the kingdom of God intended for all would-be followers of Jesus, or it is limited to a particular group and/or to a particular period of history?

"Whoever of You Does Not Renounce All that He Has Cannot Be My Disciple" (Luke 14:33)

In order to understand this text regarding the cost of discipleship and the way in which Luke adapts it for his own purposes, it

is necessary first of all to note the setting to which it belongs, vv.
25-33. Luke has obviously composed this section using traditions
from Q, Mark and his own special source.

In vv. 25-27 we have a double-saying on the radical break required for discipleship, taken from Q and Mark (Matt. 10:37-38;
Mark 8:34/Matt. 16:24/Luke 9:23). Compared with Matthew, Luke
has typically heightened the demand for discipleship in the Q saying. Luke substituted the word "hate" for the Matthean "more than
me" in v. 26 and extended this "hate" not only to one's own wife
but even to one's own life (cf. 18:29). What is the meaning of "hate"
for Luke? Very likely, Luke has taken this word from another Q
tradition, the one on the impossibility of serving two masters (Matt.
6:24/Luke 16:13). In both, he uses it to emphasize the uncompromising character of the call to serve or follow Jesus. It is either/or.
Either one leaves the old loyalties behind, or one does not. And this
includes the willingness to bear one's own cross (v. 27). This saying,
too, has been much misunderstood. Whatever its original form and
meaning, it obviously took on a new light in view of Jesus' crucifixion, so that for the early church and Luke's readers it meant the
readiness to suffer even martyrdom, if necessary, for the kingdom's
sake. In this sense, it has nothing to do with personal hardships or
crosses people bear as a normal part of life. Rather, it reflects the
cost of discipleship, which could come even to the point of hating
one's own life, i.e. martyrdom (v. 26).

The theme of the cost of discipleship provides the link with vv.
28-33. Here we find double parables unique to Luke (L), the parable of the Tower Builder and the King Going to War. They both
make the same point: consider the cost of discipleship before responding. In the parable of the Great Banquet recorded earlier in
Chapter 14, the point was made that those originally invited to the
kingdom had refused to break with their past commitments and
hence were excluded (14:15-25). But in the twin parables, those
who are willing to make the break, or who say they are, are cau-
tioned to first count its cost, lest they fail to carry through (cf.
9:57-62/Matt. 22:11-14). Luke's point is plain: without total devo-
tion to Jesus there can be no genuine discipleship. "If any one
comes to me and does not hate . . . ," or "whoever does not bear
his own cross . . . ," or "whoever of you does not renounce all that
he has cannot be my disciple" (vv. 26, 27, 33).

The most surprising verse is the conclusion (v. 33). It is uniquely Lukan. It summarizes the preceding discussion and draws out
the primary meaning ("So therefore . . ."). In light of vv. 25-33
one expects that the call to suffering and martyrdom would serve
as the supreme example of the cost of discipleship. But instead
v. 33 contains the call to the total abandonment of one's possessions
in order to become a disciple. It should be noted that the Greek
behind the RSV translation "all that he has" means "all his possessions." Thus one more time we encounter the Lukan "all" *(panta)*
with respect to the surrender of possessions.

Why does Luke so surprisingly emphasize the abandonment of
possessions as the highest demand in the service of Jesus? The
question is important, and may provide a clue to the kind of community or persons for whom Luke writes. Apparently, Luke is not
concerned with offering a logical discussion of Jesus' call to discipleship, in which case martyrdom would be the highest demand (cf.
1 Cor. 13:3). Rather, we agree with the perceptive suggestion that
Luke has shaped the tradition to respond to a situation in his own
Christian community, where the problem of possessions was a
burning issue.[6]

To whom does Luke address these words in his gospel? Unlike
the previous traditions we have examined, according to v. 25 Jesus
is addressing the crowds and not an inner circle of followers (or
prospective ones). His words are spoken to anyone or everyone
who wants to be his disciple (vv. 26, 33). Of every potential disciple he asks the same thing, the renunciation of all they possess.
Without it, or so it seems, it is not possible to be a disciple of Jesus.

The one question that still remains unanswered is whether the
call for a total renunciation of one's possessions is intended only
for the time of Jesus or whether it is meant for all time. However
we answer that, this passage heightens the demand to surrender
one's possessions for the sake of the gospel. What does Luke have
in mind, and why does he stress this so emphatically?

"Sell Your Possessions, and Give Alms" (Luke 12:33)

Here we find yet another Lukan text issuing a call to abandon
one's possessions for the sake of the kingdom. While the characteristic Lukan admonition to sell all *(panta)* is not included, the gen-

eral thrust of the passage is in agreement with this Lukan emphasis.

All of Chapter 12 deals with the theme of Christian discipleship in the world. But the problem of possessions and trust in God occupies center stage. In vv. 13-21 we have the dispute over an inheritance followed by the parable of the Rich Fool, both illustrating the power of greed. Then in vv. 22-34 Luke introduces a passage on anxiety and trust, which concludes with the appeal to sell one's possessions and give alms. Both sections are linked together by v. 22, where the word "therefore" connects the preceding parable to the subsequent words on trusting God. Moreover, both sections speak to the topic of covetousness and its antithesis of being rich toward God. While the dispute over the inheritance and the parable of the Rich Fool portray the ultimate foolishness of those who acquire treasures only for themselves, the words that follow describe the wisdom of those who store up treasures in heaven.

Our particular concern at this point is with vv. 22-34. Luke has drawn on several sources to compose this section. In vv. 22-31 he has taken up the Q tradition shared with Matthew, only he has given it a different context.[7] The meaning of these verses is plain. In contrast to the attitude of covetousness so evident in the example of the Rich Fool, the disciples of Jesus are counseled to trust the fatherly care of God for their basic needs. The Father so abundantly provides for his creation, "how much more" will he provide for his own! Hence the repeated counsel not to be anxious, which concludes with the assuring words, "seek his kingdom and these things shall be yours as well" (v. 31).[8]

In vv. 32-34 Luke has combined at least two independent sayings from his own special source. Together they provide a second response to the problem of covetousness, the response of giving to the poor. The disciples are designated "little flock," and told not to be afraid because the Father intends to give them the kingdom.[9] Undoubtedly behind this term "little flock" stands a realistic awareness of the earthly needs of the disciples and their lowly social, economic and political status in the world. Yet they are promised the kingdom. But how do they inherit this promised kingdom?

The answer is given in vv. 33-34. "Sell your possessions, and give alms." This is the way they acquire treasures in heaven that will never grow old, which neither thief can steal nor moth destroy.

And in exchange for the surrender of earthly possessions, Jesus disciples gain treasures in heaven.

But is this really a command for the total abandonment of possessions? It could be argued that these verses advocate only the selling of enough to give alms. This would then be in line with Jewish teaching, in which the practice of almsgiving was enjoined repeatedly on all the faithful. However, the thrust of the passage goes far beyond the recommendation simply to follow the accepted meritorious practice of almsgiving. At stake in this passage is the life or death matter of inheriting the kingdom (v. 32), of becoming "rich toward God" (v. 21), of realizing one's life does not consist in the abundance of possessions (v. 15), of seeking the kingdom and trusting God for daily needs (v. 31), of looking inward to discern whether the treasure of one's heart lies in God or mammon (v. 34). Therefore the meaning of the command to sell one's possessions and give alms would seem to be the same as it was in the earlier passages we have examined, i.e. a command to sell all in the service of the kingdom and the discipleship of Jesus. By selling all, one becomes free for the new life of the kingdom. This interpretation agrees, too, with Luke's use of the simple past tense for "sell" and "give," which normally indicates a once-for-all act. The command to give alms indicates the use to which one's possessions should be directed. Alms are given for the poor, the needy, the orphan, the widow and the stranger. Thus we again meet the theme so familiar in Luke, the theme centered on his portrait of Jesus' mission to the poor, as we have examined earlier.

To whom are the words of Jesus intended? According to v. 22, Jesus addresses them to the disciples, who in v. 32 are described as the "little flock." This might seem to indicate that only the circle of the Twelve (or Seventy) are included. Yet the entire section deals with the broad theme of discipleship, something not limited to the few. Luke also adds that Jesus speaks these words in the presence of the multitudes (vv. 1, 13, 54). Therefore it seems best to interpret these words as intended for all who would follow him, i.e. disciples in the broadest sense of the term. If this is correct, it means that in this passage as in 14:33, the challenge to surrender all one's possessions is directed toward everyone who call themselves followers or disciples of Jesus. And if this is the case, then it raises the question all the more urgently as to how Luke understands this command for his day, and why he places so heavy a stress on it. Does he intend to limit it to the time of Jesus or does it have special importance for his own day as well?

The Widow Who Gives All (Luke 21:1-4)

The final texts we will consider are not as directly related to the Lukan stress on the total abandonment of possessions as the previous passages, yet they also teach the same theme by way of example.

Luke shares the story of the poor widow with Mark (Mark 12:41-44). He retains the same order and context as the Markan tradition and stresses the same provocative point. In both, the poor widow is contrasted with the scribes "who devour widows' houses," and with the rich (Luke 20:47, 21:1).[10] As was customary, the rich brought their gifts for the poor to the treasury area of the Temple courtyard. These gifts were part of the poor tithe commanded by law of all Jews. For the rich, the tithes may have been a substantial amount. But as Jesus notes, they had much to give. In stark contrast, the poor widow drops in an offering of only two copper coins, the smallest denomination of coins. Yet it was everything she had. Hence the pronouncement of Jesus: "Truly, I tell you, this poor widow has put in more than all of them; for they all contributed out of their abundance, but she out of her poverty put in all the living that she had" (v. 4).

The words "all the living that she had" imply that she gave away everything she possessed. Even though she was one of the poor and even one of those under the special divine protection of Yahweh (widows, orphans, strangers) she held nothing back. Hence her action becomes an example of sacrificial giving, giving that shares unconditionally with the poor. It also serves as the point of contrasting judgment against the rich, who though they may give from their abundance, do not go beyond or even anywhere near the point at which their abundance might be threatened. Only the poor widow grasps the spirit of unlimited love.

While Luke has not reshaped this tradition in any significant way, the reason seems obvious. It already expresses his own attitude toward wealth so well, that he lets it speak for itself. The example of the poor widow is another Lukan challenge to the unconditional

surrender of one's possessions. How literally Luke intends her example to be taken, remains to be discussed. But it is nevertheless
consistent with the attitude expressed in the previous texts we have
already examined.

The Poverty of Jesus and His Disciples
(Luke 9:3, 58; 10:4)

While the example of the poor widow provides one way of teaching the lesson of unconditional sharing of one's wealth, the gospels
direct our attention to an even more powerful example in Jesus
himself.

According to the synoptic tradition, Jesus spent his entire public
ministry as an itinerant preacher/teacher, moving about from place
to place without a permanent residence or supportive occupation.[11]
He broke with home, family, and job to devote full-time to his
proclamation of the in-breaking rule of God (Mark 3:31-35). He
likewise called a select group of followers to share his life of
voluntary poverty (Mark 3:13-14). Their means of support was
undoubtedly the charity of others.

We know that the rabbis in Jesus' day also relied to a considerable extent on the goodwill of others, especially on the gifts of their
pupils. Yet most, if not all, of the rabbis had their own trade or
craft as well, of which Paul is the best-known New Testament
example.[12] Hence Jesus' own life-style differs distinctly from that
of the rabbis and this is also true of his gathering of a select group
of disciples to join him in his itinerant, possessionless life. From
what little we know, they lived from a common purse, a purse
supported by the gifts of followers and others. This common purse
must have provided for their daily needs and provided the means
to pay the Temple tax and offerings for the poor (Matt.17:27, John
13:29). Apparently Judas Iscariot was appointed to supervise the
fund's use (John 12:6).

These traditions are confirmed by the so-called missionary journey of the disciples found in the synoptics (Mark 6:7-13/Matt. 10:1-
15/Luke 9:1-6). Common to each is the instruction of Jesus to take
nothing for their journey, including no bread, bag, or money (Mark
6:8). They are also commanded to stay in only one home as long
as they are welcomed, and to live off the charity offered by this

home (Mark 6:10).[13] In essence, the disciples are told to continue
living as Jesus himself did and as they had lived in his company.
This simple life of poverty is also reflected in a Q tradition on
discipleship (Matt. 8:19-22/Luke 9:57-62). According to this text,
Jesus responds to the enthusiastic words of a prospective volunteer,
"I'll follow you wherever you go," with the warning about its cost.
"The Son of man has nowhere to lay his head." Here again it is clear
that earthly discipleship with Jesus involved the giving up of any
claim to permanent possessions or place. Once more we are confronted by the example of Jesus and his disciples, who have left all
for the kingdom's sake (cf. Mark 10:28).

What we find to be the case with respect to the synoptic tradition
as a whole, is equally true of Luke's gospel. Luke has taken over
the common tradition described above, and has done nothing to
dilute it. In fact, at several points he has strengthened this tradition.
For example, with respect to the manner in which Jesus is supported
by others during his ministry, Luke alone mentions a group of
women from Galilee, who were his constant companions and who
provided for the disciples out of their means (Luke 8:1-3).[14] In the
dark hours of his trial and crucifixion, these women were still present and doubtless were part of the nucleus of followers from which
the early church originated (Luke 23:49, 55-56; 24:1-11; Acts 1:14;
2:1).[15]

Luke also has added to the Q tradition on discipleship the demanding saying on the need to decide decisively for the kingdom
without looking back (9:61-62). But perhaps most striking is the
inclusion of a second missionary journey found only in Luke's gospel (10:1-12).[16] In this oft-described "Gentile journey" Jesus com-
missions seventy other disciples to go before him and prepare the
way for his coming. What catches our attention is that these seventy
are given almost identical instructions as the Twelve received earlier. They are told to carry no purse, bag, or sandals and to remain
in the same house until their work is completed (Luke 10:3-8).
Similarly, they are commanded to eat and drink what the host provides and this is justified by the principle that the laborer deserves
his wages (10:7-8; cf. 2 Cor. 9:14; Gal. 6:6). Thus not only Jesus,
but his disciples too practiced the life of missionary poverty, finding
their needs met by trust in God and by the daily provision that
others extended.

We find, then, that Luke both shares and intensifies the example of poverty exhibited in the life of Jesus and that of his closest followers. The demand to "sell all" for the kingdom's sake, so prominent in Luke's gospel, becomes a matter of Jesus practicing what he preaches. His life of poverty along with that of his disciples are the prime exhibits of a life free of possessions and their hold upon human life. Luke, even more than the other evangelists, presses this point home.

Summary: What Does It All Mean?

We now need to ask how we should interpret Luke's intent with regard to his repeated emphasis upon the total abandonment of possessions. The fact that he has not merely taken over this theme from the tradition, but heightened it as well, proves that it had considerable importance for him. But what might have been the situation in his own community that led him to stress this theme? And what did Luke want to communicate by it? Was Luke actually advocating the total renunciation of possessions as the Christian ideal, if not norm, as a few commentators have suggested? [17] Or is there another solution more appropriate for interpreting this theme in his gospel?

There have been several recent attempts to answer these questions which need to be considered.

1. One explanation begins with the recognition that there are actually two strains of thought in the Lukan writings on possessions. [18] On the one hand, there is the call to a total surrender of one's possessions reflected in the traditions just surveyed. On the other hand, there is the repeated demand for the proper use of possessions, a theme we will develop in Chapter Six.

On this basis it is then argued that the demand for a total surrender of possessions in Luke's gospel is limited to those who are full-time earthly disciples of Jesus, like the Twelve and the Seventy, while the demand for its proper use is intended for the people in general. Applying this same dual-level understanding to the church in Acts and to Luke's own time, it is further argued that Luke aims his radical demand for a total abandonment of possessions at the church leaders of his day, who in effect represent the disciples, while the Christian believers, who are challenged to use their possessions wisely and liberally, represent the people in general.

But does this argument fit the evidence in Luke-Acts? We will eventually have no quarrel with the recognition of the two strains of thought regarding possessions in Luke-Acts. However, the attempt to interpret both themes by creating two distinct groups with separate demands seems artificial and finally impossible. Already in the gospel we observed how the call to abandon one's possessions is not limited simply to the Twelve or the Seventy or any similar select group, but is addressed to everyone who desires to follow Jesus (14:33; 12:33; 18:29; 9:57). Although in actual fact Jesus and his disciples seem to be the only ones who practice the life of poverty, it is not intentionally limited to them, as others are called to share it as well.

The situation is similar in Acts. There seems to be no distinction within the community with respect to the matter of possessions. Whatever abandonment of goods is described in Acts, a question we will discuss later, it is attributed to the whole community and not limited to its leaders. Even the designation "disciple" is not restricted to the few but applied comprehensively to all believers (Acts 6:7). While the Twelve apostles and seven deacons are singled out for special mention by virtue of their respective functions as evangelists and waiters-on-table respectively, their use of earthly possessions is not noticeably different from any others within the early fellowship. What we find instead is that Luke's description of the practice of sharing in the early church points to an action by the whole community, in which all acted together as one heart and soul in possessing their goods in common.[19] Therefore the attempt to explain the sayings calling for a total surrender of possessions as something intended only for the apostles and their successors in the early church fails to match the evidence either in Luke's gospel or Acts. It appears to be a forced attempt to read back later theology and practice into the Lukan writings.

2. Another interpretation has sought the answer to Luke's intensification of the demand for total abandonment by appeal to a context of persecution.[20] It too has recognized the two strains of thought on possessions in Luke-Acts, yet they are explained as the consequence of threatened or actual persecution within the Lukan community.

According to this explanation, Luke writes at a time when many Christians were faced with the loss of their possessions if they publicly confessed loyalty to Christ. Luke meets this threat by underscoring the need to be ready, if necessary, to give up everything for the faith as part of the cost of discipleship. Hence the strengthened call to abandon one's possessions. At the same time, he encourages those Christians who have not suffered the loss of their goods to make them available to the needy, thereby assuring those who suffer that their basic needs will be met. Thus the admonition to share one's wealth freely. The sum of this argument is that Luke's heightened demand to surrender all earthly possessions for the sake of Christ belongs to a specific situation of crisis, in this case a period of persecution. A further argument is that total abandonment is not meant to be a form of discipleship valid for every time and place.

How persuasive is this? There is considerable validity in the attempt to consider the effects of persecution on the problem of possession. A few passages in Luke's gospel do, in fact, bring them closely together. For example, the Lukan beatitudes pronounce God's favor on the persecuted as well as on those who are poor, hungry and weeping (6:20-23). There is also a connection between the willingness to renounce all one's possessions and the possibility of martyrdom in 14:25-33. We know too that the story of the early church in Acts is narrated under the threat of persecution from both the synagogue and the state, so that it is quite possible that the call for total abandonment and total sharing of goods are related to it.

Nevertheless, it is highly doubtful that the context of persecution was the major reason for the strong Lukan emphasis on the complete surrender of one's possessions. Within the gospel itself, the demand to leave all is often unrelated to persecution. More fundamentally it is a response to the problem of covetousness (12:33), or is the final stage of response in the call for discipleship (5:21, 28; 14:33; 18:22). Nor, we would argue, did the early church develop its communal life-style and its shared community of possessions in response to persecution. It evolved rather as the outgrowth of its common experience of the Spirit's activity in its midst, patterned after Jesus' own life and teaching. It may be that the clouds of persecution intensified the problem of possessions. But they do not seem to be the chief motivation or occasion for the Lukan call to the complete surrender of possessions.

3. In our judgment a third recent interpretation offers the most persuasive way to understand Luke's intent.[21] It argues that the call to poverty or abandonment of possessions is limited for Luke only to "earthly discipleship in Jesus' time." [22] Ever since the resurrection/ascension, Jesus himself is no longer present, so that a new form of discipleship is called for (cf. Luke 22:35-38). But if this requirement belongs only to Jesus' time, one might reasonably ask why Luke has stressed it so emphatically and why, in fact, he has made it the highest demand of discipleship (14:33)? While this question is unavoidable, the very fact that Luke himself has expanded this theme shows, according to these interpreters, that it has become an ideal for Luke, something more than simple historical fact. But why this ideal and what is its meaning?

The authors respond by arguing that Luke is dealing with an urgent problem within his own community. His aim in stressing the theme of total abandonment on the part of Jesus and his earliest disciples is to offer a powerful criticism against wealthy Christians in his own time. By presenting this ideal so forcefully, Luke hopes to spark a dialog with rich Christians, in which the model of Jesus and the disciples will be the motivating power to the right use of their own wealth. Luke does not intend this model to be emulated slavishly by contemporary Christians, but he does propose its use to create a grateful willingness on the part of rich Christians to share substantively of their possessions with the poor and needy.

We find that this view has much to commend it. We agree with the understanding that limits the demand to sell all to the time of the ministry of Jesus. As we will see later, Luke does not make total abandonment a once-for-all mark of Christian discipleship. It belongs uniquely to the time of Jesus and to those called by him to discipleship. Luke's own special tradition in 22:35-38 appears to serve as a word of Jesus legitimizing a new form of discipleship after his departure, when a purse, bag, and sword may be needed. Yet we want to be very cautious lest we create too sharp a separation between the time of Jesus and the time of the church, particularly with respect to possessions.[23] Luke's description of the early church's life in which they shared "all things in common" is not far from Jesus' call to "sell all and give to the poor." Nothing should be allowed to blunt the radicality of the word about possessions, even if it does not always involve a literal abandonment. The early church at least followed the spirit of Jesus on possessions, if not the letter.

Of greatest importance is the suggestion that for Luke the call to total surrender of one's possessions during Jesus' earthly ministry is a critique aimed at wealthy Christians in his community. Surely the willingness of the early disciples to deny themselves, to leave all, and to trust their needs to a loving Father at the call of Jesus must have been heard as a similar call for unlimited sharing directed to the community of disciples in Luke's day. In particular, it must have been heard as such by well-off believers in the Lukan church. To what degree Luke may have addressed his gospel as a whole to those with possessions remains to be seen. For the moment we can at least accept the thesis that Luke's portrait of the first followers as those who left all for his sake is intended for the wealthier Christians of his day, who are thereby sharply challenged with the need to wrestle more seriously with their own use of possessions as followers of Christ. Perhaps it is possible that this theme can function the same way for our own twentieth-century communities of faith.

5

The Dangers of Wealth

In the previous chapter we have examined those passages in the third gospel that call for a total surrender of one's possessions in the service of Jesus. As this chapter will demonstrate, Luke also preserves an impressive number of passages which warn against the dangers of wealth. It is this theme that we now want to explore. As we do, we believe it will become increasingly obvious that the problem of wealth is no dead historical question for Luke, but an issue very much alive in his own community.

"Woe to You That Are Rich" (Luke 6:24-26)

The Lukan attitude toward the danger of possessions finds one of its strongest expressions in this passage unique to Luke. Moreover, by including it as part of the opening section of his Sermon on the Plain, it is apparent that Luke intends to underscore its thematic importance in his gospel as well.

This already became evident when we examined the Lukan beatitudes in Chapter Three (Luke 6:20-23). As we observed, the beatitudes continue Luke's development of the theme proclaimed by Jesus in the synagogue at Nazareth, the announcement of "good news to the poor." [1] The woes in effect announce the reverse side of the coin, the bad news to the rich.

We should also remember that the beatitudes in Luke announce God's blessing upon the poor, who are understood in the most literal sense, and that this is quite unlike the Matthean beatitudes with their more spiritualized interpretation of the poor (Matt. 6:3-12). The corresponding woes reflect the same literal understanding. Judgment is pronounced upon the rich, the filled and those esteemed by others. There is no attempt at spiritualizing their condition. It describes a privileged social and economic status. The woes only state with striking certainty that the future will bring about a complete reversal of conditions, in which the present status of the wealthy will be taken away.

Origin. What is the origin of these "woe-sayings?" Whether they belong to the original Q tradition along with the beatitudes, or whether they come from Luke's special tradition (L), or whether they are his own creation is much debated.[2] Perhaps a majority favor a Lukan adaptation of his L source. Whatever the origin, it is significant to note that Luke is responsible for their placement in this opening portion of Jesus' sermon; it is also important to note that Luke has shaped the woes as a literary and theological anti-thesis to the beatitudes.

In form, they are familiar to certain prophetic oracles of judg-ment in the Old Testament and the intertestamental literature (cf. Isa. 1:4-5, 5:8-23; Amos 5:18; 6:1; E. Enoch 5:7; 99). Elsewhere in the Gospels we find prophetic-like woes in Jesus' indictment of the "scribes and Pharisees" (Matt. 23). But the Lukan woes have a different group in mind. They focus on a particular social and economic class, the rich. It is to this group that Luke addresses his word of warning and threat.

Content. What is the specific content of each woe? The first woe against the rich has its antithesis in the blessing upon the poor (v. 20). Each are given a reward. The poor receive the kingdom of God, while the rich receive their consolation. But in what sense are the rich consoled? The verb in the first woe is in the present tense, in contrast to the future tense of the next two woes. This observation, when combined with the literal meaning of the verb which refers to the "receipt for a deal completed," points to the interpretation that the rich have already obtained their reward, that is, they possess what they desire in their present life of com-fort and ease. They are not accused of any extraordinary injustice or dissipation. It is simply a matter of fact that they have had it good in this life and so will receive no further good in the coming age. They have used up their portion of consolation here.

The second and third woes further characterize the life of the rich in contrast to the poor. The "filled" and "laughing" are the antithesis of the "hungry" and "weeping." Yet a new element is

introduced, namely, the coming eschatological reversal. The future
tenses announce this eschatological dimension, which is both a
promise and a threat. It is a promise to the poor, who now hunger
and weep, but will then be satisfied and laugh (vv. 21-22). But it
is a threat to the rich, who now are filled and laugh, but then
will hunger and mourn and weep. Twice the emphatic "now"
foreshadows the complete reversal of conditions in the coming age
(vv. 25, 26). The social realism of the words is especially pronounced. No specific charges are raised against the rich for glut-
tony or dissipation or oppression, yet somehow their whole life
stands under divine judgment, so that they will one day be brought
low while the poor are exalted.

The last woe is directed against people held in high esteem by
their contemporaries. They are the antithetical counterparts of those
hated and despised by men (v. 22). Both groups find their biblical
parallels in the prophets. Those presently hated and despised, as
followers of the Son of man (v. 22), are experiencing the same rejection as the authentic prophets of old. Those presently held in esteem
are compared to the false prophets of old, whose life and message
were eagerly welcomed by the people. Luke is particularly fond of
his comparison with the prophets and uses it more than once to
explain the rejection and death of Jesus. For in Luke's view, Jesus'
death marks the tragic climax of a long history of Israel's rejection
of God's authentic messengers (Luke 13:33-35; 11:47-51; Acts 7).

But is there any direct link between the woes against the rich
and the last woe against the esteemed? At first glance they seem
unrelated, especially since the context of persecution seems to dominate the last woe. Yet there may be a connection through the reference to the prophets. We know that the false prophets accommo-
dated their message to the rich and the powerful and defended the
status quo; the authentic prophets, on the other hand, spoke against
the status quo and condemned Israel's unfaithfulness to the covenant
and the resultant social injustices. Is this the link?

In Luke's gospel as a whole Jesus causes the gravest offense by
associating with the marginal people, the outcasts and sinners, and
by offering good news to the poor and the exploited. Could this be
the reason for the hatred and persecution of Jesus' disciples as well?
Perhaps like the true prophets, and like the Son of man himself,
they spoke and acted on behalf of the outcasts and sinners, the poor

and the needy and against the privileged who profited from the injustices of the status quo. At least this interpretation seems possible within the context of the woes against the rich and the whole of Luke's gospel and his concern for the poor. The least one can say is that divine judgment lies close at hand whenever one acts in a way that flies in the face of God's call to service in the kingdom on behalf of the poor and the needy. While the last woe contains no explicit warning of an eschatological reversal, its corresponding beatitude does ("your reward is great in heaven," v. 23), so that one can infer the same meaning here as well.

Intention for Luke. Taken as a whole, these woes sound a trumpet note of warning to the rich at the outset of Luke's gospel. Through these woes, Jesus, as God's final messenger, announces the dawn of the kingdom of God, of which the poor are the blessed recipients and from which the rich are excluded. Although the rich may prosper now, the coming kingdom will bring an end to their present status of privilege and prosperity.

But we must still pursue the question more carefully, who are these rich for Luke?

If these woes are part of the original Jesus tradition, they would most likely have been directed against those who opposed Jesus' association with the outcasts and sinners and those who rejected his demand for a radical separation from possessions as the cost of discipleship. In fact, a few interpreters have used this text, among others, as evidence that the historical Jesus called for an ascetic lifestyle and a total rejection of wealth as sinful.[3] However, the evidence is overwhelmingly against Jesus' advocacy of asceticism and questionable at best with regard to his total denial of possessions.[4] This life-style would be more characteristic of John the Baptist or Qumran (7:33-34).

How did Luke interpret these woes? If they represent his own reshaping of the Jesus tradition, whom does Luke have in mind by the rich and filled and satisfied and esteemed?

A few have dared to suggest that Luke was essentially hostile to the rich and powerful and so here preaches a message of eschatological revenge against them.[5] Other texts in Luke's gospel, however, will show that he does not reject the rich outright, only their misuse of possessions. Moreover, the idea of an eschatological revenge is not in the text. It is true that there is an eschatological reversal of conditions in the coming age. But it is a matter of justice, not revenge. The poor find their needs met while the rich now experience what the poor once lacked. The rich are not destroyed, nor are they made to suffer anything more than the poor have suffered. It is a matter, that is, of divine justice.

Other recent commentators have tried to interpret the "rich, satisfied and laughing" as false teachers in Luke's community.[6] But the evidence scarcely supports the view that Luke has a doctrinal dispute in mind, or that one should import a spiritualizing interpretation into this text in defining the rich.

We believe Luke's intention is open and clear concerning his intended hearers. We would argue that Luke is thinking of the rich in social and economic terms, with reference to the believing community of his day. It should be noted that both the beatitudes and woes are spoken to the disciples of Jesus (v. 20). No change of focus from disciples to others is mentioned in the text. It is our judgment, therefore, that Luke addresses these woes to wealthy Christian adherents (or would-be adherents), who have not yet freed themselves from their love of possessions or status.[7] The woes are thus a word of warning to these rich Christians, to the effect that they must change their way of life or find themselves ultimately excluded from the kingdom.

In sum, the beatitudes and woes contain both a promise to "poor Christians" who have abandoned their trust in earthly securities and accepted the call to radical discipleship, and a warning to "rich Christians" that discipleship and wealth are fundamentally in conflict. The announced reversal of roles between the rich and the poor in the coming age serves to underscore the warning and heighten the promise.

Choked by Riches (Luke 8:14)

This passage is a part of the well-known parable of the Sower, originating in the Markan tradition (Mark 4:1-20/Matt. 13:1-23). As it presently stands in the synoptics, it consists of the original Markan parable (Mark 4:3-9), followed by an allegorical interpretation which the majority of scholars attribute to the early church.[8] Luke has taken over both the parable and its interpretation from Mark, so that our concern lies chiefly with the Lukan modifications.

Generally Luke's version does not differ greatly from Mark, yet he makes a few telling changes with regard to v. 14 that are worth noting.

First Luke alters the sentence structure in v. 14, so that, unlike the first two examples cited in vv. 12-13, it is not the seed/Word that gets choked, but those persons who are tempted by wealth. What tempts them specifically are the "cares and riches and pleasures of life," a list essentially the same as Mark. These temptations obviously represent the sum of the dangers inherent in the accumulation of riches.

Second, and more important, is the alteration found in the words "as they go on their way" and "their fruit does not mature" in v. 14. Mark states simply, "it proves unfruitful" (4:19). In effect, Luke's version concentrates on the continuing seductive effect of possessions on the life of disciples.[9] His words are aimed at readers involved in an on-going struggle over possessions and its effect on their own life. His warning is blunt: Beware, lest your concern for material things and the pursuit of pleasures gradually chokes your loyalty to the kingdom! ·

Take Heed of the Cares of Life (Luke 21:34)

Each of the evangelists preserves a body of traditions that deal with the end-time events. While this material as a whole follows the so-called "Markan Apocalypse" of Mark 13, each author adopts and shapes the material in line with his own interests and the needs of his community (Matt. 24, Luke 21). If the current consensus of scholarship on Luke is correct, Luke has shifted his interest from the future expectation of Christ's return to the present life of the church in the world. Accordingly, even though he still retains the core of the apocalyptic traditions from Mark, his attention centers on the here and now. This is brought out by the admonition of v. 34. His readers are warned to beware of specific temptations that could endanger their readiness for the unknown end. The temptations are called "dissipation" and "cares," which plainly describe the life of the rich. Hence, even at the end of his apocalyptic discourse, Luke points to the temptations of wealth as a critical danger to believers, who wait patiently for the time of the Son of man's return.[10]

The Rich Fool (Luke 12:13-21)

The parables of Luke are especially powerful in their portrayal of the dangers of wealth. In the familiar parable of the Rich Fool we encounter the first of such parables enunciating this theme. This parable stands within one of three complexes of L traditions in the central section of Luke's gospel (the so-called travel narrative, Luke 9:51–18:14), each of which deals with the subject of possessions (12:13-34; 14:12-33; 16:1-31). Whether or not this material has a common source is unknown, but it is striking how abundant the material is. The question of possessions clearly occupies a high priority on Luke's agenda of concerns.

The parable itself has a parallel in an ancient gospel that was found among a recently discovered Gnostic library at Nag Hammadi in Egypt.[11] The Gnostics were an early Christian heretical movement, which attracted many followers with their intellectual mythic structures and their deep sense of alienation from the created world. This particular gospel, the *Gospel of Thomas*, contains a scattered collection of Jesus' sayings, supposedly given to the apostle Thomas by the risen Lord.[12] Most of the sayings are "variations on a Gnostic theme" and require a Gnostic mind-set to understand. A few interpreters have theorized that an independent oral tradition lies behind this gospel, but more likely it has borrowed from the synoptic traditions.

The *Gospel of Thomas* version of our parable contains both the request of Jesus to arbitrate the inheritance dispute and a much abbreviated parable. The parable reads like this: "Jesus said: There was a rich man who had much money. He said: 'I will use my money that I may sow and reap and plant and fill my storehouses with fruit, so that I lack nothing. This was what he thought in his heart. And that night he died. Whoever has ears let him hear" (Logion #63).[13]

The changes are not drastic, yet the sharpness of the parable is blunted and a somewhat unreal quality permeates the whole. We do not feel as strongly the futility and stupidity of trusting in one's possessions as we do in the Lukan parable. Let us look now at the Lukan version.

Covetousness, an age-old temptation. The key to understanding Luke's intention is v. 15. Here we find a direct warning against covetousness. Both the dispute over the inheritance and the parable are meant to illustrate this danger. In v. 15 the double imperatives "take heed" and "beware," along with the typical Lukan emphasis on "all" covetousness, serve to place a decisive emphasis upon the sin of greed. Similarly, the dominical saying in v. 15b, "a man's life does not consist in the abundance of his possessions," exposes the false claim of covetousness, namely its attempt to evaluate human worth in terms of material prosperity. "What is he worth?" is not the measure of human life, regardless of what many claim. To think so is to be a fool in the ultimate sense of that word, that is, one who is ignorant of the true meaning of life and its origin in God.

Dispute over an inheritance (vv. 13-14). The request of Jesus to arbitrate this dispute gives us a vivid glimpse into a real life problem, then and now. Two brothers are quarreling over their inheritance. According to the Old Testament law, the eldest son inherited the family lands, plus a double portion of all other possessions (Deut. 21:17). The remainder was divided among the younger brothers.

In this particular dispute, Jesus is asked to mediate a complaint of the younger brother against the elder, who either wants to keep all the inheritance for himself or at least more than his share.[14] The younger feels he has a just claim and expects Jesus to act on his behalf. That Jesus was asked to function as a mediator is not surprising, since it was normal for rabbis to serve as interpreters of the law in both religious and civil matters. It may also be correct to observe that Jesus may have enjoyed the favor of the people and especially the poor *am haaretz*, if he was asked to side with the the younger brother.[15]

What is surprising is Jesus' refusal to get involved. Why doesn't he? Some have suggested Jesus refuses because he is not an officially qualified rabbi. However, this does not prevent Jesus from acting and speaking with considerable authority on other matters and occasions. Others suggest Jesus doesn't want to bother with such mundane issues as dividing possessions, since his role is to preach the kingdom, similar to the disciples in Acts 6. One must be careful with this argument, however, since Jesus concerned himself deeply with the daily needs of the poor and the dangers of wealth. In our judgment, the clue to understanding Jesus' refusal is found in

v. 15. The quarrel over the inheritance illustrates the way in which greed and covetousness can divide families and people. No mediation of one dispute will solve the deeper problem of the human heart. So Luke has Jesus avoid getting caught with the surface issues and instead goes straight to the nub of the matter, i.e., human covetousness and the false evaluation of human life in economic terms. Disputes like this, as with the lawsuits between Christians at Corinth (1 Cor. 6), only expose the greedy heart and obscure the question of what human life is finally all about. "A man's life does not consist in the abundance of his possessions."

The Rich Fool (vv. 16-21). This parable deepens the discussion and reveals the ultimate foolishness of seeking security in one's possessions. We agree with those interpreters who regard vv. 16-20 as the pre-Lukan form of the parable and v. 21 as a Lukan addition. In v. 21 we have an exhortation for Luke's readers to become rich toward God, and this is further explained in vv. 33-34 in terms of selling one's possessions and giving to the poor. Moreover, the exhortation offers a sharp judgment against the rich farmer, whose life was centered in self and possessions.

What can we surmise about the situation of the rich farmer from the parable? He is obviously one of the wealthy landowners in first century Palestine. He lives from the labor of others. We are not told that he acquired his lands unjustly, even though many large landowners did gain their land by wheeling and dealing and by cheating the poor and ignorant peasants. A bumper year of crops confronted him with the decision of what more to do. He decided to store the crops as security for an early retirement and a life of ease. So he tore down his old barns and built new and bigger ones.[16] The treasure in his barns would be his life-long security.

A recent commentator has argued that the farmer's intent was even more devious and shrewd than it appears. He was actually storing the grain for a time of scarcity and then, when the prices had been driven up, he would sell it at an exorbitant price, thus profiting handsomely from the needs of others.[17] If this is so, then the sin of the rich man was not just selfish hoarding of his wealth, but an act damaging to his society as well, an act planned deliberately and maliciously to profit at the expense of others. A shrewd businessman, perhaps, yet his act has both injurious personal and social dimensions as greed usually does.

His sense of anticipated security and enjoyment of life is succinctly stated in v. 19. The words "eat, drink and be merry" do not necessarily imply a life of moral dissipation, since it was a common proverb. What he was undoubtedly after was the good life, doing what he wanted, when he wanted, and that's exactly what he believed his wealth had now assured.

But God's verdict upon his life abruptly intervenes in v. 20. The verdict is one word, "Fool!" Biblically, the fool is one who lives de facto without God (Ps. 14:1). The fool thinks and acts under the illusion that there is accountability to no one but self. This has been the grand illusion of the human race since its beginning. Yet the rich and the powerful are more tempted and trapped by this illusion than others. Hence the parable seeks to shatter its seductive hold upon the rich, so evident in the life of this land owner. The rich man "does not take God into account, and fails to see the sword of Damocles, the threat of death, hanging over his head." [18] The hour of death becomes the shattering moment of accountability. Now he is face to face with the fact that he has lived chiefly for himself, that he has worshiped and served the god Mammon and that his whole life has been built upon a lie. And it was his possessions that most deceived him. The final indictment is thus that he laid up treasures for himself and was not rich toward God (v. 21). Altogether, the judgment against him can be summarized in this manner: a) He was basically self-centered, separated from God and neighbor by his love of possessions; b) He falsely assumed human life could be measured and secured by the amount of his possessions; c) He regarded his life and property as his own, thereby violating God's lordship and his own role as a responsible steward.

While the parable in its present form points to the moment of death as the time of accountability, some conjecture that in its original form it was an eschatological parable, in which the coming of the kingdom was the time of crisis. [19] In view of the kingdom's advent, the wealthy were urged to reorient their lives and possessions before it is too late. Then, when v. 21 was added, the emphasis shifted from the coming kingdom to the time of death and to the exhortation to become rich toward God in the present. We find this to be a helpful insight. For it shows that by adding v. 21, Luke wants to focus on the present warning to the rich and not on the future. His point is not simply the ancient proverbial wisdom of how stupid it is to spend your life on something you can't take with you, nor is it a delight in the coming judgment of the rich. Rather, Luke's charge to the rich is, "Change your life before it is too late. Stop living for yourself and start accumulating riches toward God." And the meaning of this is spelled out by Luke in the section that follows, where vv. 23-31 instruct believers to seek God's kingdom first and trust his fatherly care for their basic earthly needs and where vv. 32-34 add to this by urging the selling of one's possessions and the giving of alms as evidence of the right use of one's wealth for human needs.

Finally, to whom is Luke addressing this parable in his own community? The exhortation of v. 21, combined with the word to the disciples in vv. 22-34, seems to confirm the fact that Luke has Christian possessors in mind. Their possessions have become a hindrance to following Jesus. Hence they should "avoid like cancer" [20] the sin of covetousness displayed in the life of the rich fool and in the dispute over the inheritance. Instead they should find their true riches in a life of trust in God and in the radical sharing with the poor. If they don't the warning is clear: God's verdict of "fool" will be the end verdict upon their lives too.

The Rich Man and Lazarus (Luke 16:19-31)

Here is a second challenging parable from Luke's special source (L) that deserves our careful attention. Like the previous parable of the Rich Fool it is found within a block of material that has the subject of possessions as its major theme (16:1-31): the parable of the Dishonest Steward (16:1-13), the indictment of the Pharisees as "lovers of money" (16:14-18), and the present parable (16:19-31). Only vv. 16-18 appear out of context, although there may be some link between these verses and the reference to "Moses and the prophets" in the parable. All of the material is Lukan with the exception of vv. 16-18, so that we again see Luke's preoccupation with the subject of possessions.

Form and Tradition in the Parable. Every interpreter recognizes that the parable has two distinct parts: vv. 19-26, the theme of the great reversal; vv. 27-31, the theme of repentance. However, it is much debated how these two parts relate to one another in the history of the tradition.[21] Perhaps a majority would find the original parable in vv. 19-26 and an addition by the early church in vv. 27-31.

The main argument for viewing vv. 27-31 as a later interpretation centers on the reference to one rising from the dead in vv. 30-31, and its link with Moses and the prophets. A Christian reader of the gospel could not help but hear in these verses a reference to Jesus' resurrection and a word of polemic against the Jews, who refuse to repent and believe in spite of the resurrection. Thus the present form of these verses, especially v. 31, may be due to Lukan redaction. A comparison with two passages in Chapter 24 strengthens this possibility. Here, in two successive resurrection narratives, Luke has the risen Lord using Scripture to interpret to his disciples the necessity of the Messiah's suffering and resurrection. In Luke 24:25-27, "Moses and all the prophets" are mentioned as proof of the Messiah's suffering and glory. In Luke 24:44-47, "the Law of Moses and the prophets and the psalms" are said to foretell the suffering and resurrection of the Messiah and the subsequent preaching of repentance and forgiveness of sins to all nations. Even the same verb is used in both 24:44 and 16:31 to refer to the resurrection. Thus Lukan redaction in Luke 16:30-31 is hard to deny.

Nevertheless, it needs to be emphasized that the main point of the second half of the parable is not the resurrection of Jesus or the failure of the Jews to repent and believe in spite of his resurrection as foretold in Moses and the prophets. This enters in only tangentially at best and to concentrate on this would both sever the connection between the two parts of the parable and miss its main point. It would also isolate the second half of the parable from its context in Chapter 16 and the theme of possessions. Further it fails to do justice to the special Lukan interest in possessions and Luke's frequent warnings to the rich regarding the misuse of their wealth. Hence we are inclined to agree with those interpreters who find an original connection between the two parts of the parable and who thus interpret the second part as a warning to the rich in light of the coming eschatological reversal.[22] One supporter of this view, who adds the observation that in double parables the main part is always found in the second half of the parable, has therefore suggested renaming this parable, "The Parable of the Six Brothers." [23]

Interpretation of the Parable. An initial observation is the fact that within Luke's gospel this parable serves as a vivid illustration of the beatitudes and woes (Luke 6:20-26), with their promised blessing for the poor and woes against the rich.

The Coming Reversal, vv. 19-26. The dominant theme in the first half of the parable is the complete reversal of roles in the next life. This is developed in two stages. In vv. 19-20 the great social disparity between the rich man and poor Lazarus is artfully described with a minimum of words. At the one extreme is the rich man, whose clothing, mansion, and style of life, especially the daily feasts, breathe the atmosphere of upper-class affluence. To get a feel for his lavish life-style in contrast to others in first century Palestine, one should not only compare it with poor Lazarus, but with the average tenant farmer or craftsman. A feast, e.g., was normally unthinkable, except for weddings, when the parents of the bride did their best, often at great sacrifice, to feed and entertain large crowds of relatives, friends, and villagers. The daily diet was a simple fare of soup, bread, and fruit, while clothing was limited to a couple of garments, one of which was usually reserved for the Sabbath. Houses too were small, cramped side by side or joined, quite bare inside, with animals running in and out. Life was minimal for the vast majority. Hence the parable would have startled its original hearers with the reminder of the rich man's luxurious existence and probably even caused them to murmur, if not curse, under their breath at such extravagance, while they had to sweat and scrape just to get by.

At the opposite extreme, dramatizing the social poverty of the masses, is poor Lazarus. A beggar, probably crippled, he survives on leftovers from the daily feasts of the household.[24] His emaciated and filthy body is covered with sores, which pesky dogs continually irritate and infest. Although extreme, the scene was not uncommon, especially in the larger cities, where begging was a way of life. Every detail thus etches the misery of poverty unforgettably on the mind. Once seen, it can't be forgotten. Only one ray of hope appears, namely, the fact that the beggar is given a name, the only character in all of Jesus' parables so named. Lazarus means, "God helps."

Verses 21-26 describe the great reversal between the rich man and poor Lazarus. Lazarus dies and is immediately carried by the angels into the bosom of Abraham. Though buried without funeral, he has God on his side, as his name implies. For a devout Jew, no greater hope or comfort could be imagined than to rest secure in the bosom of Abraham at the heavenly banquet. Lowly Lazarus thus receives the highest goal of the faithful.

The rich man also dies and is properly mourned and buried. But he finds himself in Hades, the interim place of the dead and a place of torment. And now he begins to experience the "hell" that poor Lazarus had known in his lifetime. The roles have completely and irreversibly changed. Despite the pleas for mercy to Father Abraham, there is nothing more to be done. The die is eternally cast. The great chasm is fixed (v. 26). Verse 25 summarizes the reason: "You in your lifetime received your good things, and Lazarus in like manner evil things; but now he is comforted here, and you are in anguish." Divine justice is done. In a society where poverty is commonly regarded as a punishment for sin, and wealth is considered a blessing, Jesus' concept of divine justice seemed to turn everything upside down.

How shall we interpret this powerful parable? Whatever we do, we cannot ignore its concrete social and economic realism. The problem it describes is poverty and riches, and the horrible inequities that exist between human beings, individually and corporately. There is no way to gloss over these stark facts by some kind of spiritualizing of this text. Luke, too, unmistakably intends to focus on the problem of riches and poverty, since he relates the parable to Jesus' indictment of the Pharisees, who justify their love of money (vv. 14-15).

What exactly does the parable teach about riches and poverty? This has been a question of considerable dispute. A few have argued that the original meaning of the parable is found in the law of compensation. By this they mean that the grounds for the rich man's punishment and the poor man's reward is not a moral one, i.e. the one was virtuous and the other evil, but due simply to a divine law in which the next life removes the inequities of this life.[25] They point to the fact that the parable contains no condemnatory word against the rich man, nor does it say anything about Lazarus' piety.

We must not dismiss this argument out of hand, since the parable does concentrate on the social/economic discrepancies and not moral ones. Moreover, God's justice and compassion for the poor as poor, apart from their individual piety and his verdict against the rich as rich, is clearly present. Yet, there is more. For how could anyone hear the vivid descriptions of the gross discrepancy in social conditions as anything other than a devastating critique against the rich who exploit the poor and live in selfish luxury, unmindful of the dying beggars at their gate? Moreover, God's decisive siding with the poor is not only alluded to in the name Lazarus, i.e., God helps, but in the great reversal which brings moral judgment. For the rich man is not just deprived of his possessions, he is punished (vv. 23-24), while Lazarus enjoys the eschatological blessings of the faithful elect. Hence we conclude that it is not just the great social inequity which results in judgment or blessing, but also the way of life associated with both. Though a law of just compensation is at work, it does not operate in a moral or spiritual vacuum. Nevertheless, the emphasis on the great disparity between the rich and poor raises the question acutely whether the rich as rich can avoid the eschatological reversal in the coming age. Or to put it in Jesus' own words used later in Luke's gospel, "How hard it is for those who have riches to enter the kingdom of God!" (18:24.)

Some who think that vv. 19-26 form the earliest core of the parable have argued that these verses were originally spoken as a word of comfort for the poor, who were promised the coming righteousness of the kingdom.[26] They further note that the parable does not breathe a spirit of revenge against the rich, in spite of the strong judgment. In fact, v. 26 implies a desire to help the rich man.

Still, though it is true that the parable does bring comfort and hope to the poor and oppressed, the bulk of it seems directed to the rich. The comfort of poor Lazarus in the next life is only the background for the judgment against the rich man. It is his irreversible fate in the eschaton, despite his plea, that becomes the focus of the parable. Therefore we find it impossible to hear it any other way than as a warning to the rich. Even apart from the second half, the challenge is already hurled at the possessors, "Redeem your life before it's too late. Remember Lazarus and pity the poor at your gate. Watch out, lest the kingdom of God be forever closed to you."

The Need to Repent, vv. 27-31. That Luke has interpreted the parable as a word of warning to the wealthy becomes plain in vv. 27-31. Here the theme of repentance is directed specifically to the rich. According to the second part of the parable, the rich man recognizes his own fate and so seeks to warn his five brothers to change before it's too late. That the wealthy need to be warned and need to repent shows that there is a clear moral judgment now assumed concerning the life of the rich. But not only do they need to repent, in order to repent they need to hear "Moses and the prophets." Twice the phrase "Moses and the prophets" is repeated. What is meant?

Since the hearing of Moses and the prophets is linked with a "messenger from the dead," interpreters have too quickly jumped to the conclusion that Luke is now importing the whole controversy about Jesus' messiahship. We earlier agreed that this may lie in the background. But it is not primary, either within the parable or in Luke's mind. Luke concentrates throughout the parable, as throughout Chapter 16, on the problem of possessions. In v. 30, the messenger from the dead is Lazarus. His purpose is to exhort the five brothers to repent, in view of the sixth brother's fate. Yet Abraham's response is that they already have the means to repent, namely Moses and the prophets. The reference is clearly to the Scriptures.

What can be learned from their own sacred book? The answer is clear—nothing less than to do good, to practice justice, to love the neighbor as oneself, to care for the poor. Or to put it another way, to be humane. "If a man (says Jesus) cannot be humane with the Old Testament in his hand and Lazarus on his doorstep, nothing will teach him otherwise." [27] The requirement of charity toward the poor and needy stands at the heart of the Old Testament Law. And that is the essential meaning of Moses and the prophets in this text. Thus the demand for a sign from the dead becomes a sheer evasion of plain duty toward one's neighbor enshrined in Scripture and embodied above all in the ministry of Jesus. So too, both in the parable and in Jesus' ministry, his contemporaries are offended by the good news of God's grace to the poor.

This means that the repentance urged in the parable is not repentance and faith as outlined in the later kerygma of the church (e.g. Luke 24:47; Acts 2:38). It is a repentance aimed at the rich man and his five brothers, an ethical and religious reversal of their lives in which the vast discrepancy between their wealth and the poor is removed and the principles of justice and mercy are accepted and practiced. No attempts to avoid this conclusion by some kind of spiritualizing exegesis should be allowed to blunt the powerful social and ethical force of the parable.

Let us now briefly summarize its meaning. The central focus of the parable is the issue of wealth and poverty and the related theme of justice. The Old Testament is affirmed as the norm for justice which the six brothers have violated (cf. 16:17). Their extravagant wealth and Lazarus' dire poverty is the condition of inequality which needs rectification. God himself will make things right in the end. That is comfort to the poor and warning to the rich. Yet there is still opportunity for the violators of God's justice to hear Moses and the prophets and to repent. That is the note on which the parable ends. Without repentance, however, the fate of the rich is sealed.[28]

The Needle's Eye (Luke 18:24-30)

The final text we want to consider on the dangers of wealth is potentially the most explosive. We have already touched briefly on this text in connection with the call to the abandonment of one's possessions, as it appears in the story of the rich ruler.[29] Now, however, we want to take a closer look at these verses, since they bring to a climax the Lukan emphasis on the dangers of wealth. In fact, this passage raises the central question of the Lukan attitude on possessions, namely, are wealth and discipleship at all compatible? Or more bluntly, can the rich be saved?

This series of sayings on wealth and discipleship is not distinctively Lukan. It is found in all three Gospels as the sequel to the story of the rich ruler (Mark 10:23-31; Matt. 19:23-30). Luke undoubtedly took it over from Mark, with only minor editorial changes. Yet it is evident that Luke found it highly congenial with his purpose of setting forth Jesus' attitude toward wealth. This is so not only because of its clear warning about wealth, but becomes most evident in the way Luke relates this text to the Zaccheus passage in 19:1-10. As we shall observe in the next chapter, the question about possessions raised acutely in these verses is responded to in the subsequent story of Zaccheus. Let us now examine the central theme of this text.

The Camel Hyperbole, vv. 24-27. The discussion in vv. 24-30 expands the problem of possessions from the story of one rich man to that of all rich people. Just as riches were an insurmountable barrier into the kingdom for the rich ruler, so riches, according to vv. 24-25, constitute a nigh-impossible obstacle for all the rich. Jesus' pronouncement, spoken in Luke's version directly in the presence of

the rich ruler, "how hard it is for those who have riches to enter
the kingdom of God" (v. 24), is then intensified by the familiar
camel saying of v. 25, one of the hardest sayings of Jesus in the
Gospels. Perhaps few texts have so revealed the way in which the
hard sayings of Jesus have been ingeniously interpreted to avoid
their plain meaning as this one. The oft-quoted explanation that
there was a "needle's gate" in the city wall of Jerusalem, and that it
was necessary for the long-legged and awkward camel to stoop
on its knees to get through is unfortunately such an explanation.
No such gate is known to exist.[30]

Rather the camel saying is a typical Hebraic hyperbole, i.e. an
exaggerated metaphor. The intent of the hyperbole is to arouse the
hearer to catch the point and to respond. In this instance, the point
of the hyperbole is the basic incompatibility between the abundance
of riches and faithful discipleship.[31]

This is clearly the way each of the evangelists understood it. In
all three the question is immediately raised, "Who then can be
saved?" The assumption is that the rich cannot be saved. The response in v. 27 further underscores this assumption: "What is impossible with men" (the salvation of the rich) "is possible with God."

This saying also needs careful interpretation. How shall we understand it? It is tempting here as well to try and find an easy way out
of these strong words. One could attribute the saying, along with
the whole section, to exaggerated speech and so not take it seriously
as realistic truth. Or one could try to find a word of reassurance to
the wealthy in spite of the seemingly harsh words. "Yes, you've got
a real problem on your hands in your wealth, but don't fret over-
much; God will find a way for you to remain a Christian and still
keep your wealth intact." Or one could even try a theological way
out by noting that Jesus merely states a general theological truth,
which Paul later develops, to the effect that no one can save themselves. Salvation, entry into the kingdom, discipleship, these are all
gifts of a gracious God and not the result of human effort. Hence
the wealthy, though they face a peculiar temptation, are really in
no radically different position than anyone else. And this argument
can be strengthened by noting that in v. 26 the question is not "Can
the rich be saved?" but "Who can be saved?", a statement that says
everyone needs a miracle of God for salvation.

Unfortunately, all of these responses seem to contradict Luke's clear intent. The subject throughout vv.18-30 is the problem of wealth in relation to the kingdom. The surprise evoked by Jesus' strong words in vv. 24-25, and the question of the hearers in v. 27, "Then who can be saved?" likely presuppose the belief that wealth is a sign of God's blessing and not a crippling handicap. Thus Jesus has once again turned the scale of values upside down. As we learned elsewhere and especially in Luke's gospel, it is the needy and the poor, the sick and the sinners who enter the kingdom first, and it is the wealthy and the powerful, the righteous and the loveless who find themselves standing outside. Hence we would interpret the saying in v. 27, "what is impossible with men is possible with God" to mean that only through a special miracle of God's grace will the rich enter the kingdom. That is to say, riches represent such a barrier, they are so tough for the human will to let go, that it is indeed a miracle when a rich person lets go and becomes a disciple! As we interpret it, the point of v. 27 is not that a few rich people get in with their wealth intact, but that only a few, by a miracle of God, will receive the strength to abandon their trust in their possessions and take whatever steps are necessary to live a life freed from its bondage and free for the service of God and man. Though it is true, of course, that all Christian discipleship is an act of God's grace, Luke is not preaching that sermon here. The subject here is the question of possessions and its role as a primary temptation to be overcome by would-be Christian disciples.

"We have left our homes" (vv. 28-30). Peter and the disciples represent those who have overcome the temptation of possessions and left their past way of life for the service of Jesus.[32] Their actions stand in sharp contrast to the rich ruler and all others with wealth. They are a living witness to Luke's readers that possessions can be abandoned by the grace of God for the kingdom's sake.

In response, Jesus' words assure those who would surrender their material goods and follow him that God will supply all their present needs as well as give them the certainty of sharing in the coming age. These words restate in their own way what was promised in the saying, "Seek his kingdom and these things will be yours as well" (12:31). Only they make it more specific, with Luke characteristically adding to the list that of "wife." Sometimes controversial and misunderstood is the assurance that the disciples who follow Jesus in this way will receive "manifold more in this time" (cf. Mark 10:30, Matt. 19:29). Behind this promise is not a guarantee of wealth and abundance in the tradition of Job, who received double of what he lost. What the Gospels have in mind is life in a new community where the needs of one person are met by the gifts of another, where there is a common sharing of possessions according to need, where a supportive community suffers and rejoices with one another, and where one can trust God without fear or anxiety over earthly needs.[33] Luke will later describe this new community for his readers as he tells of the early church in the first chapters of Acts, as we will discuss below.

By way of summary, these verses that form the sequel to the story of the rich ruler present more forcefully than ever in Luke's gospel the dangers of wealth for would-be disciples. "How hard it is for those who have riches to enter the kingdom of God" sounds the theme, which is then relentlessly carried through. Only those who have left their goods behind are offered the promise of the kingdom. Therefore there seems scarcely any way to avoid the conclusion based on this text and others that we have examined, that wealth and discipleship are conflicting terms. The dangers of wealth are so great the question seems appropriate: Can the rich be saved at all? Or is the only answer to sell one's possessions and give alms.

Is there any hope for possessors? That's the question we want to explore in the next chapter. Up to this point the Lukan attitude toward possessions has been "abandon" and "watch out." Is there also a right use of possessions possible for would-be disciples of Christ?

6

The Right Use
of Possessions

Up to this point in our study we have looked at those Lukan texts which either call for a total abandonment of possessions or warn readers concerning the grave dangers of wealth. But what is Luke actually advocating among Christians of his day? Is he asking that they sell all they have and live off the charity of others, or that they pool their material resources into some kind of common fund, from which the needs of the community and the poor are met? We have earlier argued that Luke interprets the command to "sell all" as a call limited to Jesus' time, though it still functions with exemplary force for wealthy Christians in Luke's day. Similarly, the strong warnings about the danger of possessions, culminating in the camel saying, serve as cautionary lights to rich Christians about the precariousness of their position; but they do not necessarily lead to the conclusion that possessions themselves are inherently evil.

We now want to examine another group of texts that deal with the possibility of a right use of possessions. We believe that these texts reveal the primary and practical goal of Luke's presentation on the subject of possessions. What he seeks to create is a radically new evaluation of possessions and their proper use by Christians. His purpose is not to advocate some form of Christian asceticism on the one hand, or some kind of Christian communism on the other. Rather, Luke attempts to define and encourage a *discipleship of one's* material gifts in the service of love. But lest we breathe too deep a sigh of relief, Luke does not let us forget the other texts we have just studied, with their costly demands and urgent warnings. It may even be that his call to a proper use of one's wealth cuts far more deeply than we expect or are ready to hear.

At any rate, we now want to explore those texts reflecting Luke's positive approach to the question of possessions under the theme, "Make friends with your wealth."

Jesus' Affirmation of Possessions

Wealth constitutes a major obstacle to doing the will of God. Yet the Gospels as a whole recognize that possessions are both necessary and good gifts of God, a view that emerges in the Lukan portrait of Jesus as well. Despite his life of itinerant poverty, Jesus was no ascetic nor did he advocate an ascetic life-style. This in itself set him apart from his predecessor, John the Baptist and from groups such as the wilderness community of Qumran. Jesus enjoyed the fellowship of banquets with good food and drink (Luke 5:29; 7:36; 14:1, 15). The harsh accusation of his critics that he was a glutton and a drunkard reveals his open life-style in sharing the daily life of his contemporaries, even those on the border of social and religious acceptability (Luke 7:34; 15:1-2). Jesus knows people of wealth and spends time with them (Luke 7:1-10, 36-50; 19:1; 23:50). His favorite image of the coming age was that of the eschatological feast, where joy reigns supreme and the Messiah and all the redeemed share in the heavenly feast (Luke 14:16-24; 15:11-24; 16:25; 22:18). Jesus describes his own ministry as a time of festivity. That is why Jesus' disciples, unlike those of the Baptist or the Pharisees, did not fast. The new wine required fresh wineskins (Luke 5:33-38). Luke's portrayal of Jesus' life depicts a person who rejoices in life and accepts the goodness of God's creation, including some of the things that only money can buy.[1]

Nor was Jesus unaware of basic human needs. The Lord's Prayer preserves the petition for daily bread (Luke 11:3). In the very same text which sets forth the ultimate priority of the kingdom and its righteousness, we find the promise that God will provide our daily needs for food, clothing, and shelter (Luke 12:31).[2] Similarly, the future promise to the poor in the Lukan beatitudes states specifically that their present hunger will be satisfied and their present mourning turned to joy, a theme echoed in the Magnificat as well (Luke 6:20-21; 1:53). Jesus' response to Peter's assertion, "Lo, we have left all and followed you," promises a community of disciples in which mutual assistance and sharing supplies everyday human needs and companionship (Luke 18:28-30). The life of the poor, therefore, with all their hardship and suffering, is not an ascetic ideal in Luke's gospel, nor is it in harmony with the will of God. God intends daily bread sufficient for all of life's needs, even for the wicked and ungrateful (Luke 6:35). Clearly, poverty is not from God!

Yet the awareness of the goodness of God's gifts and the recognition that God wills enough for everyone does not place a blanket endorsement on the accumulation of wealth or justify one person's abundance overagainst another's lack. The traditions we have already surveyed on the grave dangers of wealth, along with those that summon disciples to give up their possessions, forbid this kind of conclusion. In fact, they raise the question acutely about the compatibility of an abundance of possessions and the Christian life. Although possessions are not inherently evil and though God wills enough to meet life's basic needs for all people, neither the desire for possessions nor their accumulation reflects his will. What then is the right attitude toward possessions?

Make Friends with Your Wealth (Luke 16:1-13)

This unique Lukan parable demonstrates in a striking way Luke's concern for the right use of possessions. It should be noted at the outset that this parable of the Dishonest Steward has been notoriously difficult to interpret. Questions still remain, yet a sufficient consensus has emerged among interpreters in recent years, so that its meaning can help illumine for us Luke's attitude toward wealth.

Our reflections will be based on a form-critical analysis of vv. 1-13, which finds the original parable in vv. 1-8, and a series of additional interpretive comments in vv. 9-13. Even this division is somewhat uncertain, since the identity of the master in v. 8 is disputed. Is it the master of the parable (v. 1), or does Jesus himself commend the steward of the parable at this point? [3] Our own understanding is that the original parable ends at v. 8a and that v. 8b begins the earliest interpretation of the parable. In spite of these and other uncertainties, we find that this entire passage memorably illustrates the way in which an original parable of Jesus has been taken over by the early church and transformed into an exhortation on the wise use of one's possessions.

1. The Parable of the Dishonest Steward, Old and New Interpretations, 16:1-8. The fly in the ointment for all commentators has

been Jesus' commendation of the steward's apparently dishonest action. On the assumption that the steward had no legal or moral right to remit his master's debtors by 50% or 20%, the question naturally arises as to how Jesus could commend his downright dishonest and skin-saving action. Two answers have been given.

The older interpretation agrees that in no way does Jesus approve the dishonest action. Rather, the point of the parable lies in the steward's wise decision in his time of crisis.[4] Aware that his future depended on his quick response, the steward acts wisely, shrewdly, and decisively in the critical situation. Viewed within the context of Jesus' own ministry, the parable stands as a warning about the imminent arrival of the kingdom of God and urges Jesus' hearers to act with equal decisiveness before it's too late. Already in his own ministry, the critical either-or is present, in which a decision for or against Jesus is a decision for or against the kingdom. Thus the wicked servant is not an example by his scandalous behavior, but by his decisive action to save himself. And it may be that in v. 8b, we already hear the lament of the early church that the "sons of light" are not as wise as the "sons of this world" with respect to their separate goals. That is, the believers are not as committed or prudent for their great cause as the unbelievers are for theirs. Even though the old world is quickly passing away, Christians live with no grave sense of urgency. Therefore the appeal to more devoted living.

However, the basic assumption that the steward's action in remitting the debts was in itself immoral has recently been challenged, with wide acceptance.[5] The change in assumptions is due to a recent study of social and legal customs in the first century, which reveal that the servant's actions may well have been within legal limits. We know that much land in Palestine was owned by wealthy landowners, who sublet their land to persons like the steward of our parable, who in turn would let it out to others. Normally, payment was made to the steward, who then paid the owner his rightful due. But it was not unusual for the steward to also lend some of the owner's money to the poor who worked the land, and to charge additionally an exorbitant interest, which went into his own pocket. Applied to the parable, it would mean that the steward, accused of mismanaging his master's property and finding himself dismissed, shrewdly called in the poor debtors and cancelled his own share of the interest on the loans. This then, is the wise action praised in the parable. Although the original debt remained, he made friends for the future by giving up his own profit. Accordingly, the reference to "the wicked steward" does not refer to an illegal remittance of debt, but to his original mismanagement and profiteering by usury. If this interpretation is correct, a major stumbling block in interpreting the parable is removed and the original parable becomes more persuasive.

2. The Exhortations to Use Possessions to Make Friends, vv. 9-13. If the original parable and its first interpretation (v. 8b) taught the necessity of urgent, decisive action in view of the coming kingdom, we quickly realize that the interpretation of the parable moves in quite a different direction in vv. 9-13, a direction that is in line with Luke's own special interests. This shift in direction is evident in two ways. One, the original eschatological thrust of the parable is largely removed and the additional verses become instruction (parenesis) for the early Christian community; two, the subject of possessions, which was secondary in the original parable, now becomes the primary focus of attention.

One scholar has aptly written that these verses read "like notes of an early church preacher or teacher, who used the parables for Christian indoctrination and exhortation."[6] An analysis of vv. 9-13 shows that at least three separate sayings have been brought together: v. 9 introduces the new theme of making friends with mammon; vv. 10-12 are linked by the words "faithful" and "dishonest" with regard to "unrighteous mammon"; and v. 13, a Q saying (Matt. 6:24), demands a choice between God and mammon. The train of thought hinges on the catchword "mammon" and its proper use. Yet the connections are somewhat artificial, and the final admonition to choose between God or mammon stands in tension with the exhortation in v. 9 to make friends with mammon.

In our judgment the key to understanding this section is v. 9. This seems indicated already by the introduction, "But I say to you," which always betokens authoritative words of the Lord (cf. Matt. 5:22, 28, 32). This formula thus paves the way for a new understanding of the Lord's parable stated in what follows: "make friends for yourselves by means of unrighteous mammon. . . ." This new interpretation continues through v. 13.

What is the precise meaning of the exhortation to make friends

by means of unrighteous mammon? The fact that mammon is
called "unrighteous" has caused some to argue that Jesus, or Luke,
viewed money per se as evil and so to be dispensed with.[7] This is
highly unlikely, however, in view of Jesus' own use of money and
in view of the texts we are now discussing in this chapter. That the
disciples are exhorted to make friends with mammon seems to imply
a matter of right or wrong use, not total rejection. Mammon is unrighteous then, either because it is so often acquired wrongly or because it represents such a grave seduction for humanity.

But how does one make friends with unrighteous mammon? This
is not spelled out directly in these verses. Yet the fact that mammon
is to be an instrument for making friends, comparable to the steward's action in the parable, indicates it is to be used in human service. The steward gained friends by sharing his profit and helping
out poor debtors. Many other characteristic Lukan passages will
show that those who have possessions are encouraged and invited
and even warned to share their possessions with the poor and
needy. To put it simply, the way to make friends with mammon is
to use one's wealth in the service of love.[8] In so doing, one is thereby assured of a welcome in the "eternal habitations," or as Luke
puts it elsewhere, one has laid up treasures in heaven (12:33).[9]
This is the primary lesson that Luke seeks to derive from this difficult parable for his readers.

Thus the emphasis has shifted from the parable as a word of
warning or encouragement to act decisively in the face of the coming eschatological crisis, to a word of exhortation on the right use
of one's possessions. Likewise the steward's prompt and shrewd
action in meeting his imminent hour of crisis is reinterpreted as a
prudent example of using one's money to secure one's future. It
seems that for Luke, the lesson to Christian readers is plain: "Go
and do likewise. Use your possessions now to help others, and so
be assured of your heavenly reward."

The remaining verses only serve to strengthen the admonition to
the proper use of wealth. Verses 10-12 stress faithfulness in the use
of one's possessions. The principle that loyalty is tested in small
things in v. 10 is applied to mammon in vv. 11-12. If persons aren't
faithful in unrighteous mammon, how can God entrust to them
the true riches, the kingdom of God? Or if they, like the steward
in the parable, are not faithful in managing the property of another,

how can God give them something of their own to manage? In each
case the point is the same: the use of one's possessions is a kind of
testing ground for the kingdom, a place where ultimate loyalties
are revealed.

This opens the way to the concluding exhortation in v. 13, the Q
saying which poses the need to choose between the two competing
loyalties, God or mammon. Of itself, the saying insists on an uncompromising service of God or mammon. No middle ground is
possible. This could lead to the conclusion that possessions are to
be abandoned or avoided at all costs. However, by placing this
saying in the context of the parable and the call for faithful use in
vv. 9-12, Luke gives it a different interpretation. Here it stands
not as an uncompromising call for the abandonment of possessions, but as an uncompromising call for the right use of wealth.
This means to make friends with it in such a way that the kingdom is gained, not lost. Moreover, there is a sense in which this
call is no less radical than the call to abandon everything, since it
asks for undivided use of one's wealth in the service of God and
humanity. How this call works itself out in real life for Luke remains to be seen. But already in Chapter 16 it excludes the charging of exorbitant interest for personal gain and it rejects those who
seek to justify their love of money (vv. 14-15) and those who ignore
the needs of the poor in their midst (vv. 19-31).

We conclude that the parable of the Dishonest Steward and its
sequel are interpreted by Luke as a summons to free oneself from
the bondage of mammon and to participate boldly in the worldly
service of making friends with your wealth. Luke is undoubtedly
speaking to Christians in his day and challenging them to put their
possessions to work for the service of humanity.

Zacchaeus—the Lukan Paradigm for Rich Christians
(Luke 19:1-10)

We regard the story of Zacchaeus as the most important Lukan
text on the subject of the right use of possessions. We further suggest that Luke intends this text as the paradigm par excellence for
wealthy Christians in his community. It represents the Lukan response to the tough question posed in the previous chapter, "Can
the rich be saved?" Even more broadly, it takes up the subject

raised by the parable of the Dishonest Steward, namely, how does one act to make friends with one's wealth?

There are several arguments that converge to demonstrate the unique role of this narrative in Luke's Gospel. First of all, the fact that Zacchaeus is a tax collector and sinner (vv. 2, 7) reminds us that we are dealing with one of Luke's favorite topics, Jesus' association with outcasts and sinners. This story sums up this vital part of Jesus' ministry.

Second, the placement of this story at the end of Jesus' public ministry underlines its symbolic and summary significance for Luke's presentation of Jesus' mission. In the subsequent text (19:11-27), the subject switches to the delay of the parousia, prompted by the proximity of Jerusalem, the goal of the extended Lukan travel narrative. Immediately thereafter comes the entry and the story of the passion. So this narrative is the last event in Jesus' public ministry according to Luke.

Third, the Christological statement in 19:10 lends further confirmation regarding its special role, since this statement effectively summarizes the Lukan view of Jesus' entire ministry. It points to the Zacchaeus story as the final witness of the Son of man's rescue mission to the lost. Hence Zacchaeus' repentance is no isolated event along the way, but the paradigmatic Lukan example of how salvation takes place and what authentic salvation involves.

Fourth, as we will argue in our discussion, the Lukan theme of possessions here receives its fullest treatment and presents Zacchaeus as the model for all well-to-do Christians.[10] We find this text, therefore, to be uniquely Lukan, representing in many respects what is most essential and distinctive in his portrait of Jesus' ministry.

There is little doubt that Luke found the core of this tradition in his own rich storehouse of special Jesus-traditions (L). But he has done much to rewrite the tradition in such a way that his own unique theological interests come frequently to the fore, as we will observe in our interpretation. This again indicates the extent to which Luke regards this text as a prime vehicle for his interpretation of Christian discipleship. Let us now examine it more closely.

The Story of Zacchaeus

Luke describes the story in three acts. Act I depicts Zacchaeus and his desire to see Jesus (vv. 1-4). Two features about Zacchaeus are stressed; he was a chief tax collector and he was rich. That Zacchaeus was a chief tax official means that he administered the collection of taxes within a set geographical area, with the aid of tax assistants. How large his territory was, or how many he employed we are not told, yet Jericho was an especially prosperous oasis city along the Jordan rift, renowned for its balsam-wood, fruit, figs and other agricultural produce. As an important toll-station leading into Arabia, one can imagine Zacchaeus supervising the tax-collection in the district of Jericho at considerable profit.

Thus Luke's observation that Zacchaeus was rich is almost super-fluous, though it typically heightens the stress on his wealth. The one shadow on his life was his occupation; it made him an outsider, socially and religiously. Even though a Jew, he was not considered a legitimate "son of Abraham" (v. 9). Act I ends with a brief, picturesque portrayal of his desire to see Jesus. Short of stature and unable to see over the crowd, he ran ahead and climbed a sycamore tree to catch a glimpse of the famous rabbi. What follows changed his whole life.

Act II describes the encounter between Jesus and Zacchaeus and the resultant criticism (vv. 5-7). Jesus' words to Zacchaeus, particularly, "I must stay" and "today" are suggestive of Luke's theological intent (v. 5). The "today" of salvation is announced here and even more emphatically in v. 9. It is one of Lukes favorite ways to express the presence of God's salvation in the person and ministry of Jesus.[11] This concept is further strengthened by the words "I must stay," for behind the "must" of Jesus' presence stands the will of God operative in the whole life and death of Jesus (Luke 4:43; 21:9; Acts 1:16; 3:21; 4:12).[12] So Jesus' presence before Zacchaeus is no accident. Rather, it belongs to the redemptive plan of God at work in his ministry. Zacchaeus becomes for Luke a symbolic recipient of the grace of God toward lost humanity. The joy of Zacchaeus' response to Jesus echoes the joy in heaven when one sinner repents, or the joy of the lost who are found, or the eschatological joy of the messianic banquet, the latter already anticipated in the meals of the church (Acts 2:46). But of course every time Jesus sits at table with tax collectors and sinners, his critics are there to object (Luke 5:30; 15:2). For his conduct cut deep against those who would limit the grace of God. The words of Jesus in vv. 9-10 are in part directed against these critics.

Act III portrays the climax and heart of the story, the repentance of Zacchaeus. Without any statement about Jesus' conversation at table with Zacchaeus we hear only the result of Zacchaeus encounter with Jesus. He makes a two-fold vow: to give one half of his goods to the poor and to repay four-fold those whom he has defrauded. In turn, Jesus' response highlights the new spiritual status of Zacchaeus: "Today, salvation has come to this house, since he also is a son of Abraham." Once again, Luke sounds the joyful note of the today of salvation in the ministry of Jesus. The word "house" probably includes the whole household of Zacchaeus, as it does in Acts (Acts 10:2; 11:14; 16:15, 31; 18:8). By virtue of his repentance he evidences the fact that he is still a true son of Abraham and he thus rejoins the community of faith that had ostracized him. The closing Christological statement encapsules the entire mission of Jesus according to Luke: "The Son of man came to seek and to save the lost" (cf. 4:21; 5:32).

One-Half to the Poor

We now want to look more carefully at the surprising way in which the salvation of Zacchaeus is described. One might have expected Zacchaeus to stand up and announce something like this: "Lord I believe in you as the one who is to come. I ask your forgiveness for my past life and I promise from now on to follow you wherever you go." However in this story the stress is not placed upon Zacchaeus' faith in Jesus, nor is the story a call to full-time discipleship. Apparently Zacchaeus remains at his tax office. The emphasis lies rather upon the results of Zacchaeus' reception of salvation. This is a matter of crucial importance to observe. We interpret this to mean that Luke's understanding of salvation is comprehensive. By that we mean that salvation for Luke includes both repentance, the turning away from a life of sin to a new life with God, and the fruits of repentance, i.e., the ethical-social consequences of the new life. In this text we see the ethical fruits of Zacchaeus' repentance (cf. Luke 3:10-14).

Yet this is not all. It is also noteworthy that Luke chooses a tax collector and a rich man as his paradigm for one who finds salvation. For in his Gospel, the two are normally at opposite poles in their response to Jesus. While the tax collectors gladly respond, the rich find it all but impossible to become disciples. Here, however, the presence of Jesus makes possible what is humanly impossible. A wealthy man gets through the needle's eye! But not without some radical change.

What is the significance of the radical change promised by the rich man? The promise to make fourfold reparation of those defrauded falls within Old Testament and rabbinic law, though it was limited to only a few acts of wrongdoing and was the extreme amount that could be exacted for stealing.[13] Among the rabbis, restitution was a sign of true repentance. A similar restitution may also be in line with Roman law regarding robbery.[14] Thus Zacchaeus agreed to make full recompense according to the law, as part of his new life.

But Zacchaeus also announced that he would give one-half of his possessions to the poor. This is the unprecedented act that has no parallel in Old Testament or rabbinic literature. Almsgiving, of course, is enjoined on every faithful Jew toward the poor. But nowhere do we find any suggestion that it might be consistent with the will of God to share one-half of one's possessions with the poor. In fact, in the rabbinic literature there is a limit of one-fifth of one's entire wealth placed on the first sharing and then an equal limit of one-fifth for one's annual income.[15] So here is a radically new standard, a new paradigm for the godly person. The "today" of salvation present in Jesus is here shown to mark out a new way with respect to the disposition of one's wealth on behalf of the poor.

This new way is not a new legalistic prescription. It is made freely, voluntarily, joyfully in response to God's initiative of grace and acceptance in Jesus. But by underscoring Zacchaeus' act of giving one-half to the poor, Luke forcefully informs his readers that the new way of discipleship goes beyond what any law can require, that it is much more than a token gift, that, in fact, it is a total commitment of one's wealth for the poor and needy. The consequences of such personal sharing in the life of the Christian community are pictured by Luke in the book of Acts. Here, Luke holds up the example of Zacchaeus for all his readers to consider.

Let us now summarize our discussion. We concluded the previous chapter with the challenging question "Can the rich be saved?" Zacchaeus is the yes-answer to this question. He is the opposite of the Rich Ruler who could not get through the needle's eye. Nevertheless, the Zacchaeus example offers no easy way for those with possessions to enter the kingdom. It calls for a repentance and the fruits of repentance that cut deep. It is true that not all of one's possessions must be surrendered. Yet it is clear that a radically new style of life should begin. This new life involves concrete restitution, where possible, of wrongs committed against others by economic cheating or fraud. It involves above all the grateful sharing of "one-half" of one's wealth with the poor and needy. Little wonder this kind of repentance is beyond the ordinary human capacity to fulfill and so seldom seen. But Luke boldly sets it forth as the challenge of Christian discipleship and the way to make friends for eternity with one's wealth. Zacchaeus, then, is the paradigm par excellence for Luke of how the rich can enter the kingdom of God. And he has in mind readers in his own time who need to break with the service of mammon and become free for the service of God, with all they possess!

Almsgiving, the Practice of Charity

The Lukan attitude toward the proper use of possessions can be further illustrated by a number of other texts that urge a genuine concern for the poor. In the remainder of this chapter we shall seek to touch on most of these passages in one way or another, so that the fullness of Luke's interest in this subject is felt.

A number of these passages deal with the practice of almsgiving. Their importance for Luke can be recognized by the surprising fact that apart from Matthew 6:2-4, only Luke-Acts in the New Testament mentions almsgiving.

The practice of almsgiving was deeply rooted in Old Testament law and every pious Jew took it to heart. As an expression of compassion to the poor, it had its ultimate source in God's compassion for his people. In late Judaism, almsgiving was regarded as a highly meritorious work, able to cover a multitude of sins.[16] Both individual and corporate almsgiving was practiced in Jesus' time with great effectiveness for the aid of the poor, the widows, and the orphans.

Matthew's discussion in the Sermon on the Mount confirms its social and religious importance, since it is one of the three main religious duties to come under Jesus' critical scrutiny, along with fasting and prayer (Matt. 6:2-4). Jesus does not condemn the practice, only the motive to be "praised by men" (6:2). Contrary to such public displays of charity, a secret practice of almsgiving is recommended, known only to God and the giver. All of this Matthean discussion, however, falls within normal Jewish practice and seems limited to Jesus' immediate followers.

But in Luke, almsgiving is discussed in a much broader context and is understood as part of the on-going practice of the early church. The Lukan portrait includes the following texts.

In Luke 11:41, Jesus dines with a Pharisee who takes offense at Jesus because he eats without performing the cultic washing before meals. Jesus in turn accuses the Pharisees of an outward piety, in contrast to their inner "extortion and wickedness." The reference seems to indicate a greed and lust for money that leads to all sorts of injustices (cf. 16:14). So the remedy, Jesus counsels, is to substitute almsgiving for greed and thus become clean.[17] That the problem in mind is the misuse of wealth seems confirmed by v. 42, where despite legalistic tithing, the Pharisees are indicted for neglecting justice and the practice of love. Thus the practice of almsgiving is recommended as consistent with inner fidelity to the law, if done from genuine motives.

Two additional gospel texts advocate the giving of alms, Luke 12:33 and 18:22. While alms are not specifically mentioned in 18:22, it is apparent that "distribute to the poor" is a Lukan substitute for alms. In each case, to sell one's possessions and give alms is the mark of true discipleship.

Even in Acts, the practice is encouraged. Peter and John would have helped the poor beggar with alms at the Beautiful Gate near the Temple, if they had had money (Acts 3:1-11). Most interesting is the story of Tabitha, who along with other widows is involved in the practice of good works and charity, i.e. almsgiving (Acts 9:36-43). The almsgiving could mean either gifts of money or other types of care for the needy. It is possible that a special class of Christians has developed, in this case widows, whose primary purpose is doing works of love for the poor.

In the pivotal story of Cornelius, whose conversion officially authorizes the Gentile mission, great stress is placed on two religious activities, prayer and almsgiving (Acts 10:2, 4, 31). In fact, Luke seems to suggest that these pious acts are the reason God dealt favorably with Cornelius. As a God-fearer, one of many such Gentiles attracted to the Jewish faith by its monotheism and high moral-ity, Cornelius was taught to practice almsgiving. According to Luke, he took it to heart, giving alms liberally and praying constantly (v. 2). His gifts were given to the people, likely meaning the poor among the synagogue adherents. As a centurion, he was a man of considerable wealth and status. Hence Luke holds him up as a model of piety and generosity for Gentile Christians, since it is obvious that his activities did not cease after he joined the Christian community.

The final mention of almsgiving occurs in Paul's defense speech before Felix (Acts 24:17). Here Paul describes his collection for the church in Jerusalem, mentioned often in his letters (Gal. 2:10; Rom. 15:26), as his alms and offerings to my nation. Since the collection was intended for poor Christians in Jerusalem and Judea, by "my nation" is probably meant Paul's fellow Jewish Christians.[18]

It has often been debated whether or not any well-organized form of charitable distribution existed in the early church, similar to that of Judaism and its synagogue-centered activity for the poor. One thinks immediately of the daily distribution in Acts 6; yet beyond this, the evidence is slight in Acts. The Tabitha circle may hint of an identifiable group that distributed alms and clothing; otherwise the giving is largely through individual gifts.

The result of our survey of almsgiving texts shows that Luke commends it as a basic Jewish practice of providing for the poor which should continue on in the life of the church. Prospective disciples of Jesus are challenged to sell all and give alms to the poor; Gentile God-fearers and converts are praised for their generosity; among works of love in widow's circles were alms; and the church's greatest missionary hero ends his active ministry with a collection of alms for the needy in Jerusalem. Thus almsgiving constitutes an essential part of the Christian ethical life for Luke. Here again we meet the Lukan challenge to those who have, to share with those who have not.

Doing Good with One's Wealth—Some Examples

While much of what Luke offers as a positive guide for the Christian use of wealth is quite general, he also provides a number of practical examples, which illustrate further possibilities for Christian disciples.

Debts and Loans

The first of these everyday examples can be discussed under the heading of debts and loans. Some commentators have tried to trace this material back to the Jubilee theme in Jesus' teaching.[19] While we earlier denied any direct link in Jesus' preaching with the legal prescriptions of the Jubilee Year, the presence of the Jubilee vision in the foundational, eschatological announcement of Isaiah 61 may mean that traces of the Jubilee prescription for remitting debts are present in these Lukan traditions.

Lend gratis (Luke 6:27-36)

Although the Lukan Sermon on the Plain has many similarities with the Matthean Sermon on the Mount, Luke creates his own sermon with its distinctive emphases. We already saw this in the opening beatitudes and woes, with their announcement of God's love for the poor and condemnation of the rich.[20] In the next section of the Sermon, which is framed by the command to love your enemies (vv. 27, 35), three closely related themes are bound together: love your enemies, do good, lend to those in need (vv. 27-36). It is the latter which Luke particularly develops in his own way. In fact, it has recently been argued that the entire section is dominated by Luke's interest in possessions.[21] Already in vv. 30-31 Luke stresses, contrary to Matthew 5:42, that the disciples of Jesus should not seek to get back what is taken from them and the golden rule is then quoted to support this willingness to give freely to others (cf. Matt.7:12).

But especially do we find Luke's concern for gratis giving in vv. 32-36. Here the exercise of genuine love is put to the test by the challenge to give and act without any hope of return. Three examples are cited. The first two, also found in Matthew, have to do with general axioms, namely, to love those who love you or to do good to those who do good in return. Neither is the mark of a disciple, since even sinners act thus! What characterizes a disciples is to love your enemies and to do good expecting nothing in return (v. 35). The third example on lending money is unique to Luke. Sinners loan expecting a full return, no doubt with a healthy interest. But Jesus' disciples are told to lend expecting no return.[22] Not only should they forego the interest, but the capital as well. Nothing less,

that is, than sheer gratis giving. Their principle guide is agape-love,
which, since it embraces even one's enemies as well as the ungrateful and wicked, is unlimited and unconditional (vv. 35-36).

Clearly such lending is not good business practice, nor is it recommended for everyone. This is a matter of Christian discipleship.
Sinners act according to the principle of mutual reciprocity. Christians act according to the principle of agape-love. So lending without
insisting on repayment becomes a vivid illustration of how this love
can be put into practice. The reward for such action lies in the future. For the present, the disciple simply seeks to practice mercy,
even as his Father in heaven is merciful.

Give and it will be given (Luke 6:37-38)

An additional word on foolish lending in Luke's Sermon occurs
in vv. 37-38. Luke follows the Q tradition about judging others
(Matt. 7:1-2), but has his own version. He adds comments on not
condemning and forgiving and then in v. 38 he expands the saying
on giving. After the exhortation, "Give and it will be given to you,"
he has a series of words promising an abundant return to those who
give freely. "Good measure, pressed down, shaken together, running
over, will be put into your lap." [23]

Why this strong emphasis on getting back so much more than
one gives? This is certainly no appeal to selfishness, or a promise
that generous givers will reap generous material rewards in return,
as it sometimes is mistakenly interpreted. Nowhere does Christ
promise abundant material gain for a life of discipleship. If anything, he promises less! It thus seems best to interpret this in one
of two ways: Either as a promise of future reward (v. 35), or as a
word of assurance that God will fully provide for the daily needs of
those who share generously with others. In this latter sense, it advocates a strong trust in God's care to those who lend gratis, or give
liberally to the poor and needy.

The Two Debtors (Luke 7:40-43; cf. Matt. 18:23-25)

This parable, embedded in the story of Jesus' encounter with a
sinful woman (Luke 7:36-50), also says something about the Christian attitude toward debts and loans. The larger story is typical of
Lukan traditions illustrating Jesus' association with outcasts and
sinners, and as it now stands it is a controversy story defending

Jesus' activity and his authority to forgive sins (vv. 39, 47-49; cf. Luke 5:18-25).

The parable of the two debtors interprets the woman's conduct as a grateful response to her forgiveness. While the forgiveness of sins is the primary focus in the parable, God's forgiveness is portrayed in the concrete image of a creditor who willingly, freely, and magnanimously forgives his debtors when they could not pay (v. 42). This earthly activity is then held up as the image of the even greater activity of God in remitting human sin.[24] The earthly example is not thereby nullified; rather, the act of cancelling debts serves as the sign and symbol of divine forgiveness. One can therefore say that the cancelling of debts serves as the sign of divine forgiveness. And one can further say that the cancelling of debts by Christians reflects the way in which God has treated them and therefore the way in which they should treat others.

All of this agrees with the admonition articulated already in Luke 6:32-36 about lending gratis. While not a legal prescription or unqualified injunction, lending gratis and cancelling debts are concrete examples of how Christian disciples can act out of a sense of God's mercy, rather than the desire for their own profit and gain.

Inviting the Uninvited (Luke 14:7-24)

A second real-life possibility for disciples to serve God with their possessions centers on the theme of table fellowship with the poor. Chapter 14, a composite of Mark, Q and L sources, all of which are set in the context of a banquet, provides us with the most striking texts, especially in Luke 14:7-24. However, already in vv. 1-6, Jesus indicts the Pharisees because they place a concern for property over humane considerations. In the parable of the Marriage Feast (14:7-11), God's reversal of human pride echoes the theme of reversal in the Magnificat and other texts. Moreover, this pride can cause people to close their eyes to the poor and needy, as the link between those who love "places of honor at feasts" and "who devour widow's houses" in Luke 20:46-47 reveals.

The most forceful text, however, occurs in Luke 14:12-14. Jesus counsels his host, identified by Luke as a Pharisaic member of the Sanhedrin (14:1), not to invite his friends, brother, relatives or rich neighbors. The reason is the same as in 5:32-36, namely, that such action is only doing what everyone else does. You do me a

favor, and I'll do you one. Perhaps the inclusion of "rich neighbors" alludes to certain actions calculated to cultivate relations in
order to gain some favors or advantages for oneself. At any rate,
this is the norm in ordinary human relations. While such relations
are not necessarily forbidden, there is nothing specifically Christian
about them.[25] So Jesus turns the norm upside down. "When you
give a feast, invite the poor, the maimed, the lame, the blind . . .
they cannot repay you." The trouble with the old norm is that it
excluded unselfish, agape-love. The new norm of the kingdom, however, invites those who cannot repay, those who provide no advantage, those in fact who could prove to be a constant burden, since
they have so little of their own.

This is Jesus' counsel to people of means. The motivation is
agape-love for those in greatest need. Admittedly, this kind of love
runs counter to ordinary ethics, the ethics of winning friends and
influencing people, yet it constitutes the new ethic of the kingdom.
And its rewards are kingdom rewards, not material benefits or immediate rewards that one can boast of, but the reward of the eschatological gift of salvation (Luke 14:14, 6:35). Luke thereby avoids
any false motives, other than the reward of doing the will of God.

The same theme of inviting the uninvited is repeated in the parable of the Great Banquet (Luke 14:14-24; cf. Matt. 22:1-10). The
introductory verse is somewhat unclear. It could either be interpreted as a pious remark by a guest trying to affirm what Jesus had
just said, or one could speculate that the guest objects to Jesus'
statement that only those who invite the poor and needy will get in.
In either case, Jesus warns them through the parable that those who
enter the kingdom might not be those persons whom they think.

The parable itself emphasizes the wealth of those invited to the
great banquet. The purchase of a field, ten oxen,[26] even a marriage
dowry, all required considerable wealth. Whether the excuses are
real or contrived has been much debated, some arguing that almost
no one would have refused an invitation from a wealthy man, since
the advantages were so great. Even weddings were known to be
postponed in such cases. Yet the activities themselves are true to
life, and it is especially worth noting how business transactions
dominate again, warning of the danger of riches.

The key to the parable is the reaction of the host. When informed
of the refusals, he orders his servants to go out into the streets and

to bring in the "poor and maimed and blind and lame" (v. 21). These poor are undoubtedly those whom Jesus' himself came to seek, the outcasts and sinners, the persons living on the margins of society. When there is still room, others are "compelled to come in," until the banquet hall is filled. These others may be more of the poor, or they could refer to Gentile converts.

How does Luke interpret this parable? While originally it was a warning intended for Jesus' contemporaries, who took offense at his association with outcasts, the early church may have expanded its meaning to explain the unbelief of the Jews and acceptance of the gospel by Gentiles. Yet for Luke it had a third meaning, as a warning to rich Christians in his day.[27] We already saw that in vv. 12-14 the wealthy are told to invite the poor and needy to their table. In this parable, the wealthy reject God's generous invitation in favor of their own everyday pursuits of profit and pleasure. So the poor become surprised and delighted guests at the royal banquet. In effect, the eschatological reversal between the poor and rich has occurred in the parable. Thus the parable as a whole serves to warn the rich to accept God's invitation. And that means to invite the poor and maimed and blind and lame to their tables, lest God leave them out at the heavenly banquet. The section which immediately follows this parable, which closes with the call to renounce all that one possesses (v. 31), would seem to confirm our interpretation that for Luke the problem of wealth and poverty is uppermost in mind. Invite the uninvited! That's the challenge to well-off Christians from these texts.

Doing Love's Deeds (Luke 10:25-37)

No discussion of Jesus' ethics or the New Testament ethic can overlook the one command that holds center stage, the love-command.[28] There is unanimity that this command lies at the heart of the Christian ethic. From Jesus to Paul, from the early church to the twentieth century church, it has remained such, no matter how far the church or individual Christians may have strayed from it in practice.

Our purpose, however, is not to discuss the love-command in general, but to observe how Luke employs it in his gospel, and how it touches on the subject of possessions.

In the Lukan Sermon on the Plain the love-command, exemplified above all in the command to love your enemies, is embraced by the broader concept of mercy: "Be merciful, even as your Father is merciful" (6:27-36). In 10:25-28, though, Luke specifically holds up the love-command by itself as the summary of the Law and as the potential way to life. This is followed by the famous illustration of the love-command in the moving parable of the Good Samaritan. While Luke doubtless draws upon the Markan tradition in vv. 25-28, he makes his own modifications (cf. Mark 12:28-31/Matt. 22:34-40). Luke has a lawyer put Jesus to the test, both here and in relation to the parable. Most noteworthy is the lawyer's opening question. Unlike the Markan version, the love-command is not simply a matter of the greatest command, but a matter of eternal life (cf. 18:18). "Do this and you will live" (v. 28). But the sequel shows how difficult love really is. The lawyer's attempt to justify himself (cf. 16:15; 18:9-14) provides the occasion for Luke to introduce the parable and its devastating critique of loveless religiosity.

The parable itself is too well known to require extensive comment. The climate of ethnic and religious hostility between Jews and Samaritans furnishes its realistic social setting. In the choice of the Samaritan as the good neighbor, contrasted with a priest and Levite, its polemical intent is revealed. Jesus courageously exposes sensitive nerves of racism and seeks to promote "consciousness-raising," in order to overcome the centuries-old hostility and prejudice.[29] Of particular importance for us is the lavish detail that depicts the manner in which the hated Samaritan fulfills the command to love. He accepts the risk of stopping to help. He uses expensive oil and wine to disinfect the wounds. He carries him to an inn, stays with him overnight, pays the night's board and room to the innkeeper and then promises to return later and pay for any further costs. Since one denarius was the equivalent of a day's wage for a laborer, no little sum was involved. The end result is that the Samaritan becomes the unforgettable example of unconditional love for one's enemies. It cost time, money, effort and sacrifice. That a Samaritan exhibits such love only adds salt to old wounds.[30] The inclusive love and acceptance that was obviously missing in the religious leaders of Judaism is here exemplified. While Jesus contemporaries sought to put a fence around the Law—no sinners, no tax collectors, no *am haaretz*, surely no enemies such as this Samaritan—Jesus pulled the fences down and welcomed all. The conclusion is inevitable. Who was the good neighbor? "The one who showed mercy on him" (10:37). As in 6:36, the command to love becomes one with the command to be merciful.

To whom does Luke direct this parable? In a way, the parable stands as a timeless example of love in action, and of the command to love one's enemies. Perhaps Luke had no one group in mind. Yet it is not too much to hear a word directed to possessors. The parable claims that love is not words, but deeds. And these deeds involve risks, sacrifices, and sharing of one's possessions. Any well-off reader cannot avoid the implication with regard to personal wealth. Where suffering is found, where the poor and needy exist, there lies an opportunity to make friends with our wealth and to give from a deep sense of God's mercy. In fact, Luke goes so far as to say that it finally comes down to a matter of life or death to the potential "good neighbor." The ringing command of Jesus, twice echoed in this narrative, will not let the reader go: "Go and do likewise."

What shall we do? (Luke 3:10-14)

This final text which we will use to illustrate real-life possibilities for well-off Christians is a fascinating one from an ethical standpoint. It has no parallels elsewhere, but whether it comes from Luke's special source (L) or his own creation is disputed.[31] Lukan redaction is clearly present, however, as we will note below.

What is of special significance for our purposes is the way in which the comprehensive Lukan understanding of salvation is here set forth at the opening of the gospel. As we noted previously with the story of Zacchaeus, Luke inseparably links together repentance for the forgiveness of sins and the fruits of repentance. Verses 10-14 are the response to John the Baptist's demand in v. 8, "Bear fruits that befit repentance." In these verses, three groups are portrayed, each asking the familiar Lukan question, "What shall we do?" (cf. 10:25; 18:18; Acts 2:37; 16:30). For Luke, this question is always a question of salvation, of life or death (so v. 9).

The Multitudes. The response to the question of the crowd is simple: share your food and clothing with one another. The coat mentioned was actually an undergarment worn next to the body. Normally a poor person owned only two such garments, one for everyday and one for the Sabbath. Yet even with so little, the one who has two is asked to share with one who has none. Likewise with the food. With the multitudes, then, it is really a matter of the poor helping the poor. This has caused scholars to argue recently that in the original preaching of John and Jesus there was a call for solidarity among the poor.[32] That is, those in poverty were told to share with one another what little they possessed. This does seem to be a valid observation, which may also apply to Luke's description of the shared economic life of the early church in Acts.

The tax collectors. While a familiar group in Luke's gospel, it is surprising to see them appear already in John's ministry. Some have therefore suggested that Luke has read back a tradition from Jesus' ministry. Yet later, in 7:29-30, Luke refers to this text in a way that indicates that he found it in the tradition.

What are the tax collectors to do? Again, a simple response: charge no more than what is legal. To overcharge was the perennial temptation of tax collectors (19:8). Note that they are not told to leave their profession. At least for Luke, one could be both a tax collector and a Christian (cf. Zacchaeus). However within Judaism it was not the case, as tax-collectors were regarded as traitors to their people and as religious and social outcasts (19:9). According to Luke, though, the new community welcomed tax collectors into their inner circle from the beginning. Somehow one could serve both God and Caesar as a tax collector. But only if one first bore the fruits of a repentant life of honesty and generosity.

The Soldiers. This is certainly the most surprising group mentioned and historically, the most questionable. Does Luke have Roman or Jewish soldiers in mind? Since the word used for soldiers is found only here and in Romans, and since all other references to soldiers in Luke are Roman, many think the same applies here (Luke 7:1-10; 23:47; Acts 10). Yet it is possible that soldiers of Herod Antipas are meant, since the setting is Jewish and because Josephus relates how Herod regarded John as a political subversive and so had him carefully watched until he was arrested and killed.[33] If historically valid, the conversion of Herod's soldiers would have been a courageous decision on their part.

At any rate, Luke does not exclude soldiers from the church, a fact verified by other sources in the first two centuries, even though the Jesus movement was in principle nonviolent, if not pacifist.[34] Apparently in Luke's church no irreconcilable conflict was felt between the profession of soldier and the faith, provided, of course, their conduct was ethical.

What must the soldiers do as fruits of repentance? Once again, the emphasis is upon just and fair treatment of persons in the practice of their profession. They are forbidden to extort money by force —bribes, payoffs, harassment, false testimony—and to be content with their wages. As with the tax collectors, the repentance demanded is matched to the special temptations of their vocation, where violence and extortion were all too common.

What can we learn ethically from this passage? Some critics have argued that the ethical teaching here is very conservative compared to the radical ethic of Jesus elsewhere in the Gospels. For example, no one is asked to leave their profession, not even when they are associated with vocations highly suspect. Nor is the ethical response demanded anything more than simple justice, honesty, and brotherly love toward persons in need. "The fruits of repentance exist in good and just activity in the concrete situation of one's present life and calling." [35] There is nothing fundamentally new in these demands, nor do they seem to reach out into society with a vision of a new community. Critics thus speak of the "individualistic, moralistic view of repentance that Luke here exhibits." [36]

Perhaps there is some truth in this criticism. Jesus' ethic elsewhere seems to cut much deeper and to call for a far more pervasive change of motivation and orientation. Still, when compared with contemporary Jewish ethical teaching, even this section exhibits something of the radical influence of Jesus' love-centered, humanistic ethic.[37] For example, there is no call to any cultic observance of the Law or the oral traditions of Pharisaism. Instead, there is a singular focus on human needs and interpersonal relations, in which the questions of justice, integrity, and mercy outweigh all others. There is also an acceptance of persons regarded as outside the Law, along with an affirmation of their possibility to live ethically, both within their vocation and within the new community of disciples. There is even a trace of social consciousness, particularly in the sense of solidarity among the poor as they share their food and clothing, in the recognition of exploitive taxation as a problem for the poor and in the attempt to protect citizens from extortion and violence. Perhaps this is where our attention should be centered today.

Surely this passage had meaning for Luke's own time and community. It would challenge Christians who had food and clothing to share with the needy. It would sensitize persons in various vocations to the peculiar temptations of their calling and urge the practice of justice in and through them. Especially would it call for a rejection of force to gain one's end and for economic fairness. We encounter here once again, therefore, Luke's particular sensitivity to the problems and needs of the poor and powerless. And he reminds us that this sensitivity is not something optional for believers, since the fruits of repentance belong to the message of salvation announced by John, embodied by Jesus and continued in the life of God's people, then and now.

At the end of the previous chapter the question arose, are riches and discipleship at all compatible? The intent of this chapter has been to show how Luke responds to this question. As we have seen, he has preserved a rich abundance of material concerned with the right use of one's possessions. This means that in spite of his criticism of rich Christians in Jesus' call to forsake everything, and in spite of his awareness of the grave temptation of possessions, Luke affirms possessions as a necessary and good gift of God, rightly used. In Luke's estimate, possessions are to be placed radically in the service of Christian discipleship. Their proper use occurs within the context of agape-love, where caring for the poor, sharing with those in need, and doing good even to one's enemies receive the highest priority. Accordingly, Luke mounts a massive challenge for wealthy Christians to change their ways and to share their wealth more equitably with others. In particular, he points to Zacchaeus as a model worthy of emulation. Zacchaeus' willingness to share one half of all he possessed with the poor presents the strongest Lukan challenge to the rich. While the rich who hang on to their wealth cannot get through the needle's eye, by giving their wealth to the poor they are making friends for eternity and may yet find a way into the kingdom by the call and grace of God.

7

A Sharing Community

The Lukan attitude toward wealth and poverty expressed in the gospel finds its fullest confirmation in Luke's description of the life of the early church. Without this evidence, we would find ourselves hard pressed to say anything about Luke's own distinctive attitudes regarding possessions. If, e.g., Luke said nothing about possessions in Acts, after having said so much in his gospel, we would have to conclude that the topic was more pressing to Jesus than to Luke or to the early church, and that Luke was simply a faithful recorder of the tradition. Then too, our attempts to ask how Luke interpreted the gospel traditions for his own time would seem to be seriously thwarted. Or again, if the picture of the early church in Acts regarding possessions stood in conflict with the gospel tradition, we would be forced to make a hard choice over which portrait to follow, the gospel or Acts.

Fortunately, Luke has not left us in the dark about the view of possessions in the early church, nor does his presentation reveal any serious discontinuity between the gospel traditions and the early community.[1] While the number of texts on possessions in Acts is not large, this is scarcely surprising given the theological purpose of sketching the growth of the movement from Jerusalem to Rome (Acts 1:7). Nevertheless, the texts we do have are significant. In fact, what Luke preserves on this theme has proven to be controversial and challenging, for the very reason that it continues the radically new view of wealth and its proper use reflected in the gospel. Just how radical is the question often debated, especially since some commentators have coined the term "early Christian communism" to describe Luke's economic description of the earliest communities.

147

To what extent this is a fully accurate term is one of the several questions we now intend to explore.

Sharing According to Need

The two primary texts that provide us with insight into the economic life of the early church belong to the so-called "Lukan summaries" of Acts.[2] Each of these summaries describes the life and growth of the infant church and offers a birds-eye view of what that life was like.

There is much dispute about the source of these summaries.[3] Suggestions range all the way from historically reliable pre-Lukan traditions to that of primarily Lukan compositions, perhaps built upon individual case histories like that of Barnabas (Acts 4:36-37). Without denying the possibility of certain pre-Lukan sources, we find that the repetitive manner in which Luke generalizes on the early church's life and to a certain extent idealizes it, so that it becomes the model church for every age, argues for their basic Lukan origin and composition. What Luke intends is not just a historical glimpse of the earliest community, but a working vision of what every Christian community ought to be like, then and now. What is the essence of this working vision of the new community for Luke, especially in the social and economic sphere?[4]

All Things in Common (Acts 2:41-47)

This first summary is composed of two parts. In vv. 41-42 we have a general overview of the new community and in vv. 43-47 a more detailed portrait. Some scholars have argued that v. 42 preserves the earliest description of Christian worship in the New Testament.[5] More likely, however, is that each of the four areas mentioned represents a separate entity in the community's life. It is equally important to note that Luke already in this verse emphasizes the sense of oneness that permeated the community and which led to its remarkable communal life. Hence we read that they "devoted themselves to" the various aspects of their common life together.

The fuller portrait is given in vv. 43-47. Luke begins by emphasizing the presence of God's power experienced in the miracle-working activity of the apostles. Then he gets to his main point of concern, the unity of the early community. This unity is not a human creation; it is the result of believing, or better yet, it is a gift of the Spirit at work in the new community. But what is of greatest importance from our perspective is the striking way in which this God-given unity was said to express itself. Luke writes that they had "all things in common."

What does he have in mind? Its economic dimensions are spelled out in v. 45. According to Luke, those who possessed land and other property sold them and the proceeds were then distributed to the needy. However, this still does not answer all our questions. Was all private property sold and the proceeds placed into a communal fund for distribution? If so, was such action required or voluntary? If every member or family was required to sell all their possessions, then we have some form of early Christian communism. As we have noted above, some commentators favor this interpretation and have supported it with three additional observations. a) Jesus demanded full surrender of possessions to the poor; b) The early church sought to model its communal life according to Jesus and his disciples, who lived from a common purse; c) The early church also had precedent for its abandonment of possessions in the community at Qumran.[6]

Although a Christian form of communism, with its commitment to economic equality for all, does have sound biblical impulses, what Luke describes seems to be something different. Against the arguments above one must consider the following: a) Jesus' demand for a total surrender of one's possessions was limited to his lifetime and not made mandatory for all his followers;[7] b) Jesus and his disciples did not live from the proceeds of property they had sold, but from the gifts of others (Luke 8:1-3) and moreover, their life-style as depicted in the gospels, to live without permanent homes and to rely on others for food and shelter, is not the same as the early community in Acts, which owned homes and worked in secular callings; c) The Qumran attitude toward possessions was quite different. In particular, it required the surrender of all one's property, whereas, as we shall show below, in Acts the giving was voluntary.[8]

What then is the kind of economic sharing that Luke describes in v. 45? While the revolutionary quality of having "all things in common" remains, a more careful exegesis seems to show that land and possessions were sold *as the needs required*. Three arguments converge to support this conclusion. a) The use of the imperfect tense to describe the act of selling. In Greek, the imperfect tense denotes

an on-going, repeated activity, not a once-for-all act. Thus v. 45
should correctly read, "they were time and again selling their goods
and distributing them to all, as any had need." Both selling and the
distribution were carried out as the needs arose. "Whenever there
is need of money for the poor of the congregation, one of the prop-
erty-owners sells his piece of land or valuables, and the proceeds
are given to the needy."[9] b) Christians continued to live in their
homes so it is apparent that not everyone sold everything (cf. Acts
5:42; 12:12). Even in Acts 2:46, the breaking of bread takes place in
the members' homes. c) The selling of goods according to Acts is
done voluntarily, not under compulsion, as later texts will show.

What we find, therefore, in the economic sharing of the early
church is a profound commitment to the needs of everyone in the
community, along with a concommitant willingness to provide for
these needs by voluntarily selling one's possessions for the community as the daily needs required it. This willingness to make available one's possessions according to the needs was the result of their
marvelous sense of Christian community. One in the faith, they were
one in Christian solidarity; in this sense, and with the practical action
to verify it, they possessed all things in common.

The remainder of the summary in vv. 46-47 depicts this unity as
it expressed itself in daily worship and the sharing of daily bread.
In the reference to the breaking of bread in homes we very likely are
reading about the love feasts that seem to characterize the earliest
decades, until abuses required a separation between the eucharist
and the daily meals (2 Cor. 11:1ff.). What Luke wants to underscore
throughout is the vision of a believing community, alive through the
Spirit, whose sense of oneness was evidenced by their readiness to
provide for the economic needs of one another. As we will see in
the next summary, their intent was to eliminate poverty from their
midst. It was not selfishness or greed, but generosity and joy and a
sense of oneness which led them to share all things in common. And
this kind of sharing, unheard of in the Graeco-Roman culture of
their day, attracted the attention of many on the outside and became
an evangelistic arm of the community. That is what Luke means
by the phrase, "having favor with all the people" (v. 47).[10] In fact,
behind his whole emphasis on the unity and sharing of the early
church, Luke may be writing with Gentile Christians in mind, for
whom the idea of sharing was severely restricted.[11]

Not a needy person among them (Acts 4:32-39)

What was said of the community in the previous summary is here repeated, only with greater detail and emphasis. Because of the close similarity between these summaries, it has been conjectured that Luke's description for both may have originated from one source, probably represented by these verses. Whatever their origin, the theme of unity is again announced, which then serves as the basis for the church's remarkable economic life, once more expressed by the principle of "everything in common" (v. 32).

How Luke understands this principle is amplified in several verses. In v. 32 he explains this to mean that "no one said that any of the things which he possessed was his own." If we take this literally, it would seem to say that all believers were willing to share their possessions unreservedly with the community; yet it still implies ownership of possessions. At first reading, however, this verse appears to be in tension with v. 34, since we are told in v. 34 that those who did have possessions were actually selling them and bringing the proceeds to the apostles, who then supervised the distribution according to existing needs, implying they did relinquish all their property.[12] But the two verses can be reconciled. Since the imperfect tense is again used throughout, Luke wants to stress the on-going nature of the sharing. Hence the purpose of v. 34 is simply to illustrate the fact that the willingness to share, expressed in v. 32, was put into action. This same point is made even more explicit in the example of Barnabas which follows, and negatively with Ananias and Sapphira. Thus it is best to understand this text in the same way as we interpreted Acts 2:43-47. What Luke has in mind is not a total selling of all one's possessions at one time and then living off the proceeds from that moment on, but a continual selling and sharing as the needs emerged or as the treasury became low.

Furthermore, the major purpose of this summary is to illustrate the way in which the community, bound together in the unity of faith, saw to it that the economic needs of each one were met. Verse 34a expresses the goal of the community: "there was not a needy person among them." This goal itself is echoed in Deuteronomy 15:4, where the intent of the Sabbath Year is interpreted with the words, "there will be no poor among you." To fulfill this goal meant a redistribution of wealth in the community, in which the wealthier members made their possessions available to the poorer members.

This did not, according to our interpretation, require the total abolishment of private property or possessions or the adoption of a strictly communal life-style by all Christians. Nor is there any poverty ideal set forth. But what it did mean was the abolition of the proprietary spirit, combined with the willingness to share with those who had less. In fact, one can go so far as to say that the possessors voluntarily gave up their right to own and control their own possessions for the sake of the greater good of the community. In effect, they convenanted together so that there would be no poor among them.[13]

Two Case-Histories (Acts 4:36—5:11)

In the section immediately following the second summary, Luke offers his readers two examples, one good and one bad, of how the community cared economically for one another.[14]

The good example of sacrificial giving is Joseph Barnabas, identified as a Levite and a Cyriot.[15] How he acquired his property and whether it was located in Cyprus or Palestine is not stated. What remains significant is his example. As Luke tells it, he decided to sell a piece of land and bring the entire profit to the apostles. The act is done voluntarily, yet out of a sense of solidarity with Christians in need. No doubt this act represents what Luke means by sharing all things in common. Its closest parallel would seem to be the action of Zacchaeus in the gospel, when he gave one-half to the poor. By his decision, Barnabas demonstrates his freedom from the bondage of wealth and makes friends with it before God.

Because Luke singles out Barnabas for special mention, some commentators suggest that Barnabas was the exception rather than the rule in the community.[16] To what degree Luke reflects actual historical reality is impossible to say. Yet we can ascertain that Luke presents Barnabas as a model for believers to imitate. He wants to set forth Barnabas' costly sharing as the norm for the whole community, since this would allow the Spirit of Jesus to shape its life through and through. If this would happen, then no one would be suffering from need, and mutual sharing would be the way of life among believers.

That not everyone expressed the same spirit is brought out forcefully by the story of Ananias and Sapphira (Acts 5:1-11). They are the counterparts to Barnabas and a sharp warning to all Christians of means. Their fate foreshadows the fate of those who remain attached to unrighteous mammon.[17] What was their failure? Their guilt was not in the fact that they withheld some of the proceeds from the sale of their land. Verse 4 makes it evident that they were free to sell or not sell and that they were also free to give all or only a portion of the profit to the community. Everything was voluntary, not under compulsion. But this couple had mutually conspired to claim they were giving the whole profit, when in fact they held some back. So what appeared publicly as an expression of generosity and community was really a deception and a lie. Their greed had broken the Spirit-centered unity of the fellowship, a most grievous offense in Luke's eyes.

Therefore their frightful fate was meant as a clear warning signal to other Christians of how sacred and inviolable was the trust and love and unity within the fellowship. Note how the sense of "great fear" is twice repeated (vv. 5, 11). The message is to be on your guard, since God knows your hearts! (v. 4). The fact that Luke chooses a case of economic misuse to make this point about the fellowship only goes to demonstrate all the more how for him the use of possessions constitutes a preeminent test-case of Christian discipleship. In this respect, Luke has carried through his theme of the danger of riches and the importance of serving God rather than mammon.

Economic Crisis in the Early Church

In addition to Luke's challenging picture of the early community and its economic care for one another, we catch other glimpses throughout Acts of the way in which the question of possessions was treated. Each of these, as we shall see, lends further weight to our argument that Luke's overall description in Acts confirms what we have already learned from the gospel about its central importance to the Christian community.

The Problem of Fair Distribution (Acts 6:1-7)

That life in the early church was not always ideal, as the story of Ananias and Sapphira already revealed, and that even the spirit of sharing according to needs was not always carried out, is verified by the events related in Acts 6:1-7. Notice that the first recorded dispute in the early church occurs over money. Is Luke perhaps warning his readers once again about the dangers of wealth? The fact that the church has established a fund and the daily distribution was made to widows indicates that a type of organizational structure had been formed to administer the money and care for the needy and that some groups, like widows, were regularly in need. Luke seems to attribute the problem, at least partially, to the growing numbers in the community (v. 1). But we know from the Pauline letters that the church in Jerusalem remained poor and this was undoubtedly due to a variety of reasons.[18]

The main point of controversy, though, was the claim of the Hellenists that their widows were being unfairly neglected in the daily distribution and the Hebrew widows favored. The exact identity of the Hellenists, as well as the whole question of "Hebrews and Hellenists" in the early church has been much discussed.[19] Current consensus understands the Hellenists as Greek-speaking Jews, probably from the diaspora, who had returned to live in Jerusalem. Evidence indicates that these Hellenistic Jews often maintained their own identity, established their own synagogues and generally socialized within their own circles. Apparently this social isolation continued within the Christian community, at least in part. Stephen, the outstanding example of a Hellenistic Jew, reveals in his famous speech that his views on the Temple and the history of his people were quite different from Palestinian Jews. Very likely, it was the same Hellenistic Jews who were the first to begin missionary work among non-Jews, a step their Hebraic brethren feared to take. Thus the controversy noted by Luke, though erupting over the fair distribution of funds, probably went deeper and included theological differences as well.

How was this potentially divisive conflict handled? In response to the complaint of inequality the apostles requested the whole body of believers to appoint seven persons to wait on tables, i.e., to administer the daily distribution.[20] This they did, setting them apart for this work by the laying on of hands. A division of labor between the apostles and the seven is established. But that more was involved for the seven than equitable administration of funds to the needy becomes evident in the requirements stated for the task and the subsequent stories of Stephen and Philip. A combination of spiritual and administrative abilities are laid out for all (vv. 3, 5).

At this point in Acts, however, Luke concentrates on the social and economic task of caring for the poor in a just and equitable manner. An appointed office is even established for this task. One further observation about the seven is that they all have Greek names. This may indicate that all seven were Hellenists, i.e., they belonged to the minority group.[21] At the least one can say that the group discriminated against was well represented on the newly-commissioned supervisory committee.

One can only admire Luke's honesty in narrating this event. It offers an admission that the God-intended unity of the fellowship was not always a living reality. Hence it becomes an example of how to deal with crises in the church, through both spiritual and practical action. But most important for our purposes, it emphasizes the requirement for social justice and equality within the church and the need to take appropriate steps to implement this requirement. Discrimination against the poor, favoritism of one group over another, the dominance of the wealthier members over the poorer, even the large gap between rich and poor, none of these belongs to the nature of Christian community. True, the church has always been far from perfect; yet this never negates the sinfulness of its imperfection, or the need to take action to remedy the wrongs. Perhaps, too, this text shows that the willingness to share "all things in common" must have as its counterpart the concern for a structure that will insure the faithful and just administration of funds. Both are here deemed necessary. At any rate, we find in this text that the question of "fair and equitable" distribution of benevolences within the community is for the first time decisively and wisely encountered.

The Problem of Global Distribution (Acts 11:12-30; 24:17)

Another economic crisis occurs during a time of worldwide famine. According to Luke's account, Christian prophets came from Jerusalem to Antioch, and one of them, Agabus, who reappears in Chapter 20, predicted a coming famine throughout the world. Luke adds parenthetically that this famine occured during the reign of the Emperor Claudius (A.D. 41-54), a fact verified by other sources.[22] Palestine was especially vulnerable and hard hit, so that it must have suffered much. Therefore, recognizing the great need of the community in Judea, the church in Antioch of Syria made provisions to share its greater abundance with its suffering neighbors. Thus the first "world-relief" program in the church's history was begun.

The program itself is briefly described in vv. 29-30. Two principles emerge from this description. The first is that of giving relief according to their ability. That is, the aid was given in proportion to the wealth of the giver. Thus Luke recognizes differences between both the wealth of the members and their ability to give. Without becoming legalistic, one could say that the earlier principle of "sharing according to need" in Acts 2 and 4 has a parallel principle of "giving according to ability."

Yet this principle can easily be misused if it is not kept in proper Lukan perspective and by that we mean within the context of the Lukan imperative for a radical sharing of one's wealth with the poor. While this principle does recognize variations of basic needs and incomes among Christians and while it does not demand absolute equality of wealth in the community of faith, it does require proportionately more of those who have more. And the proportionately more kind of giving is to be costly and sacrificial. As the story of the poor widow illustrates, those who give only out of their abundance, without real sacrifice, are not giving in a way consistent with the will of God or the call of Jesus. Likewise, Zacchaeus sets the Lukan standard for the rich, in which the encounter with Jesus finds expression in giving away one-half to the poor. So the principle of giving according to one's ability should mean no less than costly, sacrificial, abundant sharing to meet the needs of a hungry world.

The second principle found in this text is that of Christian solidarity in need. The whole church stands together in a solidarity of Christian love for one another. One community of believers in one nation should come to the aid of believers in other lands. We might here echo Paul's words, "If one member suffers, all suffer together" (1 Cor. 12:26) and translate it to say, "Christians in wealthy lands are called to share with those in poor ones."

Another striking example of this ecumenical solidarity is found in Paul's offering for the poor in Jerusalem, alluded to briefly in Acts 24:17 and elsewhere in the Pauline letters.[23] It may be that Paul learned this ecumenical perspective from the church in Antioch. At least it is impressive to see how Luke recognizes the need for the emerging worldwide church to band together in practical aid for one another and how he sets this example before his church and readers. We might also note how Barnabas, earlier identified as the first Christian to sell his land and give the profits to the community in Jerusalem, is now identified with a program of giving on a broader scale and teaching Paul likewise. Joseph Barnabas is one of those tantalizing heroes of the early church, a man of faith, action, and compassion and a teacher of the one who eventually outstripped him in the annals of church history.

One problem remains with Luke's ecumenical vision. While we have focused on its global perspective, it must be admitted that the vision embraces only the Christian family worldwide, and not the whole human race. Verse 29 refers only to the brethren in Judea and not everyone suffering from famine. Even in 24:17, the reference to "my nation" probably means Jewish believers. There are no direct exhortations or examples of global concern for the poor elsewhere in Acts. How shall we understand this? Is it a sign of gross inwardness on the part of the earliest communities, or of indifference to non-Christians, or the result of blindness on the part of Luke, despite his worldwide perspective in both volumes? The answer is probably varied and perhaps in part unknown. No doubt the early expectation of the parousia had sometihng to do with this at first, but by Luke's time the delay of the end was obvious and the church's presence in the world was expected to continue. A more likely factor for this absence of global concern has to do with the smallness of the Christian communities. There was little they could do on a grand scale and so they concentrated on meeting the needs of the poor in their own communities. Perhaps too, we need to consider the primarily evangelistic thrust of Luke's purpose in writing, so that we only catch a fleeting glimpse of what was really going on in various Christian communities.

Whatever the reasons, we still catch glimpses of the fact that Luke does point beyond the Christian community itself to the needs of the world. For one thing, he models the Christian community itself, especially in the way it cares for the poor and shares its resources, as the example for the community at large. This is seen not only by the overall purpose of Luke-Acts as a document for Gentile Christians and other interested Gentiles, but specifically in the way Luke depicts the attraction which the early community had for non-Christians. The startling growth, as he traces it, comes in no small way from the appealing practice of caring love that the communities exhibited, what we called earlier its evangelistic function.

A second point is that Luke's concept of the poor is inclusive and is not limited in any way to Jews or non-Jews, saints or sinners, disciples or nondisciples. It embraces the hungry, oppressed, sick, lost, outcasts of every kind, Samaritans and Gentiles, and thus presents a portrait of God's love for humanity, embodied in Jesus' ministry, that cannot be overlooked or negated. While especially true of the gospel, it must be remembered in the Acts narrative as well. Perhaps the natural theology of Paul's speech in Athens, which recognizes God's creative goodness for all mankind also can be extended to include the concrete deeds of love of the Christian community (Acts 17:24-26; cf. 14:16-17). Thus we are not left merely with a community, global as it is, caring only for itself, but also have pointers to the broader task of caring and sharing with all who are the hungry and oppressed of this world.

Remembering the Words of Jesus (Acts 20:33-35)

As our last witness from Acts regarding possessions, we want to look at the farewell speech of Paul to the Ephesian elders at Miletus. Luke has framed this speech as Paul's "last will and testament" not merely to the elders, but also to the church of his own day. To what extent Luke drew on sources or his own personal knowledge of the great missionary is a complex and sharply debated question.[24] Scholars have long recognized many points of contact between this speech and the Pauline letters. In our judgment, Luke is primarily responsible for its present form as a typical farewell speech, yet he obviously was in touch with the Pauline tradition.

Of special interest for our purposes is the surprise ending to the address. In the earlier part of the speech, Paul has recounted his missionary preaching of "the gospel of the grace of God" (v. 24) and has predicted he will see them no more (v. 25). He then defends his own ministry and warns them against false teachers, who will enter the church and try to lead them astray (v. 29). The address now appears to conclude with a final word of commendation "to God and to the word of his grace" (v. 32).

But it doesn't end. Once again, Paul defends himself vigorously and then finally closes by calling on the elders to remember a word of the Lord (vv. 33-35). What is the subject of this second conclusion? In vv. 33-34 it is a familiar theme from Paul's epistles, a defense of the purity of his motives for preaching the gospel. [25] Paul insists that he has not preached out of greed or love of money. Rather, he has toiled with his own hands to support himself and his companions.

The surprise comes in v. 35. Paul presents his own labor and self-sufficiency as an example to the churches. But the example is not merely that of self-support; more important, his toil has been exercised to aid the weak, the helpless, the poor. And to validate the rightness of his labor and concern for the weak, the speech comes to its climax with an authoritative word from the Lord Jesus: "It is more blessed to give than to receive." In this way, a word of the Lord regarding possessions becomes the final admonition of the church's greatest missionary teacher.

Nothing could be stronger evidence of Luke's profound concern for the poor and weak. Strangely, this saying of Jesus appears nowhere else in the New Testament or the early Christian literature. Yet its authenticity seems indisputable, as it is so characteristic of Jesus' love for the poor.[26] The beatitude form too is typical of Jesus' sayings. Within the speech itself, the saying binds together God's love for the weak with the admonition to his disciples to love in like manner, following the example of the Lord and his great apostle!

We find this word from the Lord, "It is more blessed to give than to receive," to be a most fitting conclusion to Luke's presentation of the theme of wealth and poverty and the proclamation of good news to the poor.

8

The Poor
Inherit the Kingdom

In this chapter we shall seek to summarize our study of wealth and poverty in Luke-Acts and to relate our findings to the broader context of Jesus' proclamation of good news to the poor. At the same time we shall emphasize the relevance of our research on Luke-Acts for faithful Christian discipleship.

"For Luke, the kingdom belongs to the poor, but the rich share in it by virtue of their treatment of the poor and needy."[1] We find this recent quotation to be an accurate reflection of Luke's position. Moreover, it contains both a promise and a challenge. That the kingdom belongs to the poor conveys a word of promise and hope for the poor. That the rich share in the kingdom by virtue of their treatment of the poor presents a sharp word of challenge to the rich.

The Good News to the Poor

We began our study by asking two fundamental questions: Who are the poor for Luke and what is the good news proclaimed to them? If, as we have shown, the poor includes those who belong to the lowest social and economic level, what is the good news addressed to them? We would suggest three dimensions of this good news in Luke-Acts.

The Assurance That God Is for Them

Certainly for Luke, the God of Jesus is the God of the poor and the lowly. Beginning with the Magnificat, this theme is echoed throughout the gospel. Above all, Jesus' proclaims this good news both in word and in deed. The promise of Isaiah 61 with its vision of the Jubilee finds its fulfillment in his ministry. By his acceptance of the outcasts and sinners, the poor and disenfranchised, he makes

160

the implicit claim that God likewise accepts them. He blesses the poor and hurls woes and warnings against the rich. In all of this, Jesus is powerfully portrayed as one who revives the prophetic voice on behalf of the poor and oppressed. The poor know through Jesus, that God is for them.

The Promise of the Future

The ultimate hope of the poor is the promise of the coming eschatological reversal. In the future kingdom of God, Jesus promises a complete reversal of conditions between the rich and the poor, the mighty and the powerless. The motive for this reversal is not some kind of eschatological revenge, but ultimate justice. In the present this motif serves as a word of comfort to the poor and as a warning to the rich.

But how shall we deal with our theological discomfort over the idea of an eschatological reversal? If we can believe it at all, does this not end up with the same old "pie in the sky" theology, which offers nothing for the poor in their present misery, except to pacify them enough so they won't turn against their exploiters? That's why Karl Marx called religion, at least this kind, the "opiate of the people."

If this were the only hope of the poor, it would be open to this deadly critique. Yet one should never discount the power and vitality of an ultimate vision of hope and justice for suffering and oppressed people. Such a vision can give strength to endure and can make possible a lively faith in God that gives a sense of human dignity and worth despite the most inhumane conditions.

A conviction of ultimate justice need not lead to passive acceptance of the status quo. It can also create the resolve to work here and now for the kind of world God will one day bring about. Even in Jesus' time we find this to be true. While the Essenes at Qumran adopted a passive attitude and retreated to the wilderness to await the imminent end, the Zealots with the same eschatological hope, fought valiantly to anticipate the kingdom already in this world by their actions. Jesus rejected the Qumran passivism, as well as the Zealots' violent means to attain their goal. But he did not reject their lively hope for change and renewal, in anticipation of the coming kingdom.[2] In fact, he announced the dawn of the kingdom already now in his life and ministry.

God, of course, is the One who alone effects the final reversal. The kingdom does not come by human effort. It is always and solely a gift of God. Yet Jesus still taught his disciples to pray, "Thy kingdom come," and coupled it with the command for radical obedience to God's will, including care and concern for the poor and needy. Hence there is no way to avoid the call to serve God rather than mammon, which translates for believers into sacrificial, agape-love for one another and the world. The ultimate confidence in God's justice provides the compelling reason for it all. It is the hope which keeps faith and love alive here and now.

The Promise of the Present

The hope for the poor in the present for Luke lies in the fellowship of a new community, where justice, equality, and compassion are living realities.

Already in the ministry of Jesus we see this new community emerging. The "today" of salvation present with Jesus offers good news to the poor. This good news embraces both the gift of God's unconditional love and acceptance and the fellowship of a new community of disciples. Jesus gathers around him a community consisting in large measure of the poor and needy, the outcasts and sinners. Within this community the reality of the kingdom ethic of agape-love is at work. Here even the poor and powerless are offered a status of dignity and worth and their daily needs met by a fellowship of sharing. Jesus himself promised, we should recall, that those who left all for his sake would receive "manifold" with respect to their earthly needs and human friendships (18:28-30). What Jesus meant was the support of a community of disciples who live in such a way as to share one another's needs. Even within Jesus' inner circle of disciples, we catch a glimpse of a community having "all things in common," as the disciples live from a common fund and are aided by the gifts of wealthier followers.

But it is in the Lukan descriptions of the early church that we find the most compelling portrait of a new kind of community which offers hope for the poor. Shaped by the Spirit of Jesus and mindful of his words and deeds, this community provides a fellowship not only of repentance and forgiveness, but also of unity, love, sharing, and service. Especially noteworthy for our purposes is the manner in which this new community provided for the economic needs of every person. They determined to have no poor among them and to that end they were willing to share all their possessions. The right to private property, though not abolished, was subordinated for the common good. A new spirit of equality and justice was clearly present in which the age-old division of rich and poor was abolished.

Beyond the individual community's concern for the poor in their midst, we also find an ecumenical concern to care for the whole church. When hunger and famine threaten one community, another comes to its aid. Thus a global sense of unity and compassion is emerging.

Moreover, while Luke concentrates on the economic sharing within the community of believers, he does not totally ignore the church's concern for the poor outside its fellowship. He obviously regards the Christian communities as a model for the world. Their manner of life, especially their care for one another, became a powerful attraction to others, who recognized its revolutionary new character. We might recall Tertullian's quote of surprised pagans, "See how they love one another." [3] But Luke also offers his description of the early church's radical care for the poor and needy as an alternate vision of what the human community should be like, a vision strikingly different from the Graeco-Roman culture in which he lived.

What this all adds up to is that the community of believers is to be that place in the world where the good news of God's love to the poor, embodied most fully in Jesus, is transformed into practical reality. Christian communities are intended to be centers of a living faith, where the fruits of justice, equality, and mercy are produced. They are to be places where the world can find a credible witness to a new reality at work in its midst, in which the old values of greed and love of mammon have been transformed into unselfish service of humanity through the power of agape-love. This is truly the hope of the poor in the present. To what degree the community of believers fulfills this hope remains the unanswered question.

The Challenge to Rich Christians

While the basic message of Jesus' ministry in Luke's gospel centers around the theme of good news to the poor, his extensive discussion of wealth and poverty is addressed primarily to the rich.[4] We have interpreted this to mean that Luke is using this material to speak to well-to-do Christians in his own day. What Luke has in mind is nothing less than an urgent call for a new evaluation of possessions and their place in the Christian life and Chirstian community.

The Radical Danger

As we have shown with some thoroughness in the preceding chapters, Luke has two major themes regarding possessions. The first is a warning about their radical danger to Christian discipleship. This theme occurs already in Luke's heightening of the call to total abandonment of one's possessions. While we concluded that Luke was not advocating such a step for his own day, nevertheless, the example of the first disciples who left all for the kingdom's sake served as a striking symbol of authentic Christian discipleship and as a critique upon the life-style of wealthy believers.

However, the dangers and temptations of wealth are most powerfully portrayed in the texts surveyed in Chapter Six, especially the distinctive Lukan woes and parables. The question inevitably arises, can the rich be saved? Luke's challenge offers no easy way out, as he drives to the brink the question of whether or not wealth and discipleship have anything in common. It is plain that service of God and service of mammon, treasures in heaven and treasures on earth are incompatible in the Christian life. More than a few devout believers or groups of believers through the centuries have been so stirred by these texts that they have decided to forego their earthly possessions, as far as possible, for the sake of the kingdom. Yet even without this kind of response, these texts still pose the disturbing question for serious-minded Christians, what am I doing with my possessions and what should I be doing with them? And they pose the same question for the Christian church as well. For Luke, only radical surgery can cut the attachment to possessions that opens the way into the kingdom, and only radical sharing can meet the needs of the poor and allow the rich to be saved. Thus the danger of possessions carries with it a summons for rich believers to take heed, to be on guard and to be open for the necessity of an urgent reordering of priorities in their lives.

Discipleship of Wealth

The Lukan response to possessions is not the call to total abandonment, but what we choose to term the discipleship use of one's wealth. What Luke commends for Christians in his day is a style of life in which possessions are placed radically at the service of those in need. While possessions in themselves are not evil, their true worth is to be measured by their use. The exhortations to make friends with your wealth, to lay up treasures in heaven, to give alms, to do good with your wealth and the like, all have in mind the common goal of sharing with the poor. In particular, Luke offers Zacchaeus as an example for individual believers and Jerusalem as a pattern for the community of believers.

With the example of Zacchaeus we encounter the challenge to a new standard of giving and sharing. The principle of "one-half to the poor" sets forth that standard, not as a new legalism, but as the type of discipleship-response consistent with the call of Jesus. This paradigm offers the possibility for rich Christians to be saved. But it reflects a sharing of one's wealth that is costly and reflective of one's freedom from the bondage of mammon. It means a willingness to put one's goods at the disposal of those in need and a willingness to accept the changes in life-style this may necessitate. Similarly, all the numerous other texts that deal with the right use of one's wealth in Luke's Gospel are to be understood in light of this paradigmatic call to sacrificial sharing on behalf of the poor. Clearly the great gulf between the rich and the poor, between affluence and poverty, between abundance and want is not what the God of the poor intends, nor what the followers of Jesus are to perpetuate for themselves or for society.

With the paradigm of the Jerusalem community we encounter the challenge to a new standard for the Christian community in its disposition of money and goods. We have presented this challenge at some length in our discussion above. Suffice it to say here, that it asks of all Christians and especially the rich, the willingness to share what they possess for the sake of the needy within their own community, even to the extent of voluntarily abandoning their "right" to their own possessions. But the challenge also includes a concern for the whole church throughout the world, by a sharing of the abundance of one part with the needs of another. And as we shall develop further below, it also embraces God's concern for the poor outside the community of faith, whether at our own gates or in other areas of God's world. The challenge of the Jerusalem church is thus that of a new kind of community, where there is neither rich nor poor, where economic needs are met by practical and costly action.

Contemporary Reflections

The relevance of much of what we have learned for contemporary Christian communities may seem obvious. However, at the risk of belaboring the obvious, we would like to make a number of summary observations that we feel can speak with helpful appropriateness to our own situation.

Social Dimension of the Gospel

One of the most controversial issues in the church in recent decades has been a furious struggle between advocates of the so-called social gospel and those who insist that the church's message and task is chiefly spiritual. While a more wholistic understanding of the gospel has gradually been emerging from both sides, the struggle still continues.[5] Perhaps this study can contribute in at least two ways to this debate.

First, it has been a primary aim of our interpretation to demonstrate that the "good news to the poor" in Luke-Acts was not just a spiritualized gospel, but a message of hope and comfort to persons in real situations of suffering and deprivation. These poor included the socially and economically dispossessed and the good news embraced both the assurance of divine forgiveness and the promise of sufficient of life's daily needs.

Second, we have noted how Luke's understanding of salvation is comprehensive. By that we mean that the message of the kingdom involves both repentance and the fruits of repentance; the word of forgiveness and the life of discipleship. The salvation present uniquely in Jesus or the preaching about him carries with it the ethical imperatives of discipleship and obedience. Salvation cannot be limited either to the mere word of God's acceptance in Christ or to the summons of faithful obedience. The two are simply inseparable in Luke's theology. Perhaps we can paraphrase Bonhoeffer's famous statement, "He who believes, obeys; he who obeys, believes" with the Lukan "He who is forgiven much, loves much; he who loves much is forgiven much." [6] While the divine initiative of grace cannot be removed, the call to grace-motivated discipleship is Luke's intent.

What this means for the church's mission today is that no mere "preaching of the gospel," understood as a private transaction between the believer and Christ will do; to preach the gospel in its fulness is to hear also the call to a life of discipleship and such a discipleship means the service of agape-love in all its social, political, and economic dimensions. Luke's writings do not let us get around this in any way; in particular, he calls us to agape-love on behalf of the poor and dispossessed.

Ethics as Discipleship

How can we bridge the gap of nearly 2000 years between our century and the time Luke wrote? Perhaps the answer seems self-evident: simply read, believe, and obey! But any discerning reader knows it is not that simple. Times have greatly changed, and this affects our perspective on matters. Even if we wanted to simply believe and obey, many of our pressing moral issues are not directly dealt with in the New Testament. And when they seem to be, we have been forced to take a second look and sometimes to revise or broaden our perspectives.[7]

How then do we find an authoritative word on moral issues in Scripture? The response is complex, but we want to suggest that the way out is not by a biblical literalism that binds us to words frozen in contexts not ours, nor by a flight from Scripture to sociology or psychology. What is needed is a dialog with Scripture, in which we aim to hear its basic affirmations and intentions and then apply these to our situation and time, in light of our best understandings. Theologically, this approach can be termed an ethic of discipleship, in distinction from an ethic of imitation.[8]

Let us illustrate with a couple of examples: a) Luke's gospel contains texts which call for a surrender of all one's possessions in the service of Jesus. An ethic of imitation would require such surrender literally of all disciples. Luke, however, points to an ethic of discipleship, in which not the letter but the spirit of Jesus' call is set forth so that the question becomes the right use of possessions in the service of Jesus. b) Or take the stories of the Rich Young Ruler and Zacchaeus. The ruler was asked to abandon everything, Zacchaeus was not. An ethic of imitation would be forced to choose one or the other and then find some way to justify its decision. An ethic of discipleship, we suggest, finds both possible as appropriate responses.

We think Luke himself provides the clue to his ethical understanding in 22:35-38. Here he shows how circumstances change the way in which one seeks to follow Jesus. During Jesus' earthly life, no sword or purse; yet afterward, both are necessary. Yet both were faithful responses, so long as one seeks to act in trust and obedience to the Lord.

With regard to the use of possessions, we believe Luke's ethic of discipleship says something like this: "No one rule applies. Every disciple of Jesus is called to unselfish giving and sharing; the needs of the poor cry out for help, the exploitation of the rich for condemnation. Let this be reflected in the way you live and the way you give."

Just as Luke applied the words of Jesus to his own community, so we must do the same. Faithful discipleship is to hear the words and example of Jesus and the early church and then to act in the freedom of the gospel in a way most appropriate to our time and place. Within the community of faith itself is the best place to discover what that appropriate action may be as twentieth century disciples.

As we have seen, for Luke wealth is a gift of God to be used primarily in the service of the poor and needy. On the one hand, this basic attitude represents a powerful attack upon the greed and selfishness of humanity and upon the inequities and injustices perpetuated by that selfishness. On the other hand, it leads to some specific principles whereby the sharing of wealth can be guided.

According to need. We interpret this to mean that where the needs are greatest, there the Christian community should be most active to meet those needs. This requires Christians to educate themselves concerning human needs, both locally and globally. It also requires the development of sound strategies to act responsibly and urgently. While individual giving to persons or causes remains helpful and necessary, the scope and complexity of determining needs and strategy for aid demands that Christians work together corporately and pool their resources for most effective action.[9] The goal is greater equality and justice in the distribution of wealth and possessions, i.e., the closing of the sinful gap between the rich and the poor.

According to ability. We interpret this to mean that the more one possesses economically, the more is required. This exempts no one from giving and sharing out of their means; in fact, the story of the poor widow (21:1-4) and John's word to the multitudes (3:10-11) and even the picture of the early church "sharing all things in common" point to a solidarity with the poor. Yet the primary burden of responsibility for more equal distribution of economic resources rests with the possessors. The principle of proportionate giving according to ability means proportionately more is expected of wealthier Christians. In fact, it raises two fundamental questions:

a) Is this wealth and its normal accompanying style of life consistent with Christian commitment and discipleship? If not, what should be done to scale down the inconsistency or close the gap?

b) What exploitations of others or unjust policies might be involved in the reason why there is such a discrepancy between one's wealth and another's poverty? If these are recognizable, what can and should be done about them?

To whom more is given, more is required. The gift brings with it greater responsibilities. From Luke's point of view, the challenge to wealthy Christians is the challenge of "one-half to the poor," i.e. costly and sacrificial sharing of one's current wealth and resources.

A Christian Egalitarianism? What is the ultimate goal of Christian sharing, according to Luke? Is it the goal of approximate equality of wealth, i.e. some form of Christian egalitarianism? One might try to interpret the Lukan portrait of the early church as a community that "possessed everything in common," in this manner. Many attempts at egalitarian forms of Christian community have originated from this description in the church's history. Yet it was never adopted as a general requirement for authentic community even within the New Testament itself. Even Luke's vision of the early church did not include a required form of egalitarianism, but depicted instead a voluntary community of sharing, in which the needs of the poor were met by the free gifts of the wealthier. Certain economic distinctions remained; some owned property, some didn't; some could give, others lacked; widows were cared for out of the community's common fund. What was distinctive about this community was the willingness of each member to place their possessions at the disposal of the community and their willingness even to forego their private right of ownership for the common good. In this sense one could say that it was "egalitarian in spirit" and shaped its life so as to redistribute its wealth in a way that made certain there was sufficient for all.

Luke addressed himself to the rich Christians in his day. He does not insist that they give up all their possessions, nor does he require an elimination of all economic differences in the community. But Luke does say this to rich Christians: "Your abundance and the poverty of other Christians are not in accordance with God's will or with the spirit of Jesus. You must relinquish your abundance for the sake of the poor and work toward greater economic equality in God's world." Back to the tough question once again, can one remain wealthy and be a faithful Christian? We interpret the Zacchaeus episode as Luke's no/yes response. No, in that the rich cannot go on living as before. A new ordering of priorities is necessitated. The rich cannot be saved with their riches intact. They must get free from the burden and seduction of wealth and spend themselves in the service of others. Only costly sharing of wealth will do as a response to the call of Jesus into a life of discipleship. But yes, the rich can be saved, as they are freed by God's unconditional grace in Christ to trust the Father for life's sufficiencies and as they respond in love to make friends with their wealth through wise and sacrificial giving, remembering always the poor and the powerless.

Sharing Within the Community of Believers

Luke primarily speaks to the Christian community with regard to its use of possessions. Are there some specific guidelines for action that might still be helpful today? We suggest briefly a few.

Within the local communities of faith, two points emerge. One is that each community should covenant together to have no poor among them. Each is responsible to care for the needs of its participants. Luke would find it scandalous if this were not being done. The *how* is up to each to determine; but it involves more than charity. Money, jobs, child care, sense of equal dignity and worth, are all part of it. A second point is that each community should strive for the spirit and practice of equality, so that class distinctions or discriminations based on wealth or social status are removed. The willingness to share all things in common can only lead to the lessening of the unjust inequality that all too often exists between members within the Christian community.

Within the global community of faith we might mention these

concerns. One, help your local community of faith become more aware and responsible to the needs of suffering Christians in other parts of the world. Like individuals, Christian communities all too often become turned in on themselves and preoccupied with their own perceived needs. We need a sense of global need and equity of resources to help us break out of our innate selfishness. At Antioch, it took prophets from the "third world" of Jerusalem to prick the conscience. But they did respond. Two, the same challenge of costly sharing which Luke directs to well-off Christians needs to be directed to well-off Christian communities. "One-half to the poor" would be a good paradigm for local congregational budgets! And why not, when one considers our abundance and the hunger and suffering of others? In a global age, the conviction of one Lord, one faith, one baptism needs to be translated also into practical action on a worldwide scale of sharing according to need and according to ability.

Sharing Outside the Community

The oft-quoted statement of Jesus, "the poor you will always have with you," which by the way is not preserved by Luke, should never be understood as an expression of resigned despair or as a word of indifference toward the poor. As the Father is kind and merciful even to the ungrateful and selfish, so should the sons of the Father act (6:35-36). Christian love extends beyond the bounds of Christian community to embrace all people and above all the poor and suffering. As Jesus' love went out to all, even to the forgotten and despised, so his followers are to love their enemies, do good, lend expecting nothing in return, invite the uninvited. The Good Samaritan is the classic expression of such love without regard to the social, religious or economic status of the one in need. The poor are suffering and thus deserving of our help, for our God is the God of the poor and defender of the lowly.

Luke provides us with sufficient resources to look beyond the immediate community of believers to the poor wherever they may be, next door or on the latest telecast by satellite communications. However, in his own preoccupation with the story of the church's triumphal march from Jerusalem to Rome and for other reasons, he does not give us a vision of the church actively engaged in the struggle for justice and equality on behalf of the world's lowly and forgotten poor. We suggest that this vision and its working out in our time is the distinctive mission Luke bequeaths to our generation. Perhaps the emergence of liberation theologies and theologies of hope, along with a worldwide effort in all branches of Christendom to grapple with questions of justice and poverty and oppression is a sign that the good news to the poor of Luke's Jesus is finding its unique expression today as a word of hope to all the world's poor and oppressed.[10]

A Word to Rich Christians

We have repeatedly used the phrase "rich Christians" throughout our study without attempting to define it. Now we will try. We, of course, realize that the poor of one land may be the rich of another. No income levels or other statistical data can really define rich or poor. But by rich Christians we have in mind those Christians who have sufficient and more of the basic needs of life, such as food, clothing, and shelter. It is the *more* that makes one rich and most of us living in the western lands have a disproportionate amount of the *more*. Although some have much more than others, we all share to a greater or lesser degree in a surplus of abundance. For example, we in the U.S.A. represent only a small fraction of the world's population but we use a massive amount of the world's resources. And this surplus of abundance has resulted in the creation of affluent and wasteful economies and life-styles, which all too often thrive on the past and present exploitation of the earth's population and resources.

Consequently, a community that confesses Jesus as Lord and that seeks to shape its life after his in the power of his Spirit is to do all it can to share its abundance more equitably with the world. In fact, it must begin with the basics of simply providing enough for the survival of everyone, no simple matter when we realize that two-thirds of the world's population goes to bed hungry and suffers serious malnutrition. Perhaps as individuals our efforts might seem almost comically futile to change the world's condition of want and suffering. Yet it begins with us and through us to others. In the church, individuals, congregations, clusters of congregations, denominations, national and international agencies can and do provide some hope. Other ways are available outside the church as individual Christians in decision-making roles help influence policies within businesses, corporations, governments and the like. But as-

suming that it begins with us, or at least that we as Christians have
a vital role to play if we are at all consistent with the faith we
profess, what can we do? We will make four simple suggestions:

Adopt the Zacchaeus principle for sharing wealth. Zacchaeus'
sharing of one-half to the poor means that he gave as much to the
poor as he kept for himself. Some Christians today could do better
than Zacchaeus, most of us will have to struggle valiantly just to
begin approaching Zacchaeus' example. The response to the gospel,
however, requires that we keep this kind of costly paradigm of
discipleship before our eyes. To continue to live like the rich fool,
seeking to accumulate more than enough for our own security and
pleasures or to live like the rich man in daily indifference to poor
Lazarus cannot be reconciled with faithful Christian discipleship.
We need to hear this urgently, not to create guilt, but to move us to
compassionate action in the sharing of our abundance with those
in need.

Simplify the way we live. If our present affluence cannot be justified because of the existence of the poor and needy at home and
throughout the world, then it is time to begin new life-styles. We
learned that the first communities of believers in Acts became models of caring for the society around them. Why should that not be
true as well for Christian communities today? This might be done
not only by the way we care for the poor within and without our
own fellowship but also by the way we deliberately seek to live a
kind of counter-culture life-style in contrast to the consumer oriented life-styles all around us. Such a counter-culture life-style might
mean letting go of many of our dreams of the good life or ridding
ourselves of the extras in luxuries and conveniences that we can do
without. It might mean developing consciously a better sense of
proportion about our way of living from the items we purchase to
our habits of eating out. It might mean deciding to make even
more costly changes in our life, smaller homes, cheaper and less
transportation, change of careers, or whatever steps seem appropriate in order to shift from a consumer way of life to a helping way.
Our own families could become the experimental ground where
new life-styles are modeled, and all in the name of our Christian
concern for the whole human family.

But we also need a community of support to sustain our efforts.
This community ought to be found within our various faith com-

munities. A fellowship of like-minded families could help overcome the sense of alienation and isolation and even feeling sorry for oneself that is inevitably a part of the struggle. And it could help individual families and persons make the kind of right decisions necessary and give them the incentive and support to carry through. Perhaps then we could again begin to approximate the kind of community Jesus envisioned, where the mutual support of believers provided for each others needs (18:28-30), or the kind of community in Acts, where the sense of unity was so strong that "no one said that any of the things which he possessed was his own" (4:32).

Become advocates of the poor. It must be admitted that all too often the church simply reflects the attitude of the culture around it. But surely it is called to be something other than a mirror of culture. The call is to reflect its Lord and the community of love and justice and compassion he envisioned. We have learned from Luke that Jesus preached and embodied the good news to the poor. We can do no less! In fact, as we have seen, the hope of the poor in the present is the community of faith in the world. If this community fails, where is there hope for the poor, until the coming reversal?

Yet if this is so, why is it that we so often find more compassion and concern for the oppressed and exploited among unbelievers than believers? Or why is it that a Karl Marx and his disciples have become the champions of the world's poor and not Jesus Christ and his disciples? Or why do atheistic systems like Marxism prosper among the oppressed far more than Christianity? Is it because the poor have known only a church captive to its culture, or even worse, one lending its justification to a system that perpetuates gross injustices and inequalities? Where is the prophetic voice of Jesus in the church that says with courage and integrity, "Blessed are you poor" and "Woe to you rich." Are we all too silent because we have lost so much of our integrity, or because we do not want to prophesy against ourselves? On his visit to South America in the summer of 1980, Pope John Paul made a special plea on behalf of the masses of poor and exploited who make up such a disproportionate number of its inhabitants. Especially poignant was his open-air address to crowds in the slums of Rio de Janeiro, with a background of skyscrapers and luxury hotels!

Our task is clear. We are called to stand on God's side, with Jesus, as advocates of the poor and oppressed. To be such an advocate is to be faithful to the Gospel Luke proclaimed.

Oppose systems that perpetuate social injustices and inequalities. One of the most difficult and necessary tasks for the church today is to move from a private to a public ethic. Too much Christian preaching and teaching has centered on the private and personal relations between God and the individual, and not enough on the social dimensions of the Gospel. We are slowly realizing however, that evil is entrenched not just in persons, but in systems, in "principalities and powers," in social structures that benefit the powerful and prevent changes that would aid the powerless. Inequality is not just a matter of private greed but of corporate systems.

Even our own abundance, we have come to see, has been gained in large measure through a systematic exploitation of the earth's populace and resources. Thus a necessary part of Christian discipleship is to oppose the entrenched and exploitive powers that be and to work toward more just and humane social systems.

Christians will not always agree on what specific steps should be taken, but if the goals are held in common, there is much that can be done. It needs to be remembered that no economic system is ordained of God, whether capitalism or socialism or even a Christianized communism. Nor is the status quo sacred. Change is inevitable; the only question is, in what direction? Christians are freed to pursue God's vision of a just and humane world within every society and economic system. The goal is not the perfection of social structures, a utopian goal that finally leads to despair and disillusionment; rather, it is a realistic striving for a closer approximation of the goal, keeping in mind the vision of God's coming world where perfect justice and full human fulfillment will be attained and where God's ultimate purpose for his creation, through Christ, will be completed. As of now, we share in the pilgrimage along the way.

Notes

PART I

Introduction

1. We will refer to the author as Luke without prejudice as to his actual identity. Consult the commentaries for critical discussion. The same author wrote both the gospel and Acts, cf. Luke 1:1-4, Acts 1:1-2.

2. Two pioneering works employing careful sociological methd to N.T. texts are: John Gager, *Kingdom and Community: The Social World of Early Christianity* (Englewood Cliffs, N.J.: Prentice-Hall, 1975); and Gerd Theissen, *Sociology of Early Palestinian Christianity*, trans. by John Bowden (Philadelphia: Fortress, 1977). For a critique of Gager, see Patrick Henry, *New Directions in New Testament Study* (Philadelphia: Westminster, 1978), 180-202. Two books by Howard Clark Kee, *Jesus in History: An Approach to the Study of the Gospels* (New York: Harcourt, Brace and World, 1970); *Christian Origins in Sociological Perspective* (Philadelphia: Westminster Press, 1980) are especially sensitive to sociological dimensions of the text and reflect more closely the approach of this study.

3. This quotation is my own translation from a very helpful book recently published by two German authors, Luise Schottroff and Wolfgang Stegemann, *Jesus von Nazareth: Hoffnung der Armen* (Stuttgart: Verlag W. Kohlhammer, 1978), 14. This study seeks especially to illumine the social context of Jesus' ministry, and then interpret Luke's attitude toward the poor and rich.

4. On Lukan ethics as a whole, recent commentators have sought to identify the fundamental ethical viewpoint of Luke, apart from its specific application. E.g. H. Conzelmann, *The Theology of St. Luke*, trans. by G. Buswell (New York: Harper, 1961), 231-4, finds an ethic of martyrdom developing in which Luke stresses affliction and endurance and the good confession. Victor Furnish, *Love Command in the New Testament* (Nashville: Abingdon, 1972), 84-90 suggests "doing good" as Luke's key ethical form, along with a sharing of possessions. Jack Sanders, *Ethics in the New Testament* (Philadelphia: Fortress, 1975) 34-39 also finds "endurance" and "doing good" to be key concepts in light of the delay of the Parousia. But he expresses disappointment that Luke offers overall so little ethical direction, a comment we find very strange, esp. in Luke's gospel!

5. We list the works known to us: Hans Joachim Degenhardt, *Lukas, Evangelist der Armen* (Stuttgart: Katholisches Bibelwerk, 1965), whose author, now

a Roman Catholic bishop in West Germany, made a thorough study of Luke's attitude toward possessions, but ended unsatisfactorily by concluding that Luke advocates a two-level ethic of possessions, one for church leaders and another for all others. Three authors have concentrated on Luke's use of Isa. 61:1-2 and the Jubilee year theme, with frequent helpful insights; Larrimore Crockett, *The Old Testament in the Gospel of Luke: Use of Is. 61:1-2* (Ann Arbor: Univ. Microfilm, 1966); Robert B. Sloan, *The Favorable Year of the Lord. A Study of Jubilary Theology in the Gospel of Luke* (Austin, TX: Schola Press, 1977); Donald Blosser, *Jesus and the Jubilee: Luke 4:16-30* (Ann Arbor: Univ. Microfilms, 1979. Another author focused on possessions, but offered an interpretation of their symbolic meaning for Luke which, in my judgment, blunts the social reality and sharpness of the Lukan point of view; Luke Johnson, *The Literary Function of Possessions in Luke-Acts* (SBL Dissertation Series 39, Scholars Press, 1977). Yet two other dissertations surveyed the material on riches and poverty, somewhat to the exclusion of the theme of "good news to the poor;" Timothy Hoyt, *The Poor in Luke-Acts* (Ann Arbor: Univ. Microfilms, 1975), and David Seccombe, *Riches and the Rich in Luke-Acts* (Ann Arbor: Univ. Microfilms, 1978). We found three articles stimulating, though of necessity too abbreviated; Roland Koch, "Die Wertung des Besitzes im Lukasevangelium," *Biblica* 38 (1957), 151-69; Walter Schmithals, "Lukas-Evangelist der Armen," *Theologica Viatorum XII* (1973-74), 153-67; Robert Karris, "Poor and Rich: The Lukan Sitz im Leben," in *Perspectives on Luke-Acts*, ed. by Charles Talbert (Special Studies Series No. 5, Danville, Va.; 1978). A recent popularization of a dissertation offers a helpful overview of the social position of Jesus according to Luke, but it is stronger on the political than economic theme, at times unduly softening Jesus' attitude in Luke; Richard Cassidy, *Jesus, Politics and Society. A Study of Luke's Gospel* (Maryknoll, N.Y.: Orbis, 1978). Most challenging in our estimation is the work by the two German scholars already cited, Luise Schottroff and Wolfgang Stegemann, *Jesus von Nazareth: Hoffnung der Armen*. They, along with other colleagues, are deeply involved in the quest for a more wholistic exegesis in the service of faithful Christian discipleship, and they interpret Luke's gospel as addressed to the rich Christians in Luke's community. Other current books found especially useful were Martin Hengel, *Property and Riches in the Early Church*, trans. by J. Bowden (Philadelphia: Fortress, 1974); Richard Rohrbaugh, *The Biblical Interpreter: An Agrarian Bible in the Industrial Age* (Philadelphia: Fortress, 1978); John Yoder, *The Politics of Jesus* (Grand Rapids: Eerdmans, 1972); Ronald Sider, *Rich Christians in An Age of Hunger: A Biblical Study* (Downer's Grove, IL: Intervarsity, 1977).

Chapter One

1. For another survey see Ronald Sider, *Rich Christians in an Age of Hunger: A Biblical Study*, 60-95. On the prophets consult Hans Walter Wolff, *The Old Testament: A Guide to Its Writings* (Philadelphia: Fortress, 1973), 81-100; James Limburg, *The Prophets and the Powerless* (Atlanta: John Knox, 1977).

2. *Luther's Small Catechism*, explanation to the 9th commandment (modern translation).

3. The enslavement was likely due to economic debts. See further Chapter Three.

4. On King Josiah's reforms, read 2 Kings 22-23.

5. On its implementation see the discussion in Roland de Vaux, *Ancient Israel*, I, (New York: McGraw Hill, 1965), 174-175.

6. Jeremias, *Jerusalem in the Time of Jesus*, 314, #55, and R. de Vaux, *Ancient Israel*, 177, reflect the scholarly consensus it was never observed. See John Yoder's somewhat contrary judgment in *The Politics of Jesus*, 64ff.

7. See OT context in Chapter Three. Martin Hengel, *Property*, 9, calls it a "symbol of the eschatological liberation of Israel."

8. According to most modern scholars, ch. 40-66 of Isaiah belong to a later period of Israel's history. Ch. 40-55, known as Second Isaiah (Deutero-Isaiah), belong to the Exilic period (529-510 B.C.) and anticipate the joyful return to the homeland. Ch. 55-66 may even belong to the post-exilic period after the return.

9. On the Psalter consult Leopold Sabourin, *The Psalms* (New York: Alba, 1969); or Albert Gelin, *The Poor of Yahweh* (Collegeville: Liturgical Press, 1964).

10. See Sabourin, *The Psalms*, 86.

11. Sabourin, *The Psalms*, 12; Martin Dibelius, *James*, 39.

12. Dibelius, *James*, 12; especially W. Sattler, "Die Anawim im Zeitalter Jesu Christi," *Festgabe für Adolph Jühlicher* (Tübingen: Mohr, 1927), 1-15.

13. We also include the Jewish literature of the first century A.D. An excellent survey of both the history and literature of this period is found in D. S. Russell, *Between the Testaments* (Philadelphia: Fortress, 1960).

14. The Apocrypha are a body of writings composed in the intertestamental period, which were excluded from the Hebrew sacred canon but included with the Septuagint (LXX), the Greek translation of the Old Testament dated around 250 B.C. These writings are accepted as authoritative by the Roman Catholic Church, though regarded of lesser value by Protestants. The Pseudepigrapha are additional religious writings of this same general period, of a mixed bag theologically and literarily, and not accepted as canonical. See R. H. Charles, *The Apocrypha and Pseudepigrapha of the Old Testament in English*, 2 vols. (Oxford: Clarendon, 1913).

15. On the end of poverty, *Sibylline Oracles* 3, 378; *Testament of Solomon* 10:12; *Testament of Judah* 25:4. The latter passage is very similar to Luke 6:20-21, though some scholars attribute this to Christian interpolation.

16. *Ethiopian Enoch*. A composite work, its dating is difficult. But the section on the fate of the rich probably comes from the first century A.D.

17. Hengel, *Property*, 18-19, rightly calls this a "crude desire for revenge" and notes that the idea of the righteous gloating over the torments of the rich in hell begins here and extends through Dante's *Divine Inferno*. On the other hand, Luise Schottroff and Wolfgang Stegemann, *Jesus von Nazareth*, 45, argue weakly that only political revenge is envisioned in *Ethiopian Enoch* 94-104.

18. On the Dead Sea Scrolls and Qumran in general, see Geza Vermes, *The Dead Sea Scrolls; Qumran in Perspective* (Cleveland: Collins, World, 1978).

19. See "Sharing According to Need" in Chapter Seven.

20. Josephus, *War*, II.8.4. Philo, *Hypothetica*, 11:1. Another Essene writing, the *Damascus Document*, also speaks of both private and communal property.

21. Leander Keck, "The Poor Among the Saints in Jewish Christianity and Qumran," *Zeitschrift für die neutestamentliche Wissenschaft* 55 (1965), 66-78, shows convincingly that at best the term "poor" is only a marginal self-designation.

22. See Jeremias, *Jerusalem*, 112-116, 233-245. For rabbinic literature and New Testament parallels most valuable is Strack-Billerbeck, *Kommentar zum Neuen Testament aus Talmud und Midrasch*, 6 vols. (Munich: Beck'sche, 1923-61), though it must be used with caution.

23. *Am haaretz* is Hebrew for "people of the land." They were essentially the peasant, landed population. See Jeremias, *Jerusalem*, 259, 266-267.

24. E. P. Sanders, *Paul and Palestinian Judaism* (Philadelphia: Fortress, 1977), 152-157 stresses this against Jeremias. But he recognizes conflict between the rabbis and *am haaretz*.

Chapter Two

1. The contemporary Jewish festival of Hanukkah commemorates this event. For details on the Maccabean era consult Russell, *Between the Testaments*, 13-35.

2. Josephus, *War* IV, 3.9, 10.

3. Josephus, *Antiquities*, XVIII, 2.3.

4. Josephus, *War* II, 17.6.

5. Josephus, *Antiquities*, XI, 4.8. See Jeremias, *Jerusalem*, 102-103.

6, Jeremias, *Jerusalem*, 116.

7. Ibid., *Jerusalem*, 114.

8. Dan. 4:24, Tob. 12:8-9; in rabbinic literature cf. Strack-Billerbeck IV, 536-558.

9. On limits, cf. Jeremias, *Jerusalem*, 127.

10. Ibid., 116. Also Schottroff and Stegemann, *Jesus von Nazareth*, 24.

11. E.g. Hengel, *Property*, 26-27.

12. Luke 2:22-24. Cf. Lev. 12:8.

13. In Justin, *Dialog* 88:8, written at the beginning of the second century, Jesus is a maker of ploughs and yokes. In Mark, the Greek *tektōn* is most often interpreted as carpenter or builder. Jesus made frequent use of metaphors related to building (So Jeremias, *Jerusalem*, 112, #16).

14. See Oscar Cullmann, *Jesus and the Revolutionaries*, 6-9.

15. There is much dispute over the meaning of Iscariot. See Bertil Gärtner, *Iscariot*, trans. by V. Gruhn (Philadelphia: Fortress, 1976).

16. Although looking sympathetically at Jesus, the work of Milan Machovec, *A Marxist Looks at Jesus* (Philadelphia: Fortress, 1976), finally fails to grasp the basic religious motivation and vision of Jesus' kingdom proclamation. John Gager, *Kingdom and Community*, 130-32, 140, concludes that beyond a series of favorable external circumstances, one "single, overriding *internal* factor, the radical sense of Christian community—open to all, insistent on absolute and exclusive loyalty, and concerned for every aspect of the believer's life," led to Christianity's ultimate triumph in the ancient world. However, Gerd Theissen, *Sociology*, 109-110, concludes that the basic factor in Christianity's behalf was its vision of love and reconciliation in society, with the command to love one's enemies at the core. Both of these conclusions reached via application of sociological theories to the New Testament and early Christian documents are important and probably valid, but they finally fail in our estimation to illumine the driving force and motivation of the community and its vision, i.e., the religious experience at the center. Moreover, the conclusions become too general and sweeping to be of much specific benefit.

17. See especially Gunther Bornkamm, *Jesus of Nazareth*, trans. by Irene and

Fraser McLuskey with J. M. Robinson (New York: Harper & Row, 1960), 57-62.

18. Josephus, *War* II, 13.5, VI, 5.2.

19. The high priests in Jesus' day secured their position by bribery. Jeremias, *Jerusalem*, 157-159. This interpretation of the cleansing does not view it as a call to revolution, as a few have speculated, but as a passionate, symbolic, prophetic protest in God's name against the exploiters of justice and the poor.

20. So Norman Perrin, *Rediscovering the Teachings of Jesus* (New York: Harper and Row, 1967), 102-108. While the historicity of the Mark 2:13-17 story as it now appears may be questionable, we agree with Schottroff and Stegemann, *Jesus von Nazareth*, 16, that it still provides reliable evidence that the Jesus movement attracted tax collectors and that this caused offense to its critics.

21. Jeremias, "Zöllner und Sünder," *ZNW* 30 (1931), 293-300.

22. Schottroff and Stegemann, *Jesus von Nazareth*, 25.

23. See Chapter One on Psalter.

24. Dibelius, *James*, 41.

25. See especially Raymond Brown, *The Birth of the Messiah* (Garden City, N.Y.: Doubleday, 1977), 350-355, who develops this historical background for the infancy narratives of Luke.

26. The reader should recall that the Gospel traditions existed orally for 20-30 years before assuming their present written form. In this oral period they were shaped by the preaching of the church and its missionary-evangelists. At some points we can trace a reading back of the post-Easter faith into the pre-Easter traditions, and everywhere the church's faith has made its mark on the tradition in one way or another. This does not necessarily deny the essential reliability of the tradition as a whole, but it does mean that we must seek as far as possible to distinguish between the oldest forms of the tradition and later forms. Much of our discussion in this section is influenced by Schottroff and Stegemann's discussion in *Jesus von Nazareth*, 29-43. They identify two themes in particular as belonging to the oldest tradition: a) the reversal of social status in the coming kingdom, and b) Jesus' friendship with tax collectors and sinners.

27. We are not using the "woes" as evidence of the oldest traditions, since there is serious doubt about their historical authenticity, due especially to the literary parallelism with the beatitudes and their presence only in Luke. Also, compare our discussion on Beatitudes in Chapter Five.

28. Dibelius, *James*, 42.

29. Schottroff and Stegemann, *Jesus von Nazareth*, 32, sketch these earliest hopes in this way. "Poor Jews of Palestine found themselves together as followers of Jesus. They saw their miserable condition as a scandal in the sight of God. But they believed God would shortly put an end to this disorder, and they brought this happy message to other poor. The presence of this promise did begin to change things. Even miracles occurred, which they interpreted as signs of the end-time. Thus eschatological promise revived hope for the poor!" (Author's translation.)

30. Cf. Mark 14:25; Luke 13:29; 14:15; 15:23; Matt. 8:11f.; 22:1-10; 25:10.

31. See Joseph Bonsirven, *Palestinian Judaism in the Time of Jesus Christ*, trans. by W. Wolf (New York: Holt, Rinehart and Winston, 1974), 242-244, 205-213, esp. 211-212. Schottroff and Stegemann, *Jesus von Nazareth*, 32, like-

wise call attention to the concrete hopes of the poor for the future, as well as the "creative power of utopian thought."

32. See Brown, *Birth*, 346-350, for a summary of various viewpoints.

33. Ibid., pp. 352-353.

34. We will not enter the argument over the hymn's original ascription, whether to Mary or Elizabeth. See Brown's careful discussion, *Birth*, 334-336.

35. Similarly Schottroff and Stegemann, *Jesus von Nazareth*, 36-38. They suggest the original word order is found in Matt. 20:16, in which no limits are placed on those whose status will be reversed. "First" and "last" thus designate social positions. Cf. Mark 6:21, where the first are "the leading men of Galilee."

Chapter Three

1. One recent scholar compares it to the U.S. Presidential Inaugural Address; Robert Karris, *Invitation to Luke* (Garden City, N.Y.: Doubleday, 1966), 69. Much earlier, J. M. Creed, *The Gospel According to St. Luke* (London: Macmillan, 1930), 65-66, stated that Luke 4:16-30 constitutes "a charter and program for everything that follows." Cf. Conzelmann, *Theology*, 114, 122, 139.

2. Larry Crockett, *The Old Testament in the Gospel of Luke*, 277, rightly asks, "Are the poor, captive, blind and oppressed only 'vague metaphors,' or do they have specific meaning?"

3. Conzelmann, *Theology*, 103, would limit the "today" only to the time of Jesus. Since the time of salvation inaugurated by Jesus continues for Luke in the time of the church, we agree with those interpreters who include both periods in Luke's concept of "today." Cf. Acts 10:38, where the earthly ministry of Jesus, interpreted on the basis of Luke 4:16-21, is understood as a saving ministry that continues in the church's preaching. On Luke's use of "today" cf. 2:11; 13:32; 19:59; 23:43; Acts 13:33.

4. See discussion of *Origin* in the section on "Woe to You That Are Rich" on Chapter Five.

5. E.g. Jeremias, *New Testament Theology*, 113.

6. Why does Luke omit this line? Some suggest he did so because of the proverb "physician, heal thyself," which parallels "to heal the broken in heart." Could it be that Luke wanted to avoid the spiritualized interpretation of "broken in heart"?

7. So James Sanders, "From Isaiah 61 to Luke 4," in *Christianity, Judaism and Other Graeco-Roman Cults*, Festschrift for Morton Smith, ed. Jacob Neusner (New York: Columbia Univ. Press, 1975), 89f., who discusses the rabbinic technique of enrichment.

8. See Robert Sloan, *The Favorable Year of the Lord*, 32-36, 166-173, who critiques some of the recent discussions.

9. See the discussion of the Later Prophets in Chapter One.

10. A few disagree. Some proponents of a Jubilee year interpretation of Isaiah 61 go so far as to read the verses as a literal announcement of the Jubilee's arrival: E.g. the freed captives are those imprisoned due to debts, the blind whose sight is restored are those led out of dark dungeons to sunlight, etc. As we will argue, the Jubilee imagery lies in the background of the prophetic proclamation of freedom from exile, not in the foreground as a legalistic prescription now taking effect.

11. Especially John Yoder, *The Politics of Jesus*, who has popularized the

thesis of the French scholar, André Trocmé, *Jesus and the Non-Violent Revolution*, trans. by M. Shank and M. Miller (Scottsdale, Pa.: Herald Press, 1967). Others since Yoder have been more cautious, even though supporting Jubilee motifs in this text and Jesus preaching as a whole.

12. Yoder, *The Politics of Jesus*, 74.

13. Other texts in Luke's Gospel often used to support the Jubilee theme, in addition to the ones we will discuss in this chapter, are Luke 11:4, "as we forgive our debtors" and Luke 16:1-9, the parable of the Unjust Steward. We doubt either of these are intended to reflect Jubilee motifs.

14. We find Jesus' striking freedom with regard to the Mosaic prescriptions to be one of the best-attested Gospel traditions, as well as a chief cause of offense in his ministry. Jesus also exhibits an acceptance of persons into his fellowship on the basis of an unconditional welcome, even apart from their repentance or conversion (cf. Mark 2:17). In our view, Yoder adopts a forced exegesis of selected texts under the Jubilee spotlight.

15. Sanders, "From Isaiah 61 to Luke 4," 88ff., and especially Sloan, *The Favorable Year of the Lord*, 10-18.

16. 11Q Melchizedek (11QMelch) is a commentary (pesher) on Isa. 61:1-3, which, according to Sanders ("From Isaiah 61 to Luke 4," 91), "eschatologizes the Jubilee year proclamation of Lev. 25 and Dt. 15."

17. The reasons for the Baptist's doubts are not given. If historical, as most agree, it likely centered on the nature of Jesus' activity and preaching vs. John's; i.e., while John proclaimed the imminent day of wrath, Jesus brought to the fore the imminence of salvation.

18. See the section "Outcasts and Sinners" later in this chapter.

19. While the probable origin of this text is in the Q tradition, it developed in quite separate ways, as the Matthean and Lukan versions attest.

20. Only in v. 23, where the invitation is repeated, might there be an allusion to Gentile converts. In v. 21 the outcasts are clearly in mind.

21. 1QS 2:4ff.; 1QSa 2:5-7; CD 13:4-7 are Essene texts forbidding the blemished from the community.

22. See Sloan, *The Favorable Year of the Lord*, 123-139.

23. Several scholars have even suggested a historical connection between the occasion of the sermon at Nazareth and the utterance of the beatitudes and woes. In fact, A. Finkel, "Jesus' Sermon at Nazareth" in *Abraham unser Vater*, Festschrift Otto Michel, ed. O. Betz (Leiden: Brill, 1963), 106-115, speculates the beatitudes and woes constitute the core of the sermon!

24. C. H. Dodd, *More New Testament Studies* (Manchester: Manchester Univ. Press, 1968), 4. Likewise, Jeremias, *New Testament Theology*, 112, underscores the literal meaning of the poor in Luke, in contrast to Matthew.

25. So Hengel, *Property*, 17.

26. See M. de Jonge and A. S. van der Woude, "11Q Melchizedek and the New Testament," *New Testament Studies* 12 (1966), 309.

27. Schottroff and Stegemann, *Jesus von Nazareth*, 93.

28. So A. Finkel, *The Pharisees and the Teacher of Nazareth* (Leiden: Brill, 1964), 155-58.

29. Especially Brown, *The Birth of the Messiah*, 350-355.

30. On the shame of barrenness for Jewish women, cf. Gen. 16:4; 30:1; Deut. 28:18; 1 Sam. 1:6; 2 Sam. 6:23.

31. Note Luke's interest in widows: widow at Nain, 7:11-17; widow who persists for help, 18:1-8; widow's mite, 21:1-4; widows in Acts 6:1; 9:39.

32. See R. Brown, K. Donfried, J. Fitzmyer, J. Reumann, eds., *Mary in the New Testament* (Philadelphia: Fortress, 1978), pp. 18-20, 105-177.

33. The problem of its original ascription, whether to Mary or Elizabeth, is not important to us. We think the arguments for Mary are of equal weight with those against. See Brown, *Birth,* 334-336.

34. Again, we have no need for our purposes to discuss the historical problem of the census. See Brown, *Birth,* 547-555.

35. Cf. Jeremias, *Jerusalem,* 306.

36. While historically it is probable that one should distinguish between the "poor" as a distinct group and the "outcasts and sinners" as another, for Luke they are inseparable as special objects of Jesus' ministry. The latter are related to the poor, and subsumed under the term by Luke because they lived on the marginal edge of society, socially, economically, and religiously.

37. See section entitled "Jesus' Appeal to the Poor."

38. So Heinz Schürmann, *Das Lukasevangelium* Herders Theologischer Kommentar zum NT, III (Freiburg: Herder, 1969), 85.

39. Esp. Jeremias, *The Parables of Jesus,* 6th ed., trans. by S. Hooke (New York: Scribner's, 1963), 128-132.

40. Robert Karris, "Poor and Rich," 117. He has, however, modified this position in a subsequent article.

41. Patrick D. Miller, "Luke 4:16-21," *Interpretation* XXIX (1975), 420.

PART II

1. Might it also be possible that Theophilus, to whom Luke dedicates both volumes, was a wealthy Gentile Christian? If so, it would shed additional light on Luke's purpose in preserving these traditions.

2. Why does Luke omit this scene? It may be due to the fact that he included another anointing scene earlier in his gospel (7:36-50). Yet it may also be the result of wanting to avoid any possible misinterpretation of Jesus' concern for the poor, as some commentators suggest.

3. We list here the texts on wealth and poverty which Luke includes:

Markan:	Mk. 4:19/Lk. 8.14; Mk. 7:22/Lk. 11:39; Mk. 10:17-31/Lk. 18:18-30; Mk. 12:40/Lk. 20:47; Mk. 12:41-44/Lk. 21:1-4; Mk. 21:12-13/Lk. 19:45-46.
Q:	Mt. 5:3-12/Lk. 6:12-23; Mt. 6:19-21, 24/Lk. 12:21, 31, 33-34; Mt. 6:25-33/Lk. 12:22-31; Mt. 7:2/Lk. 6:37-38; Mt. 22:1-10/Lk. 14:16-24; Mt. 23:23-24/Lk. 11:42.
Lukan (L):	1:52-53; 3:10-14; 6:23-26; 7:10-43; 10:25-37; 11:41; 12:13-21, 33; 14:12-14, 33; 16:1-13, 19-31; 19:1-10; 21:34.

Chapter Four

1. Walter Grundmann, *Das Evangelium nach Lukas,* Theologischer Handkommentar zum Neuen Testament, III (Berlin: Evangelische Verlaganstalt, 1971), 130, notes that Levi's great feast stands in tension with his previous abandonment of everything. Walter Schmithals, "Lukas-Evangelist der Armen," *Theologia Viatorum* XII (1973-1974), 155, uses this "inconsistency" to argue that by "leaving all" Luke does not mean "get rid of all," but "use your posses-

sions for others who have nothing." Schmithals even speaks of Levi's "love-feast." I doubt any tension exists in Luke's mind, since he could clearly antici-pate Levi's leaving all after the meal (cf. John's imprisonment, then Jesus' baptism in 3:18-22). However, there may be merit in the suggestion that Luke is prefiguring a love-feast of the poor and needy, with Jesus as guest (cf. Luke 14:12-14).

2. Note only Luke adds ". . . but sinners *to repentance*," which is consistent with his overall emphasis on repentance.

3. So Schottroff and Stegemann, *Jesus von Nazareth*, 99.

4. See our discussion in Chapter Five of The Needle's Eye.

5. The rewards in Mark 10:30 are "a hundredfold now in this time, houses and brothers, and sisters and mothers and children and lands, *with persecutions,* and in the age to come eternal life." Cf. Matt. 19:29.

6. Schottroff and Stegemann, *Jesus von Nazareth*, 108.

7. In Matthew it forms part of the Sermon on the Mount (Matt. 6:25-34, 19-21). Its original context is undoubtedly lost.

8. Schmithals, "Lukas-Evangelist der Armen," 154, perceptively suggests that Luke omits the word "see *first*" found in Matt. 6:33, to avoid the impli-cation that possessions are the second most important need in life.

9. In Acts 20:28 Luke has Paul designate the church as "the flock" of God. Otherwise this term is not found in the New Testament.

10. Cf. Luke 16:14, where the Pharisees are called "lovers of money."

11. While Jesus probably headquartered at Capernaum during his ministry in Galilee, he owned no home there. We do hear of the home of Peter's mother-in-law (Mark 1:29-31), however, on the site of which, according to tradition, a Byzantine church was built. Is this where Jesus stayed?

12. On rabbis and their trades, see Jeremias, *Jerusalem*, 112-116. On Paul's trade, see Ronald Hock, *The Social Context of Paul's Ministry* (Philadelphia: Fortress, 1980), esp. 20-25.

13. Behind this command is the concern not to give any suspicion of teach-ing or healing for profit. In the first centuries many itinerant teachers did try to gain a personal profit from their activity.

14. Luke names three women who must have been known in the early com-munity (Mary Magdalene, Joanna, wife of Herod's steward, and Susanna), plus others unknown by name. Note the royal household of Herod was pene-trated by Jesus' teaching. The women obviously had considerable means and the freedom to use them as they wished.

15. Not only are women part of the original nucleus of the church, they also receive the Holy Spirit along with the disciples and so fulfill the prophecy of Joel of an outpouring on "menservants and maidservants" (Acts 2:18). A parallel is found at the beginning of the gospel in Luke 2, with Simeon and Anna.

16. The origin of this tradition is much disputed. Is it a doublet of the first missionary journey, now with the Gentiles in mind (the 70 = nations of the world)? Was it created by Luke or earlier?

17. Raymond Brown, "The Beatitudes According to Luke," *New Testament Essays* (Garden City, N.Y.: Image Books, 1968), 338, writes: "In the spiritual outlook of St. Luke's Gospel, the only proper use of wealth is to get rid of it, to give it to the poor." Jack Sanders, *Ethics in the New Testament*, 37, says that Luke's main interest in money per se is to argue that it should be forsaken

in view of the coming kingdom. Similarly Heinz Schürmann, *Das Lukasevangelium*, 324.

18. The argument of Hans Joachim Degenhardt, *Lukas, Evangelist der Armen*, esp. 215-216.

19. Similarly Schmithals, "Lukas-Evangelist der Armen," 158, who argues that there was no room or need for any special denial by the church leaders, since Luke says *everyone* shared what they had in common.

20. Schmithals, "Lukas-Evangelist der Armen," 160-167.

21. Schottroff and Stegemann, *Jesus von Nazareth*, esp. 108-113.

22. Ibid., 103.

23. See Schuyler Brown, *Apostasy and Perseverance in the Theology of Luke* (Rome: Pontifical Biblical Institute, 1969), 98-107, who argues for a clear distinction between the age of Jesus and the age of the church. He suggests the *abandonment* of possessions belongs only to the former time, as we have argued, while in the age of the church there is the *willingness* to share everything. The danger of making too great a separation is illustrated by G. Theissen, *Sociology of Early Palestinian Christianity*, 65, who argues that Luke 22:35-38 rescinds all the radical sayings on possessions in the Gospel. We concur with R. Karris' rejection of this conclusion ("Poor and Rich," 115).

Chapter Five

1. See "Blessed are you poor" in Chapter Three.

2. See the discussion in I. Howard Marshall, *The Gospel of Luke* (The New International Greek Testament Commentary, Grand Rapids, Mich.: Eerdmans, 1978), 245-247.

3. So R. Brown, 'The Beatitudes according to St. Luke," 338; E. Percy, *Die Botschaft Jesu* (Lund: C. W. K. Gleerup, 1953), 93ff.; Jacques Dupont, *Les Beatitudes*. III. *Les Evangelistes* (Paris: J. Gabalda, 1973), 150, #4, who lists additional authors supporting this view. Some of these authors speak of Luke's "Ebionite" tendencies, which means the ascetic attitude of rejecting wealth per se as evil. As we shall demonstrate, this is not Luke's position.

4. See Chapter Six.

5. On the theological problems connected with the idea of a future reversal see esp. Schottroff and Stegemann, *Jesus von Nazareth*, 34, 45-47.

6. So H. Schürmann, *Das Evangelium nach Lukas*, 339; H. Degenhardt, *Lukas, Evangelist der Armen*, 53. These scholars point to other texts such as Luke 6:39-45 and Acts 20:29-30, where warnings against false teachings are found. Degenhardt also notes that Pauline opponents in 1 Corinthians are described as "rich, filled, satisfied" (cf. 1 Cor. 4:8). But none of these passages seems related to the beatitudes and woes of Luke, where the social factors are the dominant ones.

7. Similarly, e.g. Marshall, *The Gospel of Luke*, 257; Karris, "Poor and Rich," 115-116. Could Luke have in mind persons like Ananias and Sapphira in Acts 6?

8. Jeremias, *The Parables of Jesus*, 77f. Also C. H. Dodd, *The Parables of the Kingdom*, rev. ed. (New York: Scribner's, 1961), 145; Eta Linnemann, *Parables of Jesus. Introduction and Exposition* (London: SPCK, 1966), 118.

9. Compare Luke's similar emphasis on taking up the cross "daily" in 9:23 with Mark 8:34. Luke envisions life in the world far more than Mark.

10. L. Keck, 'The Poor Among the Saints in the New Testament," 109, also

comments on the characteristic nature of this admonition concerning wealth for Luke.

11. The discovery of this Gnostic library in 1948 will probably have as significant an effect on biblical studies as the discovery of the Dead Sea Scrolls. The writings have just been published in an English edition, *The Nag Hammadi Library in English*, trans. by members of the Coptic Gnostic Library Project of the Institute for Antiquity and Christianity, James Robinson, director (San Francisco: Harper and Row, 1977).

12. *The Nag Hammadi Library in English*, 117-138. For helpful commentary see Bertil Gärtner, *The Theology of the Gospel of Thomas*, trans. by E. Sharpe (London: Collins, 1961).

13. Quoted in Jeremias, *The Parables*, 164n.62.

14. Marshall, *The Gospel of Luke*, 522, suggests it is possible that the elder brother wanted to keep the family property intact, while the younger brother wants to take his share and separate it from the family ownership. Note how twice in Luke's Gospel we encounter disputes over family inheritance (cf. Luke 15:11-32).

15. So Jeremias, *The Parables*, 165.

16. According to Jeremias, *The Parables*, 165, the barns were not for drying, but long-term usage. The storehouses were often underground, walled and lined, to keep the grain dry and secure.

17. So Schottroff and Stegemann, *Jesus von Nazareth*, 126.

18. Jeremias, *The Parables*, 165.

19. Jeremias, *The Parables*, 165.

20. Phrase comes from R. Karris' pithy *Invitation to Luke*, 157.

21. The origin of the story about a rich man and poor man is usually traced to an Egyptian tale about Si-Osiris, which was brought to Palestine by diaspora Jews and then retold as a tale about a rich publican and poor scholar. Jesus, it is thought, further readopted this well-known story for his purposes. Schottroff and Stegemann, *Jesus von Nazareth*, 39, however, point out that only in Jesus' parable is there a reversal of roles due to social status. In the Egyptian tale the reversal in the next life is based on good and evil deeds in this life, apart from social status. Regarding the gospel version of the parable, R. Bultmann, *History of the Synoptic Tradition*, rev. ed., trans. by J. Marsh (New York: Harper and Row, 1968), 203ff., goes so far as to attribute both parts to Jewish sources. However, J. D. Crossan, *In Parables: The Challenge of the Historical Jesus* (New York: Harper and Row, 1973), 66-67, represents a broad consensus of scholars who attribute the first half to Jesus and the second half to the early church.

22. Most recently, Richard Rohrbaugh, *The Biblical Interpreter*, 69-85, whose entire discussion we find most appropriate and provocative.

23. Jeremias, *The Parables*, 186. Other double-parables are Luke 15:11-32 (Prodigal Son), Matt. 20:1-15 (Laborers in Vineyard), Matt. 22:1-14 (Great Supper).

24. According to Jeremias, *The Parables*, 184, the bread was not left-over crumbs, but a flatbread used to wipe the fingers before meals.

25. E.g. Schottroff and Stegemann, *Jesus von Nazareth*, 38, insist no misconduct of the rich is implied in the first half; only in the second half does Luke issue a call to repentance.

26. So Schottroff and Stegemann, *Jesus von Nazareth*, 41.

27. A. M. Hunter, *Interpreting the Parables* (London: SCM, 1961), 84.

28. The chapter on this parable by Rohrbaugh, *The Biblical Interpreter*, 69-85, contains an excellent discussion on the social dimensions of the parable and how to preach and teach it today.

29. Chapter Four on "Sell all that you have . . ."

30. See O. Michel, *"kamēlos," TDNT* III, 594. Another suggestion is that Jesus actually said "rope," not "camel," a suggestion based on the close similarity in Greek between the two words *(kamēlos-kamilos)*.

31. "Jesus is using a typical oriental image to emphasize the impossibility of something by way of violent contrast: 'Entry into the kingdom of God is completely impossible for the rich.'" Michel, *TDNT*, III, 593.

32. In Mark 10:28 Peter says we have left "all" *(panta)* and followed you. Somewhat surprisingly, given Luke's usual stress on "all," he omits it and substitutes "our homes." However earlier we noted the demand of Jesus to the rich man to "sell *all* you" have, an emphasis unique to Luke.

33. So Sider, *Rich Christians*, 97.

Chapter Six

1. For a similar description of Jesus' life consult Hengel, *Property*, 30.

2. Behind the passive tense "will be added to you" stands God as the subject. The use of the passive was a common Jewish method of avoiding the divine name, considered too holy to utter. See Jeremias, *New Testament Theology* I: *The Proclamation of Jesus*, trans. by J. Bowden (London: SCM, 1971), 9-14.

3. Most interpreters argue that "master" in v. 8 refers to the master in the parable (v. 1). But Jeremias and a few others argue that Jesus' himself speaks at v. 8, so that the original parable ends with v. 7. For a helpful interpretation of the whole parable see John Reumann, *Jesus in the Church's Gospels* (Philadelphia: Fortress, 1968), 189-198.

4. So Dan O. Via, *The Parables: Their Literary and Existential Dimension* (Philadelphia: Fortress, 1967), 161; Jeremias, *The Parables*, 45-48, 181-182.

5. Especially J. D. M. Derrett, "Fresh Light on St. Luke XVI. I. The Parable of the Unjust Steward," *NTS* 7 (1961), 198-219. J. Fitzmyer, "The Story of the Dishonest Manager (Lk. 16:1-13)," in *Essays on the Semitic Background of the New Testament* (Missoula, Mont.: Scholars Press, 1974), 161-184.

6. F. C. Grant, *Anglican Theological Review* 30 (1948), 120.

7. H. Braun, *Qumran und das Neue Testament* (Tübingen: Mohr (Paul Siebeck), 1966), 91. The term "mammon" is an Aramaic word for "money," and is in itself a neutral term. Its preservation in Aramaic may mean, however, that it had a special moral weight to Christians, who thus preserved it.

8. Luke Johnson, *The Literary Function of Possessions in Luke-Acts*, 157; Marshall, *The Gospel of Luke*, 621; etc.

9. Many other uncertainties about v. 9 remain: 1) It "fails." a. Does it mean that mammon fails because they gave it away? b. Or, does it mean when this life is over, then, if you gave money to others, these friends will receive you into the next life? 2) Who are the "friends"? a. Angels? b. The poor who were helped by them? Since for Luke the poor are the blessed who receive the kingdom, this latter seems the better explanation. 3) Only here in the New Testament is the term "eternal habitations" found.

10. Schottroff and Stegemann, *Jesus von Nazareth*, 138, also find paradigmatic motifs in this text as: a) a model of repentance for sinners, and b) a model for rich Christians.

11. We noted earlier the "today" of 4:16; cf. Chapter Three above.

12. The Greek *dei*, "it is necessary," normally refers to divine necessity in the New Testament and Intertestamental literature.

13. See Strack-Billerbeck II, 249-50. W. Grundmann, *Das Evangelium nach Lukas*, 360, states that Jewish law required only full restitution plus 20% (Lev. 5:20-26). The one exception was the case of cattle theft, where fourfold was exacted (Exod. 21:37, 22:1).

14. Schottroff and Stegemann, *Jesus von Nazareth*, 138.

15. Strack-Billerbeck, IV, 546ff.

16. G. Davies, "Alms," *Interpreters Dictionary of the Bible* I, 87-88. Cf. also Strack-Billerbeck, I, 387ff.

17. The text is extremely difficult to interpret. It could mean: a) "First clean the inside," i.e., your hearts; then you can rightly give alms. b) "Give what's inside," i.e. the contents of the cup and dish (i.e. your possessions) to the poor, then you'll be blessed.

18. Against E. Haenchen, *The Acts of the Apostles: A Commentary*, trans. by B. Noble (Philadelphia: Westminster, 1971), 627, who thinks Luke misunderstood Paul's collection and thought it was meant for the Jewish people, not Jewish-Christians.

19. See Chapter Three, "Old Testament Context."

20. Chapter Three, "Blessed are you poor."

21. So R. Sloan, *The Favorable Year of the Lord*, 121, who remarks that "even a casual reading . . . suffices to convince one that the dominant image of this passage is financial." He also argues that Jubilee and Sabbath year motifs are central. Likewise, Schottroff and Stegemann, *Jesus von Nazareth*, 144-148, pursue the provocative thesis that the command to "love one's enemies" is directed by Luke to rich Christians, who are urged to act more mercifully toward the poor in their midst (6:36). While I find the suggestion attractive, it is not fully convincing. Vv. 27-29 fit a persecution context better than a rich-poor context, consistent with vv. 22-23, 26. And while there is a decided shift in emphasis toward generous and merciful conduct toward the needy in the remaining verses (vv. 30-38), the commands seem to include a broader setting than just the problem of rich and poor Christians. It is a matter of loving and doing good to people who do not often reciprocate, who in fact remain ungrateful and evil despite the good one seeks to do for them (v. 35). This is scarcely conceivable between Christians, where help for the poor would supposedly be met with grateful acceptance and mutual love. Nevertheless, Luke has made significant changes which introduce the problem of the rich and poor into the discussion of "loving one's enemies" and "doing good" to all men. Hence I find it legitimate to interpret many of these passages as an admonition or challenge to rich Christians in Luke's day.

22. A few manuscripts have the alternate reading, "despair of no man" (or nothing). Then the saying would mean, "lend and trust God for what happens." While possible, the context clearly favors the more radical "lend, expecting nothing in return."

23. The metaphor comes from the manner of measuring out grain to insure full weight and volume.

24. Cf. Luke 11:4. Yoder, *The Politics of Jesus*, 66-67, attempts to interpret this petition of the Lord's Prayer to mean that God forgives us as we remit the debts (financial) owed to us. He bases this on Luke's use of the word "debtors" in contrast to Matthew's "trespasses" (Matt. 6:14). He also traces this

back to the Jubilee Year motif. Sloan, *The Favorable Year of the Lord*, 139-145, does the same, more cautiously. While interesting, in our judgment the interpretation hangs on too thin a thread and reflects forced "Jubilee" exegesis.

25. A number of commentators suggest that Luke is here trying to broaden the idea of philanthropy for Gentile Christians, who lived in a Graeco-Roman environment where philanthropy was limited chiefly to friends and acquaintances, and based on the hope of personal gain.

26. According to Jeremias, ten oxen work 45 hectare per day, a great amount for Palestine.

27. J. D. Crossan, *In Parables*, 71, says Luke has "moralized" the parable in v. 21, by linking it to v. 13. But he notes it doesn't quite work, since in the parable the rich are invited first and then only the poor. The *Gospel of Thomas* version omits all mention of the poor (logion 64).

28. See Victor Furnish, *The Love Command in the New Testament* (Nashville: Abingdon, 1972). Cf. Matt. 19:19, Rom. 13:9, Gal. 5:14, Jas. 2:8.

29. Compare modern-day efforts to translate this parable in light of racial tensions in the USA; e.g. *The Cotton Patch Version of Luke and Acts*, by Clarence Jordan (New York: Association Press, 1969).

30. Note that Luke takes a special interest in Samaritans: 9:52-56; 17:11-16; Acts 1:8; 8:1ff. The Samaritans are part of the group of "outcasts" Jesus came to embrace.

31. See Marshall, *The Gospel of Luke*, 141-142. A fine article by Harold Sahlin, "Die Früchte der Umkehr. Die ethische Verkündigung Johannes des Taüfers nach Lukas 3:10-14," *Studia Theologica I*, (1948), 54-68, argues that Luke is primarily responsible, though drawing on Jewish repentance themes. Bultmann, *History*, 155, rejects its authenticity because of the soldiers present, which he thinks points to a later period than John or Jesus.

32. Schottroff and Stegemann, *Jesus von Nazareth*, 138. On this basis they argue that this tradition is early, while that of the tax collectors and soldiers was added later. Yet it is highly doubtful that the tax collector traditions are later, given the offense it caused in Jesus' historical ministry.

33. Josephus, *Antiquities* XVIII, 5.2. Marshall, *The Gospel of Luke*, 143, argues for Herod's soldiers.

34. So Roland Bainton, *Christian Attitudes Toward War and Peace* (Nashville: Abingdon, 1960), esp. 66-84.

35. W. Grundmann, *Das Evangelium nach Lukas*, 104 (translation).

36. So e.g. J. Wellhausen, *Das Evangelium Lucae* (Berlin: Reimer, 1904), 5.

37. Frederick Danker, *Jesus and the New Age According to St. Luke* (St. Louis: Clayton, 1972), 46-48, particularly points to the "revolutionary" newness of the ethical demands here portrayed. "Yet the words in Luke's context are revolutionary. The haves are to share with the have-nots, for God exalts the poor and humbles the rich. . . . The ax is heading downstroke in any society that thinks these words are an invitation merely to distribute Christmas food-baskets, handouts of cast-off clothes, and dollar bills. . . ."

Chapter Seven

1. Strangely, Leander Keck, in an otherwise fine survey of the Lukan traditions on poverty, sees no connection between the material on the poor in the Gospel and Acts ("The Poor Among the Saints in the New Testament," 109). Perhaps he was misled by the fact that the term "poor," does not occur in Acts.

But we will show that what Luke has to say on wealth and poverty grows directly out of his gospel traditions, as other commentators have clearly recognized. In fact, Acts 10:38, which describes Jesus' earthly ministry, takes up the thematic Isa. 61 text of Luke 4, and in the phrase "he went about doing good" refers to Jesus' ministry to the poor and suffering. K. Lake, "The Communism of Acts II and IV," *Beginnings of Christianity*, V (London: Macmillan, 1933), 306, correctly finds a direct link between "the communistic experiment" and literal obedience to the words of Jesus.

2. The summaries are found in Acts 2:41-47; 4:32-37; 5:12-16; 6:7; 9:31.

3. See Haenchen, *The Acts of the Apostles*, 156-157, for a brief history of their interpretation.

4. For a good popular discussion consult Sider, *Rich Christians*, 98-103.

5. So Jeremias, *The Eucharistic Words of Jesus*, 64.

6. So Jeremias, *Jerusalem*, 130, #19. The only difference from Qumran, according to Jeremias, is that in Acts the giving was strictly voluntary.

7. See point 3 in the Summary to Chapter Four.

8. A good discussion on Qumran is found in Leander Keck, "The Poor Among the Saints in Jewish Christianity and Qumran," 66-78.

9. Haenchen, *The Acts of the Apostles*, 192.

10. See Sider, *Rich Christians*, 99, on the evangelistic impact of economic sharing.

11. Recent commentators have stressed this possibility, pointing out many parallels in Graeco-Roman writers to the idea of "all things in common" among a community of friends. E.g., Degenhardt, *Lukas, Evangelist der Armen*, 221-223. Karris, "Poor and Rich: The Lukan Sitz im Leben," 116-117, strongly argues that in these passages and throughout his Gospel Luke is confronting Gentile Christians of means with the need to change their former mindset, in which concern for the poor and needy was generally absent.

12. Degenhardt, *Lukas, Evangelist der Armen*, 180-84, particularly notes this tension.

13. Sider, *Rich Christians*, 98-103, states that two basic principles were at work: *Unlimited economic liability for,* and *total economic availability to* the other members of the community.

14. K. Bornhäuser, *Studien zur Apostelgeschichte* (Gütersloh: Bertelsmann, 1934), 44, observes correctly that the entire section from Acts 4:32-5:11 is a report on how the church met the needs of the poor.

15. This is our first introduction to Barnabas, who plays an important role in later missionary activity. One of Luke's favorite techniques is to briefly introduce a person, then pick up their story later (e.g., Paul in Acts, 8:1-3; 9:1ff.).

16. So Jacques Dupont, *The Salvation of the Gentiles*, trans. by J. Keating (New York: Paulist, 1979), 100.

17. Schuyler Brown, *Apostasy and Perseverance in Luke-Acts*, 107.

18. Gal. 2:10, 2 Cor. 8-9, Rom. 15:25-27. See Sider, *Rich Christians*, 102-103, for a list of reasons the church was so poor; Haenchen, *The Acts of the Apostles*, 234-235.

19. See Haenchen, *The Acts of the Apostles*, 260.

20. From the Greek *diakonein* comes the English "deacon."

21. So Sider, *Rich Christians*, 99.

22. Josephus, *Antiquities* 3:320; Jeremias, *Jerusalem*, 142-143, for critical discussion. We have no need to raise the historical problem of reconciling this visit to Jerusalem and Paul's own account in Gal. 1.

23. By Paul, Rom. 16:25-26; 1 Cor. 16:1-4; 2 Cor. 8-9; Gal. 2:10.
24. See Haenchen, *The Acts of the Apostles*, 595-598.
25. E.g., 1 Cor. 4:12; 9:15-19; 2 Cor. 11:7-9; 1 Thess. 2:9-10; 2 Thess. 3:7-9.
26. Cf. Luke 6:38; 11:9; 14:12-14.

Chapter Eight

1. Thomas Hoyt, *The Poor in Luke-Acts* (Ann Arbor, Mich.: University Microfilms, 1975), 167.
2. See Hengel, *Property and Riches*, 30, where he states Jesus, like a true apocalypticist who expects all from God, rejected the revolutionary approach to change. Cf. also his *Victory Over Violence* (Philadelphia: Fortress, 1973).
3. Tertullian, *Apol.* 39.
4. Henry J. Cadbury, *The Making of Luke-Acts*, 2nd ed. (London: SPCK, 1968), 262, already recognized that the weight of the material was directed to the rich. He even questioned whether Luke could be called a champion of the poor. On this latter point he did not see clearly enough the "good news to the poor" themes in Luke-Acts. Why not both *for* the poor and *against* the rich?
5. "Younger evangelicals" produced the socially-conscious *Chicago Declaration of Evangelical Social Concern* in 1973. Among its statements are these: "God requires justice. But we have not proclaimed or demonstrated his justice to an unjust American society. Although the Lord calls us to defend the social and economic rights of the poor and oppressed, we have mostly remained silent . . . *We must attack* the materialism of our culture and the maldistribution of the nation's wealth and services."
6. Dietrich Bonhoeffer, *The Cost of Discipleship*, 2nd ed., trans. R. H. Fuller (New York: Macmillan, 1963), 56. Cf. Luke 7:47.
7. E.g., the role of women and ordination. On the problem of the gap in time and circumstances for Christian ethics see the fine study by Larry Rasmussen and Bruce Birch, *Bible and Ethics in the Christian Life* (Minneapolis: Augsburg, 1976), esp. ch. 2.
8. From Conzelmann, *The Theology of Luke*, 233.
9. We, of course, recognize this is being done effectively on a large scale today by World Council of Churches agencies, Lutheran World Relief, Bread for the World, etc. One might add a word of caution about some agencies whose stewardship of funds is not as good as others. Ask for financial statements before giving.
10. Among recent liberation theologies we would especially mention the work of Gustavo Gutierrez, *A Theology of Liberation*, trans. by C. Inda and J. Eagleson (Maryknoll, N.Y.: Orbis, 1973).

Bibliography

Anderson, Hugh. "Broadening Horizons. The Rejection at Nazareth Pericope of Luke 4:16-30 in Light of Recent Critical Trends." *Interpretation* 18 (1964), 259-75.

Bainton, Roland. *Christian Attitudes Toward War and Peace.* Nashville: Abingdon, 1960.

Bammel, Ernst. *ptōchos. Theological Dictionary of the New Testament* VI. Ed. G. Kittel, G. Friedrich. Trans. by G. Bromily. Grand Rapids: Eerdmans, 1968. 885-915.

Barrett, C. K. *Luke the Historian in Recent Study.* London: Epworth, 1961.

Batey, Richard. *Jesus and the Poor: The Poverty Program of the First Christians.* New York: Harper, 1972.

Birch, Bruce and Rasmussen, Larry. *Bible and Ethics in the Christian Life.* Minneapolis: Augsburg, 1976.

——— *ɪhe Predicament of the Prosperous.* Philadelphia: Westminster, 1978.

Bonhoeffer, Dietrich. *The Cost of Discipleship.* 2nd ed. Trans. by R. H. Fuller. New York: Macmillan, 1963.

Bonsirven, Joseph. *Palestinian Judaism in the Time of Jesus Christ.* Trans. by W. Wolf. New York: Holt, Rinehart and Winston, 1964.

Bornhaüser, K. *Studien zum Sondergut des Lukas.* Gütersloh: Bertelsmann, 1934.

Bornkamm, Gunther. *Jesus of Nazareth.* Trans. by Irene and Fraser McLuskey with J. M. Robinson. New York: Harper, 1960.

Braun, Herbert. *Qumran und das Neue Testament.* Tübingen: Mohr (Paul Siebeck), 1966.

Brown, Raymond. "The Beatitudes According to Luke." *New Testament Essays.* Garden City, N.Y.: Doubleday, 1968.

——— *The Birth of the Messiah: A Commentary on the Infancy Narratives in Matthew and Luke.* Garden City, N.Y.: Doubleday, 1977.

Brown, Raymond et al. *Mary in the New Testament.* Philadelphia: Fortress, 1978.

Brown, Schuyler. *Apostasy and Perseverance in the Theology of Luke.* Rome: Pontifical Biblical Institute, 1969.

Bultmann, Rudolf. *History of the Synoptic Tradition.* Rev. ed. Trans. by John Marsh. New York: Harper, 1968.

Cadbury, Henry J. *The Making of Luke-Acts.* 2nd ed. London: SPCK, 1968.

193

Caird, George B. *St. Luke* (Pelican Gospel Commentaries). London: Penguin, 1963.

Cassidy, Richard. *Jesus, Politics and Society. A Study of Luke's Gospel.* Maryknoll, N.Y.: Orbis, 1978.

Cave, C. H. "The Sermon at Nazareth and the Beatitudes in the Light of the Synagogue Lectionary." *Texte und Untersuchungen* 88 (1964), 231-235.

Charles, R. H. *The Apocrypha and Pseudepigrapha of the Old Testament in English.* 2 vols. Oxford: Clarendon, 1913.

Conzelmann, Hans. *The Theology of St. Luke.* Trans. by G. Buswell. New York: Harper, 1961.

Creed, J. M. *The Gospel According to St. Luke.* London: Macmillan, 1930.

Crockett, Larrimore Clyde. *The O.T. in the Gospel of Luke with Emphasis on the Interpretation of Is. 61:1-2.* Ph.D. Diss. Ann Arbor, Mich.: University microfilms, 1967.

Crossan, John Dominick. *In Parables: The Challenge of the Historical Jesus.* New York: Harper, 1973.

Cullman, Oscar. *Jesus and the Revolutionaries.* Trans. by G. Putnam. New York: Harper, 1970.

Dahl, Nils. *Studies in Paul.* Minneapolis: Augsburg, 1977.

Danker, F. W. *Jesus and the New Age According to St. Luke.* St. Louis: Clayton, 1972.

de Jonge, M. and Safrai, S., Gen. eds. *The Jewish People in the First Century.* 2 vols. (Compendia Rerum-Judaicarum ad Novum Testamentum) Philadelphia: Fortress, 1974.

de Jonge, M. and van der Woude, A. S. "11 Q Melchizedek and the New Testament." *New Testament Studies* 12 (July, 1966), 301-26.

de Vaux, Roland. *Ancient Israel* I. New York: McGraw-Hill, 1965.

Degenhardt, Hans Joachim. *Lukas. Evangelist der Armen. Besitz und Besitzverzicht in den lukanischen Schriften.* Stuttgart: Katholisches Bibelwerk, 1965.

Derrett, J. D. M. "Fresh Light on Luke XVI. I. The Parable of the Unjust Steward." *New Testament Studies* 7 (1961), 198-219.

Dibelius, Martin. *James.* Rev. by H. Greeven. Trans. by M. Williams. (Hermeneia Series). Philadelphia: Fortress, 1976.

—— *Studies in the Acts of the Apostles.* Trans. by M. Ling and P. Schubert. London: SCM, 1956.

Dodd, C. H. *More New Testament Studies.* Manchester: Manchester Univ. Press, 1968.

—— *The Parables of the Kingdom.* Rev. ed. New York: Scribner's, 1961.

—— *The Founder of Christianity.* New York: Macmillan, 1970.

Dupont-Sommer, A. *The Essene Writings from Qumran.* Trans. by G. Vermes. Cleveland: World, 1967.

Dupont, Jacques. *Les Beatitudes.* 3 vol. I. Le probléme littéraire-les deux versions du sermon sur la montagne et des Béatitudes. 2nd ed. Louvain: Nauwelaerts, 1958. II. La Bonne Nouvelle. Paris: Gabalda, 1969. III. Les Evangelistes. Paris: Gabalda, 1973.

Dupont, Jacques. *The Salvation of the Gentiles.* Trans. by J. Keating. New York: Paulist, 1979.

Ellis, Earle. *The Gospel of Luke* (New Century Bible). London: Oliphants, 1974.

Elthester, Walther, Ed. *Jesus in Nazareth.* Berlin: de Gruyter, 1972.

Farmer, W. R. 'The Economic Basis of the Qumran Community." *Theologische Literaturzeitung* II (1955), 295-308.

Finkel, Asher. "Jesus' Sermon at Nazareth (Lk. 4:16-30)." *Abraham unser Vater.* Festschrift O. Michel. Ed. O. Betz. Leiden: Brill, 1963.

——— *The Pharisees and the Teacher of Nazareth.* Leiden: Brill, 1964.

Fitzmyer, Joseph. "The Story of the Dishonest Manager (Lk. 16:1-13)." *Essays on the Semitic Background of the New Testament.* Missoula, Mont.: Scholars Press, 1974. "Further Light on Melchizedek from Qumran 11," *Ibid.*

Foakes-Jackson, F. J. and Lake, K. Eds. *The Beginnings of Christianity.* 5 vols. London: Macmillan, 1920-1933.

Furnish, Victor. *The Love Command in the New Testament.* Nashville: Abingdon, 1972.

Gager, John. *Kingdom and Community. The Social World of Early Christianity.* Englewood Cliffs, New Jersey: Prentice-Hall, Inc., 1975.

Gärtner, Bertil. *The Theology of the Gospel of Thomas.* Trans. by E. Sharpe. London: Collins, 1961.

——— *Iscariot.* Trans. by V. Gruhn (Facet Books 29). Philadelphia: Fortress, 1976.

Gelin, Albert. *The Poor of Yahweh.* Collegeville: Liturgical, 1964.

Grundmann, Walter. *Das Evangelium nach Lukas* (Theologischer Handkommentar zum Neuen Testament, III). Berlin: Evangelische Verlagsanstalt, 1964.

——— *tapeinos. Theological Dictionary of the New Testament* VIII. Eds. G. Kittel and G. Friedrich. Trans. by G. Bromily. Grand Rapids: Eerdmans, 1972. 1-26.

Gutierrez, Gustavo. *A Theology of Liberation.* Trans. and ed. by C. Inda and J. Eagleson. Maryknoll, N.Y.: Orbis, 1973.

Haenchen, Ernst. *The Acts of the Apostles: A Commentary.* Trans. by B. Noble and others. Philadelphia: Westminster, 1971.

Hauck, Friederick. *mamōnos* and *hypomonē. Theological Dictionary of the New Testament* IV. Ed. by G. Kittel. Trans. by G. Bromily. Grand Rapids, Mich.: Eerdmans, 1967. 388-390, 581-588.

Hengel, Martin. *Property and Riches in the Early Church.* Trans. by J. Bowden. Philadelphia: Fortress, 1974.

——— *Victory Over Violence.* Trans. by D. Green. Philadelphia: Fortress, 1973.

Henry, Patrick. *New Directions in New Testament Study.* Philadelphia: Westminster, 1979.

Hill, David. 'The Rejection of Jesus at Nazareth." *Novum Testamentum* 15 (1971), 161-180.

Hock, Ronald. *The Social Context of Paul's Ministry.* Philadelphia: Fortress, 1980.

Holtz, T. *Untersuchungen über die Alttestamentlichen Zitate bei Lukas. Texte und Untersuchungen* 104. Berlin: Akademie-Verlag, 1968.

Hoyt, Thomas. *The Poor in Luke-Acts.* Ph.D. Diss. Ann Arbor, Mich.: University microfilms, 1975.

Hunter, A. M. *Interpreting the Parables.* London: SCM, 1961.

Jeremias, Joachim. *The Eucharistic Words of Jesus.* 3rd ed. Trans. by N. Perrin. New York: Scribner's, 1966.

——— *Jerusalem in the Time of Jesus.* 3rd rev. ed. Trans. by F. H. and C. H. Cave. Philadelphia: Fortress, 1967.

——— *The Parables of Jesus.* 6th ed. Trans. by S. Hooke. New York: Scribner's, 1963.

——— *New Testament Theology I: The Proclamation of Jesus.* Trans. by J. Bowden. London: SCM, 1971.

——— "Zöllner und Sünder." *Zeitschrift für die neutestamentliche Wissenschaft* 30 (1931), 293-300.

Johnson, Luke. *The Literary Function of Possessions in Luke-Acts* (SBL Dissertation Series 39). Missoula, Mont.: Scholars, 1977.

Jones, D. R. "The Background and Character of the Lukan Psalms." *Journal of Theological Studies* (1968), 19-50.

Josephus. *Antiquities of the Jews.* Loeb Classical Library. Cambridge, Mass.: Harvard University Press, 1956.

——— *Jewish Wars.* Loeb Classical Library. Cambridge, Mass.: Harvard University Press, 1956.

Kandler, Hans-Joachim. "Die Bedeutung der Armut im Schriftum von Chirbet Qumran." *Judaica* 13 (1957), 193-209.

Karris, Robert. *Invitation to Luke.* Garden City, N.Y.: Doubleday, 1966.

——— "Poor and Rich: The Lukan Sitz im Leben." *Perspectives on Luke-Acts.* Ed. by Charles Talbert (Special Studies Series No. 5). Danville, Va.: 1978.

Keck, L. E. "The Poor Among the Saints in the New Testament." *Zeitschrift für die neutestamentliche Wissenschaft* 56 (1965), 100-129.

——— "Jesus' Entrance Upon His Mission." *The Review and Expositor* 64 (1967), 465-483.

——— "The Poor Among the Saints in Jewish Christianity and Qumran." *Zeitschrift für die neutestamentliche Wissenschaft* 55 (1965), 54-78.

Kee, Howard Clark. *Christian Origins in Sociological Perspective.* Philadelphia: Westminster, 1980.

——— *Jesus in History: An Approach to the Study of the Gospels.* New York: Harcourt, Brace, and World, 1970.

Koch, Roland. "Die Wertung des Besitzes im Lukasevangelium." *Biblica* 38 (1957), 151-169.

Krentz, Edgar. *The Historical-Critical Method* (Guides to Biblical Scholarship). Philadelphia: Fortress, 1975.

Lake, K. "The Communism of Acts II and IV-VI and the Appointment of the Seven." *Beginnings of Christianity* V. London: Macmillan, 1933.

Leany, A. R. C. *A Commentary on the Gospel According to St. Luke.* London: Black, 1958.

Linneman, Eta. *Parables of Jesus. Introduction and Exposition.* London: SPCK, 1966.

Lorenzen, T. "A Biblical Meditation on Lk. 16:19-31. From the Text Toward a Sermon." *Expository Times* 87 (1979), 39-43.

Machovec, Milan. *A Marxist Looks at Jesus.* Eng. trans. Philadelphia: Fortress, 1976.

Marshall, I. Howard. *Luke: Historian and Theologian.* Exeter, Devon: Paternoster, 1970.

——— *The Gospel of Luke* (The New International Greek New Testament Commentary). Grand Rapids, Mich.: Eerdmans, 1978.

Michel, Otto. *telōnēs. Theological Dictionary of the New Testament* VIII. Ed. G. Kittel and G. Friedrich. Trans. by G. Bromily. Grand Rapids, Mich.: Eerdmans, 1972. 88-105.

—— *kamēlos. Theological Dictionary of the New Testament* III. Ed. G. Kittel. Trans. by G. Bromily. Grand Rapids, Mich.: Eerdmans, 1965.

Miller, Patrick. "Luke 4:16-21." *Interpretation* XXIX, 4 (1975), 417-21.

Miller, Marvin. "The Function of Is. 61:1-2 in 11 Q Melchizedek." *Journal of Biblical Literature* 88 (1969), 467-69.

Morris, Leon. *The Gospel According to St. Luke* (Tyndale New Testament Commentaries). Grand Rapids, Mich.: Eerdmans, 1974.

McKnight, Edgar. *What Is Form-Criticism?* Philadelphia: Fortress, 1969.

The Nag Hammadi Library in English. Translated by members of the Coptic Gnostic Library Project of the Institute for Antiquity and Christianity. James M. Robinson, director. San Francisco: Harper, 1977.

North, Robert. *Sociology of the Biblical Jubilee* (Analecta Biblica, 4) Rome: Pontificio Instituto Biblico, 1954.

Patte, Daniel. *What Is Structural Exegesis?* Philadelphia: Fortress, 1976.

Percy, Ernst. *Die Botschaft Jesu.* Lund: Gleerup, 1953.

Perrin, Norman. *What Is Redaction-Criticism?* Philadelphia: Fortress, 1969.

—— *Rediscovering the Teachings of Jesus.* New York: Harper, 1967.

Philo. *Every Good Man Is Free.* Loeb Classical Library. Cambridge, Mass.: Harvard University Press, 1956.

Rese, Martin. *Alttestamentliche Motive in der Christologie des Lukas.* Gütersloh: Gerd Mohr, 1969.

Reumann, John. *Jesus in the Church's Gospels.* Philadelphia: Fortress, 1968.

Richardson, A. *The Political Christ.* Philadelphia: Westminster, 1973.

Rohrbaugh, Richard. *The Biblical Interpreter. An Agrarian Bible in an Industrial Age.* Philadelphia: Fortress, 1978.

Russell, David S. *Between the Testaments.* Philadelphia: Fortress, 1960.

Sabourin, Leopold. *The Psalms.* New York: Alba, 1969.

Sahlin, Harald. 'Die Früchte der Umkehr. Die ethische Verkündigung Johannes des Taüfers nach Lukas 3:10-14." *Studia Theologica* I. Lund, 1948, 54-68.

Sanders, E. P. *Paul and Palestinian Judaism.* Philadelphia: Fortress, 1977.

Sanders, Jack. *Ethics in the New Testament.* Philadelphia: Fortress, 1975.

Sanders, James. "From Isaiah 61 to Luke 4." In *Christianity, Judaism and Other Graeco-Roman Cults.* Festschrift honoring Morton Smith. Ed. by J. Neusner. New York: Columbia University Press, 1975.

Santa Ana, Julio de. *Good News to the Poor: The Challenge of the Poor in the History of the Church.* Trans. by H. Whittle. Geneva: WCC, 1977.

Sattler, W. "Die Anawim im Zeitalter Jesu Christi." *Festgabe für A. Jühlicher.* Tübingen: Mohr, 1927.

Schnackenburg, Rudolph. "Das Magnificat, seine Spiritualität und Theologie." *Geist und Leben* 38, 342-357.

Schmithals, Walter. "Lukas-Evangelist der Armen." *Theologia Viatorum* XII (1973-74), 153-167.

Schottroff, Luise and Stegemann, Wolfgang. *Jesus von Nazareth. Hoffnung der Armen.* Stuttgart: Kohlhammer, 1978.

Schürmann, Heinz. "Zur Traditionsgeschichte der Nazareth Perikope Lk. 4: 16-30." *Melange Bibliques.* Essays in honor of Beda Rigaux. Ed. by A. Descamps and A. de Halleux. Gembloux: Fuculot, 1970.

—— *Das Lukasevangelium* (Herders Theologischer Kommentar zum Neuen Testament III. Erster Teil). Freiburg: Herber, 1969.

Seccombe, David. *Riches and the Rich in Luke-Acts.* Ph.D. Diss. Ann Arbor, Mich.: University microfilms, 1978.

Sider, Ronald. *Rich Christians in an Age of Hunger: A Biblical Study.* Downer's Grove, Ill.: Intervarsity, 1977.

Sloan, Robert. *The Favorable Year of the Lord. A Study of Jubilary Theology in the Gospel of Luke.* Austin: Schola, 1977.

Stahlin, Gustav. *Die Apostelgeschichte* (Das Neue Testament Deutsch) Göttingen: Vanderhoeck und Ruprecht, 1966.

Strack, H. L. and Billerbeck, Paul. *Kommentar zum Neuen Testament aus Talmud und Midrash.* 6 vol. Munich: Beck'sche, 1924.

Strobel, August. "Die Ausrufung des Jobeljahres in der Nazareth Predigt Jesu." In *Jesus in Nazareth.* Ed. by Walther Elthester. Berlin: de Gruyter, 1972.

Talbert, C. H. "The Lukan Presentation of Jesus' Ministry in Galilee. Lk. 4:31-9:50." *Review and Expositor* 64 (1967), 485-97.

Tannehill, Robert. "The Mission of Jesus According to Luke 4:16-30." In *Jesus in Nazareth.* Ed. by Walther Elthester. Berlin: de Gruyter, 1972.

Theissen, Gerd. *Sociology of Early Palestinian Christianity.* Trans. J. Bowden. Philadelphia: Fortress, 1977.

Topel, L. J. "On the Injustice of the Unjust Steward: Lk. 16:1-13." *Catholic Biblical Quarterly* 37 (1975), 216-227.

Trocmé, A. *Jesus and the Non-Violent Revolution.* Trans. by Michael H. Shank and Marlin E. Miller. Scottsdale, Pa.: Herald, 1973.

Vermes, Geza. *The Dead Sea Scrolls: Qumran in Perspective.* Cleveland: Collins, World, 1978.

Via, Dan Otto Jr. *The Parables: Their Literary and Existential Dimension.* Philadelphia: Fortress, 1967.

Vogt, J. "Ecce ancilla domini: Eine Untersuchung zum socialen Motive des Antiken Marienbildes." *Vigiliae Christiana* 23 (1969), 241-63.

Wellhausen, Julius. *Das Evangelium Lucae.* Berlin: Reimer, 1904.

Wilckens, U. "Interpreting Luke-Acts in a Period of Existentialist Theology." In *Studies in Luke-Acts.* Ed. by L. E. Keck and J. L. Martyn. Nashville: Abingdon, 1966.

Yoder, John H. *The Politics of Jesus.* Grand Rapids, Mich.: Eerdmans, 1972.